78-27

IN[...] **SHORT PLAYS, POEMS, STORIES**

Date Loaned	Signature of Student	Date Returned	Teacher	Condition
9-19-78	Kathy Scruggs			New

domains
in language and composition

WRITING INCREDIBLY SHORT PLAYS, POEMS, STORIES

James H. Norton

Francis Gretton

HARCOURT BRACE JOVANOVICH, INC.

NEW YORK   CHICAGO   SAN FRANCISCO   ATLANTA   DALLAS

JAMES H. NORTON has taught English in junior and senior high schools and in college. He has written articles and given talks about the teaching of English.

FRANCIS GRETTON has taught in private schools in England and America. He is a candidate at Columbia University for his doctorate in English.

ACKNOWLEDGMENTS: For permission to reprint copyrighted material, grateful acknowledgment is made to the following publishers, authors and agents:

BRANDT & BRANDT: From *The Quiet Man* by Maurice Walsh, copyright, 1933, by Curtis Publishing Company; copyright renewed, © 1960 by Maurice Walsh.

THOMAS STEWART BRUSH: "Birthday Party" by Katharine Brush, copyright © 1946, by Katharine Brush. Originally published in *The New Yorker*, March 16, 1946.

WILLIAM BURFORD and SOUTHERN METHODIST UNIVERSITY PRESS: "A Christmas Tree" from *Man Now* by William Burford, © 1954 by Southern Methodist University Press.

COLLINS-KNOWLTON-WING, INC. and THE EXECUTORS OF THE ESTATE OF H. G. WELLS: From *The Time Machine* by H. G. Wells, copyright © 1932 by H. G. Wells.

GREGORY CORSO: "Dialogue—Two Dollmakers" by Gregory Corso from *New American Poetry 1945-1960* edited by Donald M. Allen.

DELACORTE PRESS: "It's Raining in Love" from *The Pill Versus The Springhill Mine Disaster* by Richard Brautigan, copyright © 1968 by Richard Brautigan. A Seymour Lawrence Book/Delacourt Press. First published by Four Seasons Foundation in its Writing Series edited by Donald Allen.

J. M. DENT & SONS LTD. and THE TRUSTEES OF THE JOSEPH CONRAD ESTATE: From *The Secret Agent* by Joseph Conrad.

DODD, MEAD & COMPANY, INC.: From "The Great Lover" from *The Collected Poems of Rupert Brooke*, copyright 1915 by Dodd, Mead & Company, Inc.; copyright renewed 1943 by Edward Marsh.

NORMA MILLAY ELLIS: "Counting Out Rhyme" (adapted) from *Collected Poems* by Edna St. Vincent Millay, published by Harper & Row, copyright 1928, 1955 by Edna St. Vincent Millay.

FARRAR, STRAUS & GIROUX, INC.: "Charles" from *The Lottery* by Shirley Jackson, copyright 1948, 1949 by Shirley Jackson.

IAN HAMILTON FINLAY: "Au Pair Girl" by Ian Hamilton Finlay.

Contents

WRITING SHORT PLAYS

1 Note to the fearful   3
2 Conflict plus consequences
          equals suspense   9
3 Characterization   23
4 Stage directions   37
5 The beginning   51
6 The middle   61
7 The responsible resolution   75
8 Production notes   89

WRITING SHORT POEMS

1 Poetry: private and public   101
2 Etch and sketch   111
3 A language of your own   125
4 Imagery   141
5 Blood rhythms   157
6 Tone and mood   169
7 The shape of things   181
8 The finished product   189

WRITING SHORT STORIES

1	Introduction	199
2	Loosening up	207
3	How does it feel?: the sketch	213
4	Character sketch	221
5	Autobiographical account	237
6	Second overview	249
7	Narrative	263
8	Conflicts and climaxes	277
9	Point of view, tone, mood	289
10	Putting it all together	305

WRITING
SHORT
PLAYS

1

Note to the fearful

DID YOU SAY YOU'RE AFRAID to write a play? Do you know why? Perhaps it is because you have never tried to write a play *a step at a time.*

Today, most of what people see and use has been designed and manufactured by others. To the laymen, the electronic circuits found in a computer are beyond their comprehension. People stand in awe, wondering how anyone could imagine such a complex machine. Like most inventions, the computer was not the result of a creative insight by one man. Rather, scientists and mathematicians, working independently or in teams, began with a basic idea or a problem to solve. They conducted hundreds of experiments, some of which ended in failure, others in success. Eventually, each of the problems was solved, and the finished product evolved. The point is that anything, no matter how complex or difficult, becomes much more manageable if it is taken one step at a time.

The same is true for a play. The plays you see on television or in the theater—that is, the finished products—are the results of long hours of experimentation. Like a scientist, the playwright begins with an idea, a situation, a character, or a problem to be solved. The initial creative spark is then developed and shaped through a number of revisions. Lines are written and rewritten; situations added or dropped; characters introduced or modified. And it is not unusual that the process of revision continues into the actual rehearsal. In other words, a playwright does not create his finished play initially.

Like most things, writing a play is easier if you follow the problem-solving technique: Begin with something that stimulates your imagination, and then work out the problem through a series of steps. You are not going to be asked to write a play all at once. You are being invited to write a play, a short play at that, by attacking the problem with a definite strategy. Many of the plays in this book were written by students your own age who followed the path you are now on.

Before writing a play, or any literary form for that matter, you must discover your imagination. Everyone has one. There are some of your classmates who you think are imaginative. Many of you feel that you are not imaginative. Actually, everyone has imagination; it's just that you may not be aware of how to discover and use it. Using your imagination requires two things. First, remember that *imagination works one step at a time*. As we have said, this is the secret behind creativity. Second, free your imagination; let it go so that you can find your unique ideas. Each of you does have a unique imagination. Each of you has something to offer that no one else could possibly offer, because each of you sees life through your own eyes.

Unfortunately, many people fall into bad habits that prevent them from letting their imaginations act creatively. Eliminating these habits is essential for freeing creativity. First of all, people allow faulty assumptions to slow up or even completely stop the creative process. When your teacher mentioned the writing of plays, how many of you thought or said, "I'll never be able to"? Man would still be living in caves if everyone had accepted this as a reason for not trying to do something. What if Edison had said, "Well, we've never had electric lights so I guess I won't be able to invent one"?

Another faulty assumption is saying, "I just wasn't born with that talent." You don't know if you can do something until you try—try hard and try for a long time. The greatest writers have always trained and practiced for many years, even after they achieve success. Success is as much hard work and self-discipline as it is inspiration.

Another hindrance to creativity is poor use of existing knowledge. Everyone has past experiences on which to draw. You know a lot more than you think you do. Once again, if you approach things with a step-at-a-time, problem-solving process, things will appear less difficult.

Initially, you might tend to throw out ideas or situations that are ordinary or trite. For example, in trying to find an idea for a play, a person might say, "How about having a boy trying to date a girl who is already going steady?" Immediately this is recognized as an everyday situation. But don't reject it; use it as a starting point. Try to build from it or at least put it down to be considered later when you are working on another idea. Don't throw *anything* away, no matter how trite or seemingly unoriginal it is, until the final work is completed. Great writers have to rework their stories, poems, or plays numerous times before they can express in words exactly what they want to communicate.

The basic situations of many great plays are frequently quite ordinary. Shakespeare's *Romeo and Juliet,* for example, is the story of a girl and boy falling in love. The problem is that their parents don't approve. This is a situation that is centuries old, and yet still happens to people today. You will find that it is not the basic situation that must be original. It is your imaginative presentation of the situation that makes a play fresh and original.

Another hindrance to creativity is the failure of most persons to examine what they know closely. They are overwhelmed because they try to consider the whole idea at once instead of breaking the whole into smaller, more manageable parts. For example, how many state capitals can you list? Your first reaction may be that you know a few or perhaps none at all. But when you begin to think of individual states, you begin to remember their capitals. If you are working in a group, you will find members who can help you remember. You know a lot more than you think you do.

Dependence on previous ways of doing something also stifles creative thought: "I've always done it this way." "Mr. Jones always did it this way." "Let's see how they ran the prom last year." Always looking backward allows patterns to become rigid because previous assumptions are never questioned. Good writers are constantly questioning commonly held assumptions. Literature forces people to look at life from different points of view, to reevaluate their beliefs.

Putting labels on ideas tends to be confusing. You might come up with an idea that someone labels "way out," "ridiculous," or "stupid." Your reactions and the reactions of others in your group will most likely confuse the label with the idea. This, of course, limits the possibility of objectively evaluating the idea. As you listen to and work with other students, don't label or jump to conclusions about ideas. Write the idea down, no matter what you or the group thinks of it. You may never use it, but who can tell, the idea or parts of it may become the key to a problem that arises later on.

The point of this discussion is that the mental attitudes that exist when approaching any problem are vitally important. What makes one athletic team able to beat another in a game when on paper the two teams are equal? The team's mental attitude and its spirit and drive! Going into a situation believing that you will solve the problem successfully increases your chances of success.

ACTIVITY

On a sheet of paper, list at least three examples for each of the following:

a. *Colors*—a favorite, something weird, and something masculine or feminine.
b. *Odors*—something spicy, something awful, and a special one that no one else in the room could know.
c. *Light*—different kinds of light and darkness caused by nature or by man.
d. *Objects*—one delicate and fancy, another extremely modern, and something grotesque.
e. *Emotions*—such as hate or pity.
f. *Short sentences*—such as "I'm never going to try that again."
g. *Body movements*—one sweeping and overly polite; a second jerky, perhaps humorous; a third, strange and unusual.

Select one item from each of letters a–d. Now imagine a place that could have all four things and jot it down. This might be a unique setting for a short play. Next, choose an item from each of letters e–g. Imagine a character combining all those items. Put the character into your setting. What you have done is to create a character in a setting. And that is the beginning of drama.

~~~~~~

His Own
by Betsy Gill and Carolyn Bartoe

Characters

JEFF, a typical teen-age student
MISS RUTFORD, a young but conservative teacher
SHOAN ⎫
REMER ⎬ Imps, small lifelike creatures that live in the land of imagination called Laie
GERRI ⎭
FEAR, a shapeless object played by a dancer

(*Spotlight focuses on boy who is to the left of the stage. He is sitting at a desk trying to do an art project.*)

JEFF. Oh, geez! I don't know what to do, and this stupid project is due tomorrow. If only Miss Rutford wasn't so old-fashioned about her ideas. (*Pauses for a moment.*) I know! (*Voice getting excited.*) A blue sun, and a round house, and a triangle cloud, and red grass. Yeah! I'll show 'em some new ideas. Things don't always have to be one way.

(*Light starts fading on boy and goes on in the little village of Laie—really the imagination. All the little Imps start working on their blue sun, and red grass, and round house, and triangle cloud, while busy life of Imps continues in background.*)

SHOAN. (*Painting blue sun on mural.*) This is really neat!
REMER. Yeah! Why didn't we think of this a long time ago?
GERRI. I agree. I think it's stupid that you have to do things like they've always been done. What we need is some change around here.

(*Lights go off on the stage and on the teacher, who is with JEFF.*)

MISS RUTFORD. (*Looking at project.*) What's this? A blue sun? Who ever heard of a blue sun?

(*Lights fade off teacher and go onto Laie. Music, symbolizing fear, starts softly, getting louder and louder. Soon* FEAR *comes in, dance routine.*)

(FEAR *brings on yellow sun and tries to cover up blue sun.*)

SHOAN. Stop! What are you doing? This is our village. Leave us alone! (FEAR *knocks him down.*)

REMER. (*Stepping up.*) Quit it. Would ya . . . (FEAR *pushes him away and brings on green grass.*)

GERRI. (*Running off.*) Help, everybody. Something's destroying our project.

(FEAR *pushes* GERRI *down and busy life in background fades. Then* FEAR *pushes on frame house and perfect white cloud; lights start fading, and it looks as though* FEAR *is going to win.*)

FEAR. Oh! I'll get them. We can't let the imagination go or it will never get back.

(*Lights are dim on stage and come on spotlighting* JEFF.)

JEFF. (*Stands up and says.*) I don't care if I get it in on time, it's how well I do the project that counts. I don't want it to be a yellow sun and green grass. I want this project to be mine. All me. Nobody else's. It's going to be my project.

(FEAR *goes away, Imps continue life as usual. Lights go out as* JEFF *starts to work on project.*)

2

Conflict plus consequences equals suspense

THE FOLLOWING PLAY IS GIVEN as a model of a situation in which there is a conflict with important consequences.

Treat or Trick
by Sharon Grimm

Characters

NARRATOR	MOTHER
BILL	FATHER
TOM	CASHIER

SCENE 1: *Curtain is closed.*

NARRATOR. Two nine-year-old brothers are in their bedroom on their beds talking to each other. It is the day before Halloween.

(*Curtain opens.*)

BILL. (*Exasperated.*) We've just got to have a new sled.
TOM. Yeah. But eleven dollars is out of the question. Where would we ever get that kind of money?

BILL. I don't know, but we've just *got* to have a new sled. It's already snowed three times this winter, and we haven't even gone sledding once. That old sled of ours that's stored in the attic is practically an antique. It falls apart every time you look at it.

TOM. (*In a mocking tone.*) I know. Remember last winter when we were racing Jerry and the runner fell off? I ended up with a skinned knee and a purple bruise all over my leg.

BILL. Yeah, I remember. (*Pause.*) There must be some way to come up with eleven dollars. I'd ask Mom or Dad for the money, but I haven't had a chance to talk to them. They've both been so wrapped up in the school UNICEF program. Just yesterday I saw Mom in the hall giving out UNICEF boxes.

TOM. Yeah, so did I.

(*A long silence follows. Both boys put their chins on their hands as if in deep concentration. Suddenly* TOM *perks up as he is hit with an idea.*)

TOM. Hey, Bill! Why don't we borrow two of Mom's UNICEF boxes? She'd never know they were gone. Then tomorrow night when we're trick or treating we could ask for donations for UNICEF. Then with all that money we could buy a new sled.

BILL. (*Hesitating.*) Yeah. But isn't that sort of cheating?

TOM. Do you want that new sled or not?

BILL. Sure, (*Still hesitating.*) but I still say it wouldn't be right to do that.

TOM. Look, Bill, the money that we would collect would go to buy sleds for other kids anyway, so why couldn't it buy one for us?

BILL. Well, (*Finally giving in.*) I guess you're right.

TOM. Then it's settled.

(*Curtain closes.*)

SCENE 2: TOM *and* BILL *are seated alone at the breakfast table. It is the morning after Halloween.*

TOM. Boy, we sure got a lot of money last night, didn't we, Bill?

BILL. We sure did. Thirteen whole dollars. Finally, after all these years we'll be able to get a new sled.

TOM. You sure did a good job last night. You sounded so sincere about UNICEF you almost made me want to give you some money.

BILL. Why don't we go to Gibson's tonight and get the new sled? I can't wait to get it and try it out.

TOM. Yeah, me too.

BILL. (*Violently, almost hissing.*) Shut up. Here come Mom and Dad.

(MOTHER *and* FATHER *enter, sit down, and begin to eat breakfast.*)

MOTHER. Hi, boys. How did it go last night? Did you get a lot of candy?

TOM *and* BILL. (*At the same time.*) We sure did!

MOTHER. Well, that's nice. (*She turns to* FATHER.) I was so glad last night when I saw so many people participating in the UNICEF drive.

(TOM *and* BILL *glance at each other.*)

FATHER. So was I. I am sure that our school drive will earn a lot of money for UNICEF. I'm glad so many children are taking an active interest in other children around the world. UNICEF is such a worthy cause because it helps so many people.

(*When the conversation began,* TOM *and* BILL *had been sitting up tall and proud of themselves. As the conversation goes on, their shoulders begin to droop more and more.*)

MOTHER. Yes, I know. (*She looks at the boys.*) Boys, did you know that UNICEF buys food for starving children? You are really lucky. You have so much food while other children around the world hardly have any.

FATHER. UNICEF also buys clothing for very poor families around the world. Every day we sit here and take clothes and food for granted while other children feel lucky they even have any at all. I feel UNICEF has to be one of the greatest organizations in the world, and I'm glad to be a part of it.

MOTHER. I agree. (*Turning back to the boys.*) Would either of you like some more oatmeal?

BILL. (*Very low and sort of hoarse.*) N-no, thank you.

(*The boys sit silently with their heads drooped. After a few moments,* TOM *speaks.*)

TOM. (*Very softly.*) May we please be excused?
MOTHER. Of course, boys.

(*The boys rise and leave as the curtain closes.*)

SCENE 3

NARRATOR. The third scene takes place in Gibson's Sporting Goods Store that evening.

(*The curtain opens. The scene is that of a sporting goods store. A cashier's stand is at one end of the stage. A cashier is standing behind the stand doodling around doing something. There is a bright, shiny, new sled hanging on the wall. There are also other sporting goods items here and there. There is a UNICEF receptacle on the cashier's stand. The two boys enter from one side of the stage, talking with each other. Neither sees the sled.*)

BILL. But do you really think we should go ahead and get the sled? After what Mom and Dad said this morning, I—
TOM. (*Interrupting.*) I know! I know. I feel kind of lousy, too. I just can't make up my mind. Should we get the sled or not? We've got all the money for it, but—

(*Both boys raise their heads and see the shining sled on the wall at the same time. Their reasons for not getting the sled are forgotten. They both run to the sled and start examining it.*)

BILL. (*Really excited.*) Wow, just look at it. Isn't it a beaut?
TOM. (*Excited.*) Yeah! It's even got a steering device on it.
BILL. I bet it could even beat Randy Bowman's streamlined sled.

(*The CASHIER approaches the boys.*)

CASHIER. Can I help you, boys?
TOM. Yes. We'd like to buy this sled.
CASHIER. Fine. (*He starts taking the sled off the wall.*) If you'll just step over here, you can pay for it. (*He walks toward the cash register.*)

(*The boys follow the CASHIER to the check stand. Just as they reach the check stand they see the UNICEF receptacle. They stop suddenly and look at it for a few moments with a startled and guilty look on their faces. Meanwhile, the CASHIER is ringing up the price on the cash register. Both boys turn and look at the sled for a few seconds and then they look back at the receptacle. Finally, the boys look at each other guiltily.*)

TOM. Uh—sir—we've decided not to buy the sled after all.

(*The* CASHIER *stops and looks at the boys with a puzzled look and finally shrugs his shoulders.*)

CASHIER. Okay, if you say so.

(*Then, as the* CASHIER *is trying to get the sled back on the wall, the boys give each other one long last look, and suddenly* TOM *pulls out the thirteen dollars and puts the money in the receptacle. Then the boys turn and leave as the curtain closes.*)

Life is full of problems. As a matter of fact, one could say that life is either the successful or unsuccessful solving of those problems. The alarm goes off in the morning and disturbs your sleep: a problem. You solve it successfully by turning off the alarm and getting up to get ready for school. To some of you, this is not a successful solution. Maybe shutting it off, turning over, and going back to sleep would be a more successful solution. Of course, if you do that, then you will be either late for or absent from school, and you will have another problem to solve. The point is that you are constantly being forced to make decisions.

Some decisions are more vital than others. For instance, choosing a breakfast cereal is not an important decision. The consequences of the decision—that is, the different tastes of the cereals, whether one needs sugar, or whether the other needs to be cooked —will not make a significant difference in your life. Notice, however, how the problem is radically upgraded when you must make a decision whether to secretly date someone whom your parents have forbidden you to see. Here the consequences of being caught with that person might involve severe punishment, such as being grounded for a month.

The last situation described involves a conflict, or the struggle between two opposing forces or persons. In this case, your desire to see the other person conflicts with your parents' orders.

The greater the consequences of the decision, the greater the conflict. The consequences that follow from selecting one brand of cereal over another are of minor importance. Deciding to date a person your parents have forbidden you to see involves greater consequences—both good and bad. The same is true if the decision involves breaking the law or disobeying an officer's command while in battle.

When thinking about a short play, you should look toward the basic problem-solving pattern of *conflict and consequences.* *Conflict and the possible consequences of the conflict are the basic elements of a good play.* The audience is interested in seeing someone confronted with a significant conflict—whether to disobey some authority figure in a situation that implies drastic consequences, such as losing the use of the car, going to prison, or losing a life.

At this point, imagine yourself in the following situation: You are new to the school. You are slowly being accepted by a group of students who are influential socially in the school. In the meantime, you have won the lead in the school play. This is very important to you because someday you hope to make a career in the theater. The day before the opening performance, your friends invite you to celebrate your coming performance by skipping school with them and having a party at one of their homes. When you balk at the idea, they tell you not to worry because they have a system that will keep all of you from getting caught. You realize, of course, that the punishment for cutting a day of school is at least three days' suspension. This would prevent you from being in the play. You are now in a state of conflict. Your decision to skip school carries with it the possibility of getting caught and suspended, which, in turn, implies missing out on the play, as well as disappointing the director and the others in the cast. Furthermore, the chances of your ever getting another part in a school play will be nil, and so will be your chances of getting a good recommendation from your drama coach when you apply to drama school. On the other hand, what will happen if you turn down the group's invitation? Will you be rejected by the group, thereby destroying much of the social power you have been building up? What if the person you have been dating is also in this group? Will you lose that relationship as well?

Can you now see why conflict and the consequences of a decision is the key to exciting drama? If you put the above situation into a play, you will create suspense, which means arousing important unanswered questions. The audience is wondering what your decision will be and how you will make it. They are worried that you might get caught if you decide to cut school, but at the same time, they know you deserve to get caught. They want you to make the "right" decision. But, is there a "right" decision to make? Either way you appear to lose something of great value to you. This is another perspective from which to evaluate whether you have an effective conflict-and-consequences situation: within the conflict, *both decisions bear fairly equally crushing consequences.* No matter which way your character turns, no matter what decisions he makes, the consequences will appear foreboding —there is something he will have to lose.

In conclusion, when constructing your basic dramatic situation, keep uppermost in your mind the important concept that conflict plus consequences equals suspense.

~~~~~~

ACTIVITY

The conflict-and-consequences situation is the key to a short play. The following activity will help you recognize an incident that involves a conflict as opposed to a simpler life-problem situation.

In general, there are four main types of conflict:

1. Man versus man.
2. Man versus society.
3. Man versus nature.
4. Man versus himself.

Most times the consequences of our actions are really not earthshaking. But a play should hit that *special time* in our lives—a time when the *conflict and consequences are important. This will keep our audience in suspense.*

From the following items pick the situations that contain a conflict: identify the conflict and mention possible consequences. For the remaining items, see if you can introduce conflict with vital consequences and thus make it a dramatic incident.

a. Buying an article of clothing.
b. Waiting for a bus without an umbrella when it looks like rain.
c. Answering the telephone at home when you are playing hooky.

d. Deciding whether to have a mushroom or a pepperoni pizza.
e. Having your dad find an extra key you secretly had made for the car.
f. Choosing a book in the library.
g. Discovering in your first-period class that you are wearing shoes of two different colors.
h. Turning down a date with a person you don't like.
i. Accepting a date with a person you don't know well.
j. Taking home a report card that you know will ground you for a month.
k. Accepting a responsibility you are not sure that you can handle adequately.
l. Doing your math or your English homework first.
m. Deciding to go on a blind date while your "steady" is out of town.
n. Accepting a ride with a person who has obviously had too much to drink.
o. Deciding whether to make a layer cake or cupcakes for a party.

~~~~~~

Now that you have some understanding of a conflict-and-consequences situation, the question arises, "If the concept *conflict plus consequences equals suspense* is necessary for a short play, how can I create a situation that will fit the formula?" This is not so difficult to answer. Stop for a moment and go back over your life. Think of a time in which you had to make a significant decision. Bear in mind that, when improvising dramatic situations, you have the prerogative to "stretch" real life somewhat. Perhaps an incident with little dramatic value that happened to you can be changed into a highly suspenseful incident by modifying the incident in some way. The initial incident might be: Two students illegally enter the home of a family they do not like. They intend only to take food from the refrigerator. They are not caught, but they live with that fear while in the house. According to the discussion on conflict and consequences, this is not yet a good dramatic situation. However, in order to provide a dramatic situation, perhaps you could "stretch" the real-life incident in this way: While the students are in the house, they hear someone else breaking in.

The students hide while the other burglars steal some money. The students stay hidden for quite a while to make sure they don't confront the other burglars, and, in doing so, are discovered by the family.

Most dramas have their origin in everyday happenings; otherwise they would not be believable. And they must be believable in order to create the suspense you want. As soon as the audience doubts that the action they are seeing on stage could happen, they will no longer be interested in having any questions you may have aroused answered. The important thing to remember is that *you must heighten the conflict in order to create action that will be intense enough to keep the audience involved.*

In creating the conflict, remember that the play will be performed live upon a stage. This imposes certain limitations not found in film. A conflict involving a battle between ten thousand soldiers on horseback is possible in film, but not on a stage. A dramatic rendition of William Tell's shooting an apple off his son's head is more suited to the movies than to a live performance (to say nothing of the problem you'll have in finding someone to act the part of the son). There are many dramatic situations that are impossible to portray realistically on a stage.

In film, the background of the action is quite fluid. That means it can change rapidly or can move with the action, as in a scene set on a moving car. But a play is acted in front of a fixed set. A set, in general, shows one place at a time: for example, the room of a house, a field, or the interior of a plane. It would be almost impossible, given a limited amount of money for sets, to show a person walking from the attic to the cellar. You would have to close the curtain and change the set to show this. The action of a short play should be limited to one or two places. Try to keep in mind the restrictions imposed by a live stage presentation when you are writing your plays.

~~~~~~

ACTIVITY

Invent situations that have a conflict for several of the following:

a. A punishment.
b. An accusation.

    c. A lie.
    d. Hurting someone's feelings.
    e. Sneaking into a theater, the circus, etc.
    f. Avoiding someone.
    g. A scary situation.
    h. A theft.
    i. An encounter with authority.
    j. An encounter with a rival.
    k. A close game, match, meet, etc.
    l. An accident.
    m. Caught in a storm.
    n. Getting out of doing something.
    o. Achieving an ambition.
    p. A fight.
    q. An impulsive action.
    r. Giving something up.
    s. An embarrassing moment.
    t. An unexpected arrival.
    u. A brash remark.

If you imagined some real-life incidents, but are still having trouble "stretching" them into suspenseful situations, try adding a conflict by using some of these methods:

1. Change the color, shape, motion, sound, size, beginning, ending, etc., of something.
2. Exaggerate and/or magnify an idea, problem, character trait, etc.
3. Add something: a person, sound, weather, temperature, etc.
4. Make something less important, accurate, readable, emotional, etc.
5. Make something more important: a person, sign, etc.
6. Rearrange events: have a girl ask the boy before he gets a chance to ask her, etc.
7. Reverse the situation: have a father borrow money from his son or a mother borrow clothes from her daughter.

~~~~~~

Another effective way to create new and exciting ideas is through creative association. This is combining or relating very unlikely things. Some examples might be "the shadow of sun," words having flavors, and a football coach who loves to crochet. The key to creative association is to take something ordinary and to think of something opposite or even impossible at first glance that would relate to it. When you come up with "a sword made out of strawberry jello," you might have the beginning of a really original idea.

~~~~~~

ACTIVITY

Select a few incidents from the list of conflicts you thought of in the last activity. Try creative association. The purpose here is *not* to write a play, derive an incident, or anything that specific. You are to combine completely impossible things that might add anything to a play—a character, a prop, a setting, a lighting situation, etc.

~~~~~~

Brainstorming is another method used by most creative people. The process is simple and can be done either alone or with others. Brainstorming begins with a problem to be solved: in this case, you have been invited to write a short play, and you need a dramatic incident. If you are working alone, sit down and think of possible ideas. Write them all down, no matter how foolish they might appear at first. If you are working in a group or with another person, begin talking about whatever comes into your head. Once again, write down all the ideas. What will happen is that one idea will stimulate another idea, and in the end many possible ideas will be presented. The original ideas may be very vague. Talk about an idea mentioned, despite the fact that it doesn't seem to make complete sense. Continue to discuss it even though you are "sure" it won't work and you are tempted to abandon the idea. This is the key point to the success or failure of brainstorming: you must *not* give up when that impulse hits you. You might feel foolish explaining something that doesn't seem to fit or make sense. You must overcome your fear of having your friends laugh at you or poke fun at your "impossible" idea. This is where the power of brainstorming lies—your impossible ideas could lead to possible and original ideas. You or your partner might suddenly be hit by some part of your brainstorming, and one of you will carry it out to a workable idea. Also, be sure to give yourself enough time. You may have to come up with five, ten, even twenty possibilities before workable and original ideas come together. The point of brainstorming is to let your imagination run wild and to verbalize your ideas no matter how foolish or impossible they seem.

~~~~~~~~~~~~~~~~~~~~~~~~~~~~~~~~~~

ACTIVITY

Start with an incident containing conflict and let your mind go wherever it wants to. Remember, in terms of setting up an idea for a play, write whatever comes into your head. The purpose here is to learn how it feels to brainstorm, not to write a play.

~~~~~~~~~~~~~~~~~~~~~~~~~~~~~~~~~~

Now you know that a short play is based on conflict and consequences, and you have proven that you can recognize an everyday situation and turn it into a dramatic conflict that has vital consequences. In addition, you have practiced stimulating your imagination through creative association and brainstorming to develop dramatic incidents.

Brainstorming reveals that there are many starting points from which to create a short play. *The inspiration for a short play can come from anywhere and from anything.* Many people think that writers start at the beginning with perfect words or lines and go through the play word by word, line by line, without hesitation, without ever changing a thing. Nothing could be further from the truth. Try starting your play with whatever comes into your head. It might be a funny line around which you want to build your play. It might be a scene from your past; it might be a character. It could be a theme such as ecology that comes to mind. However, *no matter your starting point, you must build it into a dramatic incident by adding a conflict and consequences.* Your inspiration could come from anywhere. The point is to begin.

Perhaps the best illustration to demonstrate how far a creative person can break from trite and conventional ideas is Gregory Corso's poem "Dialogue—Two Dollmakers."

Let's not use eyes anymore
    A doll without eyes?
Let's use barber-shop chairs instead
    Fool! Say next no mouth why don't you!
I say no mouth—I say a zeppelin for the mouth
    And I say folly folly FOLLY!
A small zeppelin, of course; can't let the work get out of hand
    Of course!
What say you for the nose? How's about a bathtub?
    What say I? You care what I say?
Of course! We're partners no?
    No! I never be partners with nuts! You nuts!
No . . . the ears nuts; that's right, the ears walnuts!
    I say the whole business nuts!!!
And the arms . . . suitcases!
    Let's close shop right now!
And the body . . . how's about a lovely staircase?
    Why not a lovely meat truck!
Why not! Oh, Alberto, I love you! You're beginning to see!
    Hmmmmm . . . for the dress we could use a doorknob
The legs, Alberto, what about the legs
    What about them! There's always abandoned farms to use . . .

                                       (1959)

~~~~~~

ACTIVITY

    Analyze the conflict in the play "Treat or Trick" (page 9) and decide what type of conflict it is: man against man? man against nature? man against society? man against himself? What are the possible consequences of the conflict—both good and bad? Are the conflict and its consequences important?

~~~~~~

3

Characterization

CREATING INTERESTING, believable characters lies at the center of successful play writing. Often people will forget the story of a play yet remember a striking character. And since most plays deal with ordinary situations, though heightened through the introduction of a conflict, the creation of exciting characters distinguishes good plays from bad ones.

A good dramatist must know the characters in depth. This means knowing the background, economic situation, likes and dislikes, habits, beliefs, physical appearance, and all the other characteristics that make the person an individual. Naturally, all these traits will not be found in the play. Nevertheless, the playwright should know how the characters would act in any given situation. One effective way of learning about your characters is to write biographies for each one. This practice will force you to analyze the personality of each person in the play. Of course, the major characters will be more extensively individualized than are the minor figures.

There are two basic types of characters: static and dynamic. The personality of a static character remains the same throughout the play. He enters the play with certain characteristics, mannerisms, and thoughts, and he does not change during the play. The real drama of a play does not focus on this type of character.

One kind of static character is called the symbolic character. A symbolic character stands for some idea or thing. For instance, characters named "Freedom," "Justice," "Flag," and "Poetry" are symbolic. When using symbolic figures, character is developed through the qualities of the symbol; there is no attempt to give a symbolic character a human personality.

A good play centers on and revolves around a dynamic character or characters. A dynamic character changes in some significant way because of the conflict. He might abandon some belief that has been causing others to be unhappy; he might learn an important lesson about himself or about life; he might come to understand humanity more fully. The point is that some great change must take place within him or something significant must happen to him. The other characters either cause or watch the change.

There are two fundamental ways in which a dramatist can present the personalities of the characters. The first technique of characterization is to reveal personality through the character's words, actions, and reactions to events and to other persons. Usually this is accomplished in dialogue, the conversations between two or more characters. Although dialogue is the most common method of showing what a character is like, at times a character will speak to himself or directly to the audience.

In real life, you learn what a person is like from the comments of your friends. Similarly, in a play characterization is achieved through the comments of one or more characters about another. Of course, hearing about one character from another is not as effective a method as seeing or hearing the character directly. But it can help to portray a character's personality in all its complexity.

In the following excerpt from *The Importance of Being Earnest,* the playwright, Oscar Wilde, illustrates both techniques of characterization: (1) seeing and hearing a character's actions and words, and (2) hearing about one character from another.

(*Enter* JACK.)

ALGERNON. . . . What brings you up to town?
JACK. Oh, pleasure, pleasure! What else should bring one anywhere? Eating as usual, I see, Algy!
ALGERNON. (*Stiffly.*) I believe it is customary in good society to take some slight refreshment at five o'clock. Where have you been since last Thursday?

JACK. (*Sitting down on the sofa.*) In the country.

ALGERNON. What on earth do you do there?

JACK. (*Pulling off his gloves.*) When one is in town, one amuses oneself. When one is in the country, one amuses other people. It is excessively boring.

ALGERNON. And who are the people you amuse?

JACK. (*Airily.*) Oh, neighbors, neighbors.

ALGERNON. Got nice neighbors in your part of Shropshire?

JACK. Perfectly horrid! Never speak to one of them.

ALGERNON. How immensely you must amuse them! (*Goes over and takes sandwich.*) By the way, Shropshire is your county, is it not?

JACK. Eh? Shropshire? Yes, of course. Hallo! Why all these cups? Why cucumber sandwiches? Why such reckless extravagance in one so young? Who is coming to tea?

ALGERNON. Oh! Merely Aunt Augusta and Gwendolen.

JACK. How perfectly delightful!

ALGERNON. Yes, that is all very well; but I am afraid Aunt Augusta won't quite approve of your being here.

JACK. May I ask why?

ALGERNON. My dear fellow, the way you flirt with Gwendolen is perfectly disgraceful. It is almost as bad as the way Gwendolen flirts with you.

JACK. I am in love with Gwendolen. I have come up to town expressly to propose to her.

ALGERNON. I thought you had come up for pleasure? . . . I call that business.

JACK. How utterly unromantic you are!

ALGERNON. I really don't see anything romantic in proposing. It is very romantic to be in love. But there is nothing romantic about a definite proposal. Why, one may be accepted. One usually is, I believe. Then the excitement is all over. The very essence of romance is uncertainty. If ever I get married, I'll certainly try to forget the fact.

JACK. I have no doubt about that, dear Algy. The Divorce Court was specially invented for people whose memories are so curiously constituted.

Through the dialogue, Wilde not only shows something about the personalities of the two speakers but also hints at the characters of Aunt Augusta and Gwendolen. And, in a subtle way, he introduces one of the basic conflicts of the play: Aunt Augusta's disapproval of Jack's engagement to Gwendolen.

In addition to these general techniques of characterization, there are several specific methods for making your characters individuals. Pick a special word or phrase for a character to say, and don't let anyone else in the play use it, except in contradicting that character or in contrast to that character. For example, if the character, a father who drives his family quite unrelentingly, has for his favorite line "You're not trying hard enough," toward the end of the play have one of the children catch the father dodging his responsibility and say to him "You're not trying hard enough." This is especially powerful if it is the last line in the play. Doing this sort of thing will also make the line indisputably the father's. The idea is to develop strong characterization for the main character by letting him have something special to say. The audience will begin to look forward to it, and your character will grow on the audience.

Besides specific words, the kind of "voice" you give your character helps individualize him further. You can make him sound young or old, confident or frightened. You can decide that every time he gets very nervous his voice cracks or changes pitch. Does he talk through his nose or always use a megaphone? The possibilities are endless. Choosing a good language device will tell a great deal about your character to the audience.

Another technique to instill personality in a character is to present him with an unyielding attitude. The attitude may have become an obsession. Give your character some belief and never let him sway from it. For example, an old woman might firmly believe that all young people are up to no good. Of course, if your character is dynamic, the audience anticipates a dramatic change from the previous attitude to a new one.

Physical actions and appearance communicate much about a character. Everyone has significant movements, but they are usually not so exaggerated that people take notice of them. On stage, however, all motion is very noticeable. How does he carry his head? to one side, or with chin against his chest? Are his shoulders straight or slumped? Does he answer most questions with his shoulders? Does his stomach protrude excessively? Are his legs stiff or wobbly? Are his arms always in the way, or folded? Does he constantly scratch his chin? Does he move clumsily and knock things and people over? Does he constantly check his hair? Is he so athletic that he does sit-ups or deep knee bends every chance he gets? Take a specific movement, exaggerate it, and give it to a character.

Remember not to restrict your expression to the hands. The head can be used many ways. A character could raise his nose continually throughout the play to indicate his conceit, or bow from the waist to indicate humility, whether sincere or hypocritical. A character could sit or stand in a special way that indicates something significant about his personality.

Costumes and props can also be important to characterization. A pipe, a top hat, a wilted bouquet, a trumpet always in hand could be effective in adding to your characterization. You could create a character who always has to answer the telephone or always has to call in someone else for an answer to everything. Then, there are smaller, less obvious costume props, such as glasses, hats, moustaches, and key chains, that add an aura to your character. A vest might suggest something of the character. A very wide or loud tie, special shoes, or short pants might be important. When you create your character, think of props and clothes that reveal facts about him that you can use to portray him to your audience.

Remember to match a character's clothing with his personality. It is unlikely that the president of a large corporation would appear at a formal dinner wearing love beads. This is especially true for a serious play; in comedy, however, such incongruity might produce the desired humorous effect.

Finally, the physical setting can reveal the personality of a character. The decor of a character's room or office can say more about the character than many lines of dialogue. Again, the physical setting should fit the personality of the character, except when specific reasons dictate otherwise.

~~~~~~

ACTIVITY

At first, you may feel that you cannot create characters. This activity is designed to show you that you can derive original and unusual characters easily. Start going back to Chapter 1, p. 6.

List three items for letters e–g. Add three items for each of the following:

   a. A belief and/or attitude.
   b. Costume and/or prop.
   c. An obsession.

Take one item from each letter as you did in Chapter 1 and combine them to create a character. Write a brief dialogue that will reveal your character's personality. Suggest props, costumes, and specific expressions that could contribute to the characterization.

~~~~~~

Lines of a play should do two basic things: promote the action and further define your characters. Within these two purposes, your lines should sound like everyday conversation, which implies appropriate diction and length.

The audience cannot decide to ignore irrelevant or repetitious dialogue in a play as can the readers of a book. They are captive, in a sense, to the conversations you have written. However, captive or not, they can become bored, and may talk or walk out during the performance. Therefore you have the responsibility to make every line move the action of your drama. You have no room for fumbling around until you hit on the right line. By that time you may have lost the audience.

All the lines should reflect the personality of the speaker. Often people mention that such and such a line was "out of character," meaning that what the character said did not agree with his personality as it was developed in the play. While each line promotes action, this purpose should not overshadow the idea of keeping lines in character.

Another method of keeping your lines on course is to think of them as everyday conversation. This will also keep them an appropriate length. As discussed before, lines not vitally related to the action will lose your audience. This is also true of lines that are too long. When one character speaks at great length, the play begins to sound like a lecture. Also, long speeches tend to come out sounding memorized, or "canned." A canned speech can destroy the entire effect of a scene. If you are convinced that what you've written in a particular speech needs to be spoken, portion it out to several lines with another character's lines in between.

The only exception to this principle are introductions, summaries, and "phone-call speeches." Introductory or summary speeches introduce or draw together a series of actions:

> JUDGE. Will the defendants please step forward and approach the bench. (MANKIND, POWER, *and* COMFORT *step up to the bench.*) Mankind, Power, Comfort . . . you have been responsible for getting our world into a position where you might kill us all—forever! I now sentence you to fifty years of hard labor in laboratories, homes, factories, and schools, working day and night to discover solutions to your shortsighted and selfish ways. And after that fifty years, you will be retried, and if you have labored well and hard, perhaps your children and grandchildren who will be sitting in my place will be able to judge you less harshly. (*To the* POLICEMEN.) Take them away.

A "phone-call" speech implies someone at the other end of the phone who is not heard by the audience:

> DR. H. Yes, Harold, I can talk. There's no one around. (LANIE *hears this and quickly ducks behind the couch to listen.*) What? You mean those rocks that Vance brought back may contain the secret of the Sun's energy! Yes, I have them in my living-room safe. To come up with some phony substitutes? . . . About ten minutes . . . You said it! One leak to the newspaper and we'll be flooded before we can do anything. And if we're wrong . . . What? . . . But that's impossible! I ate lunch with their ambassador last week. OK, OK . . . I believe you. But Cornigbal. They've been a friendly country for years. . . . Two of their best men, huh? Well, let the spies steal the phonies from the school after the dance. By the time they discover they're phonies we'll have the experiment completed. Now, not a word to anybody. . . . Of course, Harold. Talk to you later. Bye.

Conversational or colloquial speech is also the best level from which to choose your diction. When people write, they tend to use formal diction and formal structure. This will not work for writing plays. In a play you have people in emotional situations of conflict and consequences. People caught up in their emotions don't stop to compose high-flown phrases and complicated sentences. In general, characters should speak as they would in conversation.

The best way to overcome this tendency is to read your play *aloud* as you go along. Or better yet, have someone else read it aloud. Since it's your play, you may not be able to hear how formal it sounds even after reading it orally.

The final aspect of composing lines that needs some discussion is that of tone. Much humor can be added to plays, whether intended serious or humorous, through several language phenomena.

The simplest is the use of names. Names of several syllables, such as Rollingford Tooglesworthy or Sytesmiggle Silvertonsils, should bring a humorous response from the audience. Rhyming sounds, such as Marguerita Seepalita, Mitford Witford, and Rudgley Sludgley, are humorous language devices. Humorous names often reflect the character's occupation, such as:

Doctor	Dr. Sloppystitch
Lawyer	Mr. Jurystomper
Banker	Mr. R. U. Needingany
Teacher	Miss Yellownotes
Dentist	Dr. Prymouth

A second device for humorous effect is having one character start as many words as possible with the same letter. The letters *p, b,* and *t* are especially effective when attempting to adapt this device. For example, you might change this speech: "PEMPERTONE. In the coming election, I would like to ask all of you here to vote for me" to: "PEMPERTONE. In the coming election, please place your preference positively for me, Pegglestone P. Pempertone."

Another idea is to impose a sound upon your character that isn't especially a word. Have him hiccup when a certain girl approaches. Have your heroine sneeze during crucial moments. A character could spit tobacco, "P-too," or fall off to sleep all the time, "ZzZZZzzz."

Spend some time working these into your comedies. Check a

serious play to make certain you have not used any of these humorous devices unwittingly.

To summarize, there are three rules of thumb for writing lines:

1. A line must be appropriate to all the other aspects of characterization: An erudite professor will not use poor grammar.

2. A line should sound like everyday conversation: The line "If you continue to behave in this manner, I shall fire you" would sound more realistic as "One more mistake and you're fired."

3. A line should end as soon as it has accomplished its purpose.

~~~~~~

ACTIVITY

Read each line aloud. Then do the following three things with each line, keeping in mind the discussion in this chapter on the appropriateness of lines:

1. Decide if the line is appropriate for a character.
2. If it is appropriate, then briefly describe the character who might say it.
3. If it is not appropriate, point out the aspects of the line that make it so.

Lines
   a. If you continue to perpetrate behavior similar to that which you have demonstrated the week previous, I shall terminate your employment at this establishment.
   b. Sure, I cheated to win.
   c. (*To* BOSS.) Yeah, I heard you.
   d. Gee, Walter, I was only about to request that I might be of assistance.
   e. I will do my very best, Mr. Jones, to keep everything going smoothly for you. I will try my hardest to do my best. I will keep a sharp lookout for anything that needs to be taken care of, and take care of it as soon as I can, Mr. Jones.
   f. I am certain we can admonish Larchmont Lockspur so

that he will never again be victorious in a race of motor-cycles.

g. Listen, Bob, I think you're being very overbearing.

h. That's a terrible thing. He's dead.

i. Just fine. Sunny day.

j. Gee, Mom, I was going to continue cleaning my room.

k. This is the fourteenth time I've told you to be in on time, young lady. Next time I'm going to get angry.

l. Her vocabulary test is just incredulous in terms of mitigating vicissitudes.

m. Tarnation, Hickory, you done it again!

n. My bride shall always hold a lily in her fist.

~~~~~~

The Wizard of Is
by James H. Norton

Characters

YO	LYIN
RABID	WICKED WHICH
MAD HADDER	WIZARD OF IS

SCENE: *The scene is a place of dreams, a distorted reality.* YO *is being pulled out onto the stage by invisible forces. He is fighting the forces, but gets pulled on anyway. He keeps rubbing his eyes. He is barefoot.* RABID *comes hopping in from the other side. The characters all appear wearing signs that bear their names.*

RABID. (*Stopping; laughing and pointing to* YO's *feet.*) Where're your shoes, Yo?

YO. (*Looking down.*) I thought I had them on when I left. . . . (*Looks at his name card.*) Is that my name—Yo?

RABID. Of course. What other name is there? (*Laughing again.*)

YO. Will you stop laughing at me. What's your name?

RABID. (*Showing his card.*) Rabid, of course.

YO. But you just said that there weren't any other names but "Yo."

RABID. Sorry. (*Pause.*) It's just the Wicked Which will capture you without shoes.

YO. The Wicked Which?

RABID. (*Checking watch worn on his ankle.*) Of course.—Which came first and Which drug tonight and Which . . .

YO. Wait a minute. Are you making fun of my trip?

RABID. (*Trying to hold back laughter.*) Me? I wouldn't think of it! (*He laughs; checking his watch again.*) Nuts! I'm going to be on time again. Bye. (RABID *exits.*)

(MAD HADDER *comes out walking on his knees, carrying a head under his arms. He has a huge hat on. He runs right into* YO.)

MAD HADDER. (*Very angry.*) Why don't you watch where you're going? Can't you see I'm taking this head to the Wicked Which?

YO. (*Drawing back.*) Why—that's my head! (*Frightened, feeling his own head.*) Where did you get it?

MAD HADDER. When you've spaced out on acid as many times as I have . . . (*He makes a grotesque face and laughs hideously.*) you'll be a Mad Hadder, too! (*Looking at* YO's *feet.*) I like your shoes.

YO. (*Looking down.*) I don't have any on. I mean . . . I didn't think I had any on . . . until now. . . .

MAD HADDER. (*Doubling up with laughter.*) I'm a Hadder, and you're a Had-Any. Oh, the Which will love it—love it!

YO. (*Frightened, but angry.*) Shut up! Shut up and go away! (*Shakes his head in an effort to clear it.*) I wish this whole thing would go away.

(MAD HADDER *exits.* YO *continues to walk to the opposite side of the stage. A roar is heard off stage.* YO *pulls back.* LYIN *enters, roaring.*)

LYIN. Where do you think you're going? And get some shoes on!

YO. But I was just told I had some on.

LYIN. (*Roaring.*) The Mad Hadder told you that . . . (*Coming up face-to-face with* YO.) didn't he? Didn't he?

YO. (*Pulling back.*) Well . . .

LYIN. Come on, don't lie to me. Who are you going to believe, a Mad Hadder . . . or me, Lyin? (YO *doesn't respond.*) It's a cinch you're having trouble believing yourself, though, isn't it? (YO *nods.*) Well, shape up or the Wizard of Is won't talk to you.

YO. The Wizard of Is?

LYIN. Yes. He should be here any minute. (*Looking back over his shoulder.*) I just hope he gets here before the Wicked Which.

YO. The Wicked Which?

LYIN. Of course. . . . Which escape, Which trip, Which narcotic . . .

YO. You, too?

LYIN. No! (*Points at* YO.) *Yo,* too! (YO *looks away guiltily.*) Oh, come on. *Yo* knows it. *Yo* just wants to have somebody else solve his problems for *Yo.* Just needs somebody to answer his which Which. Am I right? (*No response from* YO.) Of course, I am. You're trying to find the Wizard of Is before it's too late. Well, good luck. But the answer you get won't be what you think. (LYIN *exits.*)

YO. (*Calling.*) Wait a minute! What do you mean by that?

(YO *starts walking off the way he came, hopping and feeling his feet as he goes.* WICKED WHICH *enters, cackling.*)

WICKED WHICH. Hello, young man. What a beautiful shoe you have on.

YO. But I have two shoes on. . . . I mean, I don't have any shoes on. . . . I mean . . . do I only have one shoe on? For my sake, which is it?

WICKED WHICH. It's always which! It's never one or two or three. It's always *which!*

YO. What are you talking about?

WICKED WHICH. You know very well what which—LSD, cocaine, mescaline, heroin, speed—which Which is all that's left to you now.

YO. But I'm not hooked on anything yet!

WICKED WHICH. (*Rubbing her hands.*) Oh, Yo and I know. . . . Yo can tell me which Which. . . . Yo . . . which Which?

YO. But I'm not, honest.

WICKED WHICH. (*Getting angry.*) Look at your feet! (YO *looks.*) Which has the shoe?

YO. I'm not sure.

WICKED WHICH. Neither does, stupid.

YO. (*Confused.*) But you said . . .

WICKED WHICH. Both do, stupid!

YO. But . . .

WICKED WHICH. Only your right foot. Feel it. Tell me. (YO *feels his right foot.*) That's your left. I said right. Which is it?

(*Coming up to* YO *like a lawyer cross-examining.*) Which—which—which?

(YO *sits down, his head in his hands. The* WIZARD OF IS *enters.*)

YO. (*Jumping up.*) You! Are you the Wizard of Is?

WIZARD OF IS. Yes, I am.

YO. Then help me! Please help me! I don't know. I can't tell by myself. Can you tell me?

WIZARD. Ask your question.

YO. Should I . . . I mean, if I take . . . look, I've been fooling around with drugs, and my trips are getting worse and so are my problems. Should I stop? Should I?

WIZARD. Look at me closely, Yo. Look and tell me who I am.

(YO *comes up to the* WIZARD'S *face and looks into his eyes.* YO *points at the side of the* WIZARD'S *head.*)

YO. That's my brain in your head. Those are my eyes. You're . . . you're . . . me! (YO *steps back, dazed.*)

WICKED WHICH. Curses!

YO. You mean, I'm my own Wizard? I already know what I have to do? What I should do? (WIZARD *nods.*) But . . . but that's hard. I've always had someone *tell* me what to do.

WIZARD. You can get dope whenever Yo want to, can't you?

YO. Yes. That's right.

WIZARD. No matter how you are punished or what you are told, when it comes right down to it, who sneaks off and takes it?

YO. Me, Yo.

WIZARD. Of course. Do you really think someone can be with you all the time—every minute—every second—just to tell you what you should do? Which decision to make?

YO. No, that would be impossible.

WIZARD. Has dope solved any of your problems?

YO. No, they're even worse than before, because now I worry so much about drugs that I . . . (*He cannot finish.*)

WIZARD. I see. Well, do you have shoes on or don't you?

YO. Can't you tell me?

WIZARD. No . . . I mean, yes, if you'll make up *our* mind.

YO. Oh, I see.

WIZARD. The thing of it here in the Land of Is, is . . . *it's entirely up to you.* Your scene is *your* scene, and *nobody* else's. The thing of it is *YOU* are the Wizard of your *own* Is.

(*Through some effect—perhaps lighting or a cloak—the* WIZARD *fades away, the scene becomes clear and real.*)

YO. (*Looking around, feels his feet.*) My feet! They're bare!

(*Curtain.*)

4

Stage directions

WHILE THE DRAMATIST IS WRITING a play, he must keep in mind that the play will be acted on a stage. The actors will speak the lines in front of a set and will be surrounded by props. The playwright should imagine what the play will look and sound like when it is presented for the audience. This means (1) the setting of the whole play or of part of the play, (2) any visual effects, (3) any sound effects, and (4) the movements of the actors and the tone of their speaking voices.

The playwright gives this information to the director and to the actors through the use of stage directions. It is important to remember that the stage directions are meant for the director and the actors and not for the audience. Actually, when the play is performed, the audience will not be aware of the stage directions at all. The theatergoers will only see the sets, the props, and lighting; they will hear the lines spoken and hear the sound effects. They will not be aware of the existence of the written instructions for the actors. Because the audience will not read the stage directions, all stage directions should only indicate things that can be revealed visually, as the furniture of a room, or that can be presented verbally, as the tone of voice to be used for certain lines.

Stage directions are always written from the point of view of the actors facing the audience. The drawing illustrates the most common positions on the stage.

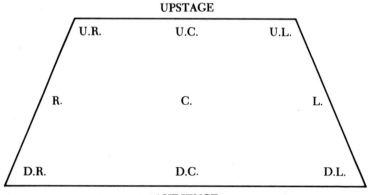

UPSTAGE

U.R.	U.C.	U.L.
R.	C.	L.
D.R.	D.C.	D.L.

AUDIENCE

U.R.—upstage right. R.—right. D.R.—downstage right.
U.C.—upstage center. C.—center. D.C.—downstage center.
U.L.—upstage left. L.—left. D.L.—downstage left.

In setting the scene, the audience should know the time and the place of the action they are witnessing if it is essential to their understanding of the play. There are four periods of time that might be indicated: the year, the season, the day, and the hour. Not all these are necessary to every play; the general rule is to supply the time of a play when it varies from the present and has a definite effect on the action.

Likewise, the audience should know the location of each scene. As a playwright, you can make the setting as general or as specific as you desire. You might want to indicate the general location of the scene: *The Hobbs's living room.* Or you might want to give an explicit description of the room: *The curtain opens on the Hobbs's living room, rather elegant in taste, but not over-done. As a matter of fact, there is a slight tightness of conservatism about the place. Everything is exactly where it belongs. At the entrance (stage right) is an archway leading to a foyer at the front of the house. Toward the back wall is a couch set in front of a bay window. There are several lamps and tables placed about the*

*room. At each side of stage front is a stuffed chair. Stage left has
a doorway leading to the hall. Downstage left has a stairway. It is
generally a bright room.*

There are various ways that you can indicate the time and
place of the play. Professional shows indicate both time and place
in the program that is given to each person in the audience. But
for your plays, this is usually too costly and time-consuming.
Occasionally, a narrator can tell the audience the time and location
of each scene. While this technique has been used by professional
dramatists, it should be avoided whenever possible. The use of a
narrator is too artificial; it destroys the illusion of reality that a play
usually tries to create. Instead of a narrator, use props and costumes
to indicate the time and the setting of the action: An artificial fire-
place and persons entering dressed in heavy coats create the impression of winter more realistically than will a narrator's stating
that it is the winter season.

Essential information that cannot be presented visually or
cannot be suggested by the actor's speaking voice must be given
in the lines of the play. For example, a stage direction might read:

SETTING: MRS. DYER *and her three children walk up the
sidewalk of the last house for rent in Vacton. Her husband
has been reported dead in the war. It is the depression
of 1972–73, and they can't afford any rent over ninety
dollars. And they are hungry. It is January 2, 1973.*

If this information is needed for the audience to understand the
action, then it must be presented in the lines of the play. Otherwise, there is no way for the audience to know that Mrs. Dyer's
husband is dead or that the family cannot afford more than ninety
dollars for rent. In practice, the student who wrote this stage
direction recognized the problem and inserted most of the information into the dialogue, as in the following excerpt:

TOM. Mom, when are we gonna find a house? My feet
hurt and I'm hungry.
MRS. DYER. We'll try this last house, and then we'll go
somewhere and see if we can find something to eat,
OK?

Although many problems with lighting are handled by specialists, the playwright is obliged to mention in a general manner

some lighting schemes that are vital to a basic understanding of the play. Following are typical situations in which a mention of lighting might be significant to a director:

1. *Character spotting.* A light shining on a character to indicate some special significance: that he is a ghost, that he has some special kind of protection, that he is marked for some future incident, or that he is especially important.

2. *Passing of time.* This is usually done by dimming or blacking out a scene, leaving the curtains open, and coming back up with lights on the scene. For example, the lights may come down to dim on a scene, and the characters exit (not that they have to). The lights come up from dim to bright, and the characters re-enter. You have changed the scene and you have never touched the curtains.

3. *Creating a scene within a scene.* Lights dim on the ongoing scene and a spotlight comes up on a scene that takes place adjacent to the previous scene, as in the following example:

> KATHY. (*Puts out her hands again and* RICK *takes them. The lights begin to fade on the coffee table, coming up on the parents' bedroom.* KATHY *gets up and walks into the new scene.*) Things were pretty good for me, I guess, until junior high. Then my parents started bugging me about everything—man, like, I mean everything. (*Black out completely on* RICK.)

4. *General effect.* This could be use of light to show something of significance, such as the moon or the star of Bethlehem in a Christmas play.

Another way for a playwright to visualize lighting is to think in terms of different colors suggesting different emotional tones. Red, yellow, and orange are warm colors that go with strong- and warm-feeling situations. They are effective in light comedies (yellow and orange) and in scenes showing anger (red) and scenes that are humorous or mysterious (red). Green, blue, and white are cold colors that fit impersonal, serious situations. These colors heighten moralistic scenes (blue and white), death scenes (green or blue), the other-world scenes (green or blue), and stark realistic scenes (white). The lighting effects can help to build the overall emotional mood of a scene.

The effect created by black light can add a dimension to your play. When a black light is on, only the special black-light paint and white clothing are visible to the audience. Both have a glowing effect. When the black light is off and the regular lights are on, the black-light paint is seen as any other flat-color paint. In one production of *The Wizard of Is,* the black light was used up until the closing scene when Yo's "mysterious world" became a back alley.

Just as basic lighting directions are necessary, so are those for sound. Because it is impossible to bring on stage large props, such as cars, airplanes, wild animals, and other such things, you must create them for the audience through sound effects. Other situations requiring sound include weather, telephones, doorbells, auto accidents, and broken windows. Music adds a dimension to your drama, as do periods of silence. If all these special sound effects are relevant to the basic action of your play, they must be included in your stage directions.

Stage directions for actors are by far the most extensive in plays. These directions can be divided into six areas:

1. General physical movement.
2. Indicating the person to whom an actor is speaking.
3. Physical indications of emotions.
4. Manner of delivering a line.
5. Handling of props.
6. Costumes.

Directions indicating entrances, exits, gestures, and crossings are some of the basic movements that must be indicated by stage directions. There are also scenes of pantomime—that is, scenes with actions but without words. Stage directions must be specific and accurate so that the director will understand the purpose of the scene even though he might alter some of the specifics. Following is an example of a scene in pantomime.

> SCENE 4: *Early Christmas morning. The* STEPHEN-
> SONS' *living room. The stage is deserted for five
> seconds. Then* B. J. *sneaks out, looks around, and
> begins to hurriedly trim the tree. He hears a sound
> and ducks behind a chair.* RUBY *comes sneaking out,
> looks around, then hurriedly begins to hang Christ-*

mas stockings. Another noise, and she ducks for cover, too. GRANDDAD *comes out, looks around, and is slightly startled that someone has started to trim the tree, but continues the job. Another sound, and he hides.* FATHER *comes out and is slightly startled to see the stockings hung, but he begins to fill them. Finally* GINNIE *comes out as* FATHER, *trying to hide, bumps into* GRANDDAD. *Everybody sticks out his head and laughs quietly. Each then puts a finger to his mouth and finishes the job he started. They complete the job, and sneak back to bed.*

Many times it is important for the sake of interpretation that the actor know that he is supposed to be talking to this character rather than that one. This kind of direction is written as follows:

MARCIA. I can't listen to this any longer. (*To* MOTHER.) Do I have to?

When necessary, an emotional interpretation may be stated to help an actor correctly interpret a line:

GREGORY. (*Clenching his teeth in hate.*) That's very funny!

However, be sure to avoid giving some emotional interpretation for almost every line because that impedes the actor's personal interpretation of the part. General instructions, such as "smiling," "frowning," or "laughing," as well as impossibly specific details, such as "really insisting on it," or "slightly raising a corner of his mouth," should be left to the actor and director to decide when the play is in production.

Finally, whenever a character handles props, stage directions are in order. They may be

1. To describe action: *"Nervously tearing open the letter."*
2. To extend characterization: *"Lifting his pizza with his little finger extended."*

However, don't try to develop character through constant directions. If a female role calls for a girl who is vitally concerned with her outward appearance, let the actress develop the physical characteristics that indicate this rather than filling up her lines with stage directions, such as when to check the mirror and when to straighten her hair.

If clothing is significant, this is usually outlined when the character first appears or reappears.

1. DR. RIBER *enters. He is dressed in suit and tie. He is impeccably dressed; nothing out of place. He sets his attaché case down and takes out a file.*
2. SCENE: *On the curtain, center stage right, are hung two props—a somewhat elegant door with a gold doorknob and gold door knocker, and to the left a many-paned window.* ROBBIE, *age twelve, is painting the door after having painted all the windows.* HILDA, *a woman over fifty, is now washing the windows and generally cleaning up around the city apartment.* ROBBIE *is dressed for the cold—a long scarf around his neck and peaked cap pulled down over his ears. The cap and scarf are too big.* HILDA *is also bundled up in worn and tattered clothes.*
3. *In the light* LES *appears dressed like a "hippie." He sports a full beard, beads, sandals, bell-bottom pants.*

As you can see, stage directions are an integral part of a play and have accepted forms. The best advice for stage directions might be to write them down as they come to you when composing, and what is missing or not needed will probably be discovered through a reading by someone else or in rehearsal.

~~~~~~

I'm Cold, Aren't You?
by Dana Smedra

Characters

JEFF PATTERSON	FLIPSY
SUZANNE HERSHEY	GLADYS
MARK KAY	NURSE
MARI	DR. BYERS
WAITRESS	

SCENE 1: *The scene takes place at an exclusive Eastern private school for the mentally disturbed.* SUZANNE *is seated alone in the recreation room.* JEFF PATTERSON *walks in.*

JEFF. Suzanne? (*She looks up at* JEFF.) That's your name, isn't it? When did you arrive? I'm Jeff Patterson. I've been here almost two years.

SUZANNE. Oh, I guess I arrived about three yesterday, but I'm just guessing.

JEFF. We usually don't have such a small number in the recreation room, but tonight's the Liberty Dance in the counselors' hall.

SUZANNE. Oh. That's very nice.

JEFF. Weren't you invited?

(SUZANNE *moves in her seat.*)

SUZANNE. No.

JEFF. That's too bad. I suppose you want to know why I didn't go?

SUZANNE. Well, I really can't say. . . .

JEFF. Well, you see—those counselors say I need a lot more therapy.

SUZANNE. Oh, that's too bad.

JEFF. Why don't you talk more?

SUZANNE. I really can't say.

JEFF. Oh. (*Pause.*) What are *you* here for?

SUZANNE. My parents say I need help.

JEFF. Oh, I see. Well, my parents are dead.

SUZANNE. Oh. That's too bad. (*She moves more; is uncomfortable.*)

JEFF. I s'pose you'd like to know how they died?

SUZANNE. No. I find that revolting.

JEFF. Oh, I didn't mean to be persistent.

SUZANNE. That's all right. I'm used to it.

JEFF. Oh, I see. (*Pause.*) Why?

SUZANNE. Why? Oh, my parents are very pushy. They always want me to have a boy friend and go to all the school dances and all, and I'm just not that type.

JEFF. Really? I hated those school socials, too.

SUZANNE. Oh, that's too bad . . . I m . . . mean that's, that's good.

JEFF. I hate this room.

SUZANNE. What? Oh, y . . . yes, I hate it, too. (*She looks around the room to examine it.*)

JEFF. I'm really not very sociable, are you?

SUZANNE. No. I don't like people.

JEFF. Do you like me?

SUZANNE. I really can't say at this point. I think I could.

JEFF. Well . . . would you like to go to the TV room with me tomorrow night?

SUZANNE. (*Perkily.*) I should say *not!*

JEFF. Oh . . . (*Pause.* JEFF *stands.*) Well, I'd better leave. I'm a very busy boy. (*He starts to exit.*) I'm . . . I'm, I'm terribly sorry.

SUZANNE. (*Gets up and follows him.*) Oh . . . Oh, Jeff—wait?! (JEFF *turns around and smiles.*) I'm sorry. Please come back and sit with me. I'm so sorry! (*She holds out her hand.* JEFF *doesn't react but follows her as they walk back to the recreation room.*)

SCENE 2: *Next night* JEFF *goes to* SUZANNE'*s room. He knocks softly.* SUZANNE *enters, wearing a casual dress.*

JEFF. (*Overanxious.*) Hi!

SUZANNE. Hello, Jeff. Are we going to the TV room?

JEFF. I was hoping you wouldn't change your mind.

SUZANNE. Oh, no! I think I'll enjoy it.

JEFF. Good! If we hurry, we can get the best chairs and first choice of programs.

SUZANNE. Oh, that's very nice! Let's hurry!

JEFF. (*Looks at watch.*) Yes—the TV room will be crowded tonight, and it's almost seven.

SUZANNE. (*Glances at him and smiles.*) I'm glad I'm going to the TV room with you, Jeff. I wouldn't go with anyone else.

JEFF. (*Shyly.*) Oh. (*Looks down at his feet.*) That's very nice of you, Suzanne. (*Looks up excitedly.*) And, I'm glad I'm going with you, too!

(*They walk together down the hall, smiling at each other. Both are silent.*)

JEFF. Well, here's the TV room. (*He looks down at his feet, biting his nails and pushes open the door.*)

SUZANNE. (*Looking around surprised.*) It's very nice. Let's sit in the front.

JEFF. I can't. (*Looks down at his feet.*)

SUZANNE. Oh. Well, let's sit down.

JEFF. Don't you want to know why?

SUZANNE. No. Let's sit down?

(*They sit quietly and a young man,* MARK KAY, *comes to ask what they would like to watch.*)

MARK. Hello, Jeff. I see you brought a friend. Mind if you introduce me?

JEFF. Oh—yes. This is Suzanne. (*He looks at her and smiles.*) Suzanne Hershey.

MARK. Hello, Sue. I'm Mark. Mark Kay. I'm *very* glad to meet you. That's what we need—some good-looking girls around this damn joint!

(SUZANNE *is silent and looks down.*)

MARK. Oh—one of the shy ones, huh? Well, anyway, Jeff, whadda wanta watch?

JEFF. Nothing!

MARK. Fine. See ya round, Sue. Bye. (*He goes to another boy.*)

JEFF. Suzanne? Are you upset?

SUZANNE. No. Let's please leave.

JEFF. (*Frankly.*) Well, just because Mark introduced himself to you is no reason why you should . . .

SUZANNE. Jeff, please—let's leave. (*She starts to sob.*)

(*She exits.* JEFF *follows. Both are now in the hall.*)

SUZANNE. Oh, Jeff! Now I've ruined your evening. I'm so ashamed!

JEFF. Please, don't be—you didn't embarrass *me!* Why I hate that Mark Kay. (*Looks toward TV room.*) He's a snob.

SUZANNE. Oh, my God—I've made a fool of myself.

JEFF. Let's go to our rooms and get some rest. You'll feel better tomorrow.

SUZANNE. Do you think so?

JEFF. What? Do ya think I'm crazy? Now come on!

(*They exit down hall.*)

SCENE 3: *The next morning at breakfast some girls,* MARI, FLIPSY, *and* GLADYS, *are gathered, talking.*

MARI. I hear that Suzanne Hershey girl has *already* gone to the recreation room alone with Jeff Patterson!

FLIPSY. Well, better still—last night they went to the TV room, and she threw a tantrum.

MARI. You don't say?

GLADYS. No, it's true! I've heard it myself!

FLIPSY. Well! *I* think it's just revolting!

(SUZANNE *walks past, as everyone is silent and watches her.*)

MARI. I bet you a dime to a doughnut she's going to Jeff's room.

FLIPSY. Oh, *my* God, no!

GLADYS. Look, she is!

(SUZANNE *turns—they all giggle and run off.* SUZANNE *comes to* JEFF'S *room and knocks softly, looking at the ground.*)

JEFF. Hello, Suzanne? I'm only half dressed, so don't come in.

SUZANNE. Well . . . I'll meet you at the breakfast table.

JEFF. No! . . . (*Pleading.*) Please wait!

SUZANNE. Well. . . . Well . . . al . . . all right.

(JEFF *enters with casual clothes on.*)

SUZANNE. You look very nice, Jeff.

JEFF. (*Looks at his feet.*) Oh . . . th . . . thanks, Suzanne; so do you.

SUZANNE. Oh, don't be silly. (*She giggles. They go to breakfast.*)

JEFF. It sure's snowy out.

SUZANNE. Oh, how lovely. Perfect weather for a snowball fight!

JEFF. Hey, yeah! Let's have a snowball fight after breakfast.

SUZANNE. Really? No! . . . I'll . . . I'll catch a cold.

JEFF. Yes! Yes! (*His mouth stuffed.*) Come on!

SUZANNE. Well, I don't think it's cold enough for me to catch a cold. . . .

JEFF. (*Pleading.*) Please?

SUZANNE. Well . . . al . . . all right, but let's dress warm!

(*Curtain*)

SCENE 4: SUZANNE *and* JEFF *are having a snowball fight. They stop, and are relaxing by a tree.*

SUZANNE. Jeff? Don't you wish we could leave? Sometimes I wish . . . that . . . that I was home with Mom and Dad, but I like being here with you, Jeff.

JEFF. Really? Suzanne ... I ... I ... like to be here with you, too. I wouldn't leave for the world! (*He raises his arms to form a world.*) Even if it is an institution!

SUZANNE. Really, Jeff?

JEFF. What ya think? I'm crazy?

(*They both laugh.*)

SUZANNE. Jeff ... I ... I think ... I love you, Jeff!

JEFF. I love you, too, Suzanne. I love every little inch of you! (*They stare at each other for a long time.*) Well, I think it's time we went in. I'm cold, aren't you?

SUZANNE. Well, sorta!

JEFF. Besides, I have an appointment with Dr. Byers. He says he has good news!

SUZANNE. Oh. That's very nice.

JEFF. *Come on,* Suzanne.

(SUZANNE *starts to run and laugh—she stops, puts out her hand and* JEFF *grabs it as they both go into the building.*)

JEFF. Well, you'd better change. I'll see you at lunch. Bye.

SUZANNE. Bye.

(JEFF *goes into* DR. BYER'S *office.* SUZANNE *exits.*)

NURSE. Go right in, Jeff. Dr. Byers is waiting.

(JEFF *walks in.* DR. BYERS *stands.*)

DR. BYERS. Well, Jeff—I'll come right to the point! ... sit down, my boy, sit down!

(JEFF *sits.*)

DR. BYERS. As I was saying ... we have decided that you can leave, Jeff.

(JEFF *jumps up.*)

JEFF. Really? (*He considers* SUZANNE, *looks down at his feet, bites his nails.*)

DR. BYERS. As I was saying, Jeff, you've progressed *so* well! (*He notices* JEFF.) What's wrong? Don't you want to leave, Jeff?

JEFF. Oh, no, I guess I *want* to leave! I'll be packed by ten.

DR. BYERS. Fine, fine. Do you think you can walk to the bus depot?

JEFF. Yes, I'll go to my Aunt Melissa's?

DR. BYERS. Yes, but you'll have to come back for checkups. All right?

JEFF. Of course, Dr. Byers!

DR. BYERS. Fine. Fine. See you tom . . .

JEFF. Good-by, Dr. Byers.

(JEFF *walks out sadly.*)

SCENE 5: *That afternoon after lunch,* SUZANNE *and* JEFF *are just finishing.*

JEFF. Suzanne! I . . . I . . . have to tell you . . . some . . . something. The . . . the . . . well, Dr. Byers . . .

SUZANNE. Jeff, aren't you feeling well?

JEFF. No! Because I have to leave!

SUZANNE. You have to leave? (*Pause.*) Oh, that's very nice. You'll have fun in the big world.

JEFF. Don't you care?

SUZANNE. Oh, yes . . . but it's your decision—you're free!

JEFF. It's not my decision! It's the doctor's!

(SUZANNE *stands.*)

JEFF. Don't you like me anymore?

SUZANNE. No! Jeff, I don't like you anymore, and everything I said this morning was a lie! A complete lie!

(*She exits.* JEFF *just sits stunned. A young lady, the* WAITRESS, *comes to clear the table.*)

JEFF. She doesn't like me! She doesn't like me anymore! I can't leave!

SCENE 6: *Next morning* JEFF *is packed, waiting and talking to* DR. BYERS. SUZANNE *enters.*

DR. BYERS. Well, Suzanne, Jeff is leaving. Aren't you happy for him? Now he'll be one of the big people!

SUZANNE. Yes . . . yes, I'm happy for Jeff. Well, I guess . . . it's not my position to say. It's Jeff's.

JEFF. Will you say good-by to me, Suzanne?

SUZANNE. Yes, Jeff. Yes . . . yes, I will.

DR. BYERS. Well, I'll let you two say good-by. I'll call you tomorrow, Jeff. Good-by.

JEFF. Yes, good-by, Dr. Byers.

(DR. BYERS *exits.*)

JEFF. Suzanne, I still love you, and I'll write you every day.

SUZANNE. Fine, Jeff. (*She moves away.*) There's not much I can say except good luck and good-by. Yes . . . bye, Jeff. (*She looks down at her feet.*) Well, you'd better hurry. You'll miss your bus.

JEFF. Yes, Suzanne. (*Pause.*) Good-by.

(SUZANNE *bends and gets his suitcase. They go out the door to the outside.* SUZANNE *hands him his suitcase as they each stare at each other.*)

JEFF. (*Still staring.*) Thank you, Suzanne, for everything.

SUZANNE. Jeff?

JEFF. Suzanne, I know you still love me, and I love you more than ever!

SUZANNE. Jeff? Let's run!

JEFF. Yes . . . Let's run!

(*They exit running, holding hands.* JEFF *leaves his suitcase behind.*)

~~~~~~

5

The beginning

A PLAY CAN BE DIVIDED into three parts: the beginning, the middle, and the resolution, or the end. The significance of this statement is clear only after looking at the idea of plot. It is the arranged pattern of related incidents and events in a play or other literary work. The plot, in turn, can be divided into several parts: (1) the initial situation that introduces the conflict, (2) the complications surrounding the conflict, which is also called rising action, (3) the climax, and (4) the final resolution or the dénouement. Usually each incident in a well-written plot is connected by a cause-and-effect relationship to the incidents that precede and follow it.

The basic purpose of the beginning of a play is to introduce the conflict. Some crisis is taking place in a character's life, and this person must make a decision that involves important consequences. When you write the beginning of a play, you are responsible for capturing the audience's attention immediately. Therefore, begin with action and/or lines that arouse significant unanswered questions in the minds of the theatergoers. Lines such as, "Oh, no, not again," will start your audience wondering what happened before and why is it so bad that it happened again. What you have done is created suspense. As discussed in Chapter 2,

the point of conflict and consequences is to provide suspense—
something that will always keep the audience wondering what is
going to happen next.

Look at the opening of *The Wizard of Is:*

> RABID. (*Stopping; laughing and pointing at* YO's *feet.*)
> Where's your shoes, Yo?
> YO. (*Looking down.*) I thought I had them on when I
> left. . . . (*Looks at his name card.*) Is that my name
> —Yo?

Immediately the audience will want to know:

1. Why must Yo have shoes on?
2. Why is Rabid laughing and pointing?
3. What kind of a place is it that has strange characters like
   Rabid and Yo?
4. Is Yo out of his element, and if he is, is he in danger?
5. What kind of a person doesn't know his name?

The beginning of a play should clearly indicate what the
fundamental conflict is and what the consequences are that will
follow from the major character's decision. In order to insure that
the conflict and its possible consequences are clearly defined for
the audience, the opening of a play should also provide an ade-
quate setting in terms of time and place. It should include any
background material that is needed for the understanding of the
play. Furthermore, all the major characters should appear in person, or be mentioned in the initial section of the play. If all major
characters are not revealed in the beginning, the audience will
feel cheated when you resolve the conflict by introducing a new
character at the end. When you introduce each character and have
him speak and act, you will begin to characterize him.

ACTIVITIES

1. Evaluate the following openings to student plays. Do they
introduce a conflict? Do they create suspense about the outcome of
the conflict? Also, write down any questions they arouse in your
mind.

a. *The curtain begins to open. The stage resembles a barnyard. Approximately thirteen turkeys are gathered around listening to an older, more distinguished turkey.*

OLD TURKEY. Nominations are now open!

FIRST TURKEY. I nominate George as president of the Save the Turkey Movement.

SECOND TURKEY. I want to nominate Marshal.

THIRD TURKEY. I say Sam Wobblegobble is our man.

FOURTH TURKEY. I move the nominations be closed.

SECOND TURKEY. I second it.

OLD TURKEY. Okay, let's vote. All in favor of George. (*A few turkeys vote yes.*) All in favor of Marshal. (*A few different turkeys vote for* MARSHAL.) All in favor of Sam. (*A majority of the turkeys vote for* SAM.) I am pleased to announce that you have elected Sam Wobblegobble as president of the Save the Turkey Movement. (*He looks around the group of turkeys looking for* SAM.) Sam, why don't you step up here and say a few words. (*The* OLD TURKEY *steps off the platform he has been standing on, and* SAM *steps up on the platform.*)

SAM. I am very honored to be chosen as president. I will try my best to save the rest of the turkeys, although there are only a few of us left.

b. *It is early in the day and the room is cluttered with moving boxes and assorted articles of furniture.* MR. *and* MRS. DAVIS *are sitting on boxes talking. Jeff sits on the window sill with tears in his eyes, watching the snow fall. Outside there is a deep blanket of snow on the ground.*

MOTHER. (*Glancing at her watch.*) Where could those movers be? They said they would be here at nine sharp.

FATHER. They're probably being delayed by the storm. You know the news report said there've already been two accidents since it started yesterday.

MOTHER. I sure will be glad to get out of this year-round blizzard, and no more delays on account of the weather.

(*The teakettle starts whistling, and* FATHER *gets up to get it.* MOTHER *notices her son and sits beside him on the window sill.*)

JEFF. (*Looking up at his* MOTHER *after a long pause.*)
Doesn't it ever snow in Florida?

MOTHER. Yes, it does, but not very often. I think their last
snow was eight years ago.

JEFF. How come we have to move somewhere where it *never*
snows? Christmas just isn't Christmas without snow.

MOTHER. You know we must go where your father can get
a job.

JEFF. But you can't have Christmas without snow.

MOTHER. We'll still have Christmas, and I tell you what, we
can get some of that fake snow and spray all over the
windows and it will be just as though we were here at
home.

JEFF. It just won't be the same, Mom.

(*The doorbell rings, and* MOTHER *goes to answer it.*)

FIRST MOVER. Hello. We're from the Acme Moving Company.
We're terribly sorry about the delay, but the roads are
completely iced over.

c. *The* COLONEL *and the* LIEUTENANT *are in a spy plane
over a Soviet-bloc country. The plane has just taken a
hit.*

LIEUTENANT. We've taken a hit, Colonel.

COLONEL. Let's get out of here. If we're still in this plane
when it crashes, we've had it.

LIEUTENANT. But, sir, if we bail out, we'll get caught and be
sent to Moscow.

COLONEL. I don't care. I'd rather be caught than die.

LIEUTENANT. Are you a coward, sir?

COLONEL. This plane is going to be totally destroyed, so
there is no need for us to get killed.

LIEUTENANT. Yes, there is, sir. We can't get caught.

COLONEL. But, what could they do to make us talk? I don't
want to die.

LIEUTENANT. You'll die before you ever get out of this plane.

2. Go back to page 14 and reread the example for an idea

for a play. Write a strong beginning for this idea. Try to:

1. Begin the action immediately.
2. Create suspense.
3. Introduce the conflict.

~~~~~~

You are now ready to try your hand at writing your own play. Up until now, you have probably been successful at performing the activities assigned you. However, if you are like the majority of students, the thought of writing an entire play will still leave you feeling helpless. And the success you have had up to now won't lessen that feeling. Consequently, seven specific suggestions are offered for deriving an idea for the beginning of a play.

1. Turn back to page 6 and repeat that activity. Derive your scene and your characters, and see if you can also relate a conflict and set of consequences that begin to work as an idea for a short play.

2. Turn back to page 18 and go over the list of general suggestions offered. Search your memory again for experiences that you can "stretch" into a good dramatic situation. Try brainstorming or creative association as two methods of discovering valuable ideas.

3. Below is a set of characters and settings. Devise some conflict and consequences for any one combination that you feel could provide you with an original idea.

Characters	Setting
Landlady and college student	church picnic
Kidnapper and spoiled nine-year-old boy	warehouse
Spy and spy's boss	a train
Hermit and sociologist	the hermit's cave
Old camper and tenderfoot	mountain
Football coach and not-too-bright player	locker room

Ghost and person who doesn't believe in ghosts	person's house
Substitute teacher and set of twins	classroom
Invader from another planet and the leader of a country	golf course

Guides
a. List the types of conflicts that might exist between a set of characters. For example, the spy might be more intelligent than his boss.
b. List the results of these problems. For example, the spy might want to be the one who gives the orders to the boss.

4. Perhaps you could attempt a play for a special day, such as Columbus Day, Thanksgiving; or for a historical incident, such as the landing of the Mayflower, the surrender at Appomattox Court House.

5. Think of a fairy tale or a nursery rhyme that might be the basis of a play for young children.

6. Try emphasizing character. Do this by answering the following questions in the order given:

a. Who is your character and what does he want?
b. What stands in the way of his goal(s)?
c. What decision does he have to make to overcome this hindrance? (Conflict!)
d. What does it look like his decision(s) will lead to? (Consequences!)

7. You could adapt a short story that you have enjoyed for the stage.

ACTIVITY

Write the beginning of your play. Spend some time going back over the activities you have already done and be ready to brainstorm and to use creative association to uncover ideas.

The Keys
by Jo Goeldner

Characters

MR. SMITH	SUZY
MRS. SMITH	TOMMY

SCENE: *In a house in city, medium income, not fancy but neat. Middle-aged lady and husband talking to babysitter.*

MRS. SMITH. Now remember, Suzy, absolutely no guests.

SUZY. Yes, Mrs. Smith. I understand. I hope you and Mr. Smith have a nice time. When will you be back?

MR. SMITH. (*Looks at watch.*) Well, the movie is out about ten-thirty, so probably, oh, about eleven.

SUZY. All right, good-by. I'll take good care of the baby.

MRS. SMITH. (*To* BABY.) Good-by, honey.

(MR. *and* MRS. SMITH *exit; Suzy closes the door and runs to the telephone, dials four digits, hangs up.*)

SUZY. Should I? (*She dials seven digits.*) Hello, is Tommy there? Oh, Tommy, the old bags are gone. Can you come over? Groovy, see you soon. Hurry!

(*Baby is in the kitchen in the highchair.* SUZY *walks into the kitchen, picks up half-empty jar of baby food, feeds baby, saying a little bit of baby talk. Takes jar to sink. Doorbell rings.*)

TOMMY. Suzy?

SUZY. Yeah, Tommy. I'm in the kitchen, come on in.

(*Tommy comes in and lays his keys on the highchair.*)

SUZY. We can go into the den. (*Exit.*)

(*Baby is in highchair playing with keys, then she starts sucking on them. She puts them completely in mouth. Takes them out. Puts them in. A choking sound. Switch to den.*)

SUZY. Hey, Tommy, I'll put on a record. What records do they have?

TOMMY. Oh, baby, there's a good one.

SUZY. Right, baby. Hey, I better go put the baby to bed.

TOMMY. OK. Hurry back. (SUZY *exits.*)

SUZY. Tommy, come here fast. (*Baby slumped in chair,* TOMMY *comes running in.*)

SUZY. Tommy, is she dead?

TOMMY. Hell no, she better not be.

SUZY. Oh, God, what can I do!

TOMMY. Listen here, Suzy, I wasn't allowed to use the car tonight.

(*They start hitting the baby on the back. Sound of a car.* SUZY *jumps up.*)

TOMMY. Should I leave?

SUZY. Tommy . . . it's your keys. Can we . . . oh, help!

(*Car door slams, voices in background.*)

TOMMY. I'll leave. No, they've seen the car already.

(*Door opens, and the* SMITHS *enter.* SUZY *runs to door.*)

SUZY. Mrs. Smith, I'm sorry. (*Bursts into tears.*)

(*The three walk into the kitchen.*)

MR. SMITH. Suzy, who is th——

MRS. SMITH. My baby, what have they done to my baby! Did they —oh, my poor baby. What in God's name did they do to you?

(MR. *and* MRS. SMITH *kneel over baby in background.*)

TOMMY. (*Quietly.*) Suzy, come here.

SUZY. Huh? (*Still crying.*)

TOMMY. Try to calm down. We are really in trouble! We've got to do something.

SUZY. But what?

TOMMY. Call an ambulance, and hurry. I'll try mouth-to-mouth resuscitation.

(SUZY *leaves for telephone, and* TOMMY *goes in and starts mouth-to-mouth.* SUZY *comes in.*)

SUZY. They're coming.

(*Faraway siren gets closer. No sounds, faces tell story. Siren pulls up. Escort* MRS. SMITH *and baby outside. Siren fades.*

Clock—nine-thirty. Clock—eleven-thirty. Ring of telephone.
MR. SMITH *answers.*)

MR. SMITH. (*In background.*) Hello, hello. Oh, thank God, I'll tell the kids. Well, Tommy, your keys are at the hospital. You can pick them up any time.

TOMMY. Thank you, sir. I don't think I'll be needing them up for quite a while.

(TOMMY *looks at* SUZY. *Blackout.*)

6

The middle

ONCE THE PLAYWRIGHT HAS a good conflict, he then has to invent some problems to extend his conflict to keep it from resolving too quickly. You know the old adage that a person doesn't appreciate anything too easily won. This same idea applies to an audience. Think of how it would be if you, as a member of an audience, saw the beginning of a movie and then the final reel showing immediately how the story ended. You would feel cheated, because part of the fun of the movie is going through the trials and tribulations with hero and heroine. When they come to the final scene, you have developed some feelings about what happens to them. The middle of a play, in other words, is the place where the audience has a chance to learn to feel for the characters.

Structurally, the middle of a short play begins as soon as the initial situation has introduced the conflict, all the major characters have been mentioned, and suspense has been created. The purpose of the middle section of a play is to intensify the suspense by adding complications. The complications are merely the actions taken by the major character or by the forces working against him. Because each of the complications increases the conflict, this pattern is called rising action. As one complication follows another, the conflict grows in intensity until something must happen. The conflict must be resolved in some way.

In a short play the number of complications you can add to a plot is limited. A short play has one basic conflict that is intensified by adding anywhere from one to three complications.

When you are thinking about complications to add to your play, keep the following guidelines in mind. First, the complications of a serious play should be probable. In life, many unusual things are possible, but serious plays are based on complications that are likely to happen. In other words, look for complications that are probable rather than possible. For example, in *The Keys* (p. 57), the conflict is intensified by having the baby swallow a set of keys. Knowing that babies put almost everything they can reach into their mouths makes this complication both possible and probable. Another possible complication might be as follows: a criminal, just escaped from prison, recognizes Tommy's car as that of the doctor who was responsible for having the convict's parole turned down. He breaks into the house and threatens to kill the baby if Tommy does not drive him out of town. While this complication is possible—it could happen—it is not likely that it would. In this case, the probable event is more effective as a complication than the event that is only possible.

Second, the complications of a serious play should be well motivated. This means that what happens in the play should, in general, follow from the personality of the major character or characters. The complications should be the consequences of certain decisions made by the major figures or by forces opposed to the major characters. And the decisions should be in keeping with the personality of the person making the decision.

Complications in a comedy are not limited as severely by these two restrictions as are the complications in a serious play. Comedy can be based on sudden changes in character, improbable events, sudden strokes of good fortune. Many successful comedies resolve their plots by revealing hitherto unsuspected information. While these sudden changes and improbable events would weaken the effect of a serious play, comedy thrives on surprise and on having the unexpected happen.

The point is that the complications should follow a definite pattern. Because the scope of drama is so broad, there is no one pattern that will apply to every play. The basic pattern for a serious play is a linking of events together by means of cause and effect. The critic and novelist E. M. Forster briefly illustrated what is meant by a cause-and-effect relationship between events. Forster said that the statement "The king died and then the queen died" narrated two events. However, the statement "The king died and then the queen died of grief" is a plot. It is a plot based on the cause-and-effect relationship between two events: the death of the king caused the death of the queen. Each complication should carry out the implications of what has gone before.

Another pattern is the addition of complications united thematically. Each complication presents a variation of the central theme. This pattern is called the episodic plot.

ACTIVITIES

1. Read the following "middles" of student plays. Each represents a different complication pattern. Describe the pattern used in each.

  a. *Initial situation:* Any increase in air pollution will cause the death of all living creatures. The two prisoners do not realize this, and they are surprised that the people do not use fire or work in factories. The people have been reduced to a primitive existence.

   In the factory. All dark, light on prisoners.

JULES. (*With conviction.*) Those people are crazy as bedbugs. Where are we anyway? I think it's some kind of paper mill.

HARRY. (*Looking around.*) I've been trying to remember something, and now I remember it. I read in a magazine —oh, way back in 1970, that if the pollution didn't stop, in twenty years we'd all be crazy or deaf. I . . . I guess they're all crazy. God, it's cold. See you in the morning.

   (*Next morning.*)

JULES. Hey, I've been thinkin' 'bout last night. We gotta help those guys. I don't wanna be one of the only sane people in the world.

HARRY. Yeah, like help 'em start a fire or . . . I got it! We'll
start the factory for them. But first we gotta help them
with the fire.

(*They walk out to see the people huddled around, eating
raw meat.* JULES *walks up to the* PROFESSOR, *takes a
match out of his pocket, and starts to light the fire. With
a shriek, the* PROFESSOR *grabs* JULES's *arm, shouting.*)

PROFESSOR. No Black. It is death! No more. (*The savages
leap to their feet and yell in unison.*)
PEOPLE. No Black! Professor say no!

(JULES *is astounded, then he regains his confidence.*)

JULES. What the hell do you think you're doing?

(JULES *shakes free and trys again. The largest savage
starts toward* JULES *in fury.* JULES *and* HARRY *run back
to the protection of the factory.*)

HARRY. What do they mean "No Black"? Who's this professor?
JULES. And why can't they light a fire? It's for their own
comfort!
HARRY. Damned if I know. Remember, they're crazy. All of
them.
JULES. The sooner we start this, the better. I think I know
how. I used to work in a paper factory once.
HARRY. Yeah? Well, let's get those guys to help us. I'll go
get 'em.
JULES. Once they start working, we'll be able to get them
civilized; hurry it up and get them.

(HARRY *opens the door and goes to get the* PROFESSOR.
Meanwhile, JULES *starts the smokestacks. Black smoke
pours out.* JULES *walks around adjusting gadgets, when
he hears a mob outside.* HARRY *dashes in exhausted, pant-
ing.*)

HARRY. Run, run, they're going to kill us!
JULES. What?
HARRY. Hurry! It's the smoke. They'll kill us.

(*Convicts are panic-stricken and run around in horror.*)

b. *Initial situation:* Tom and Bill decide to use the money they have collected for UNICEF to buy a sled.

TOM *and* BILL *are seated alone at the breakfast table. It is the morning after Halloween.*

TOM. Boy, we sure got a lot of money last night, didn't we Bill?

BILL. We sure did. Thirteen whole dollars. Finally, after all these years we'll be able to get a new sled.

TOM. You sure did a good job last night. You sounded so sincere about UNICEF you almost made me want to give you some money.

BILL. Why don't we go to Gibson's tonight and get the new sled? I can't wait to get it and try it out.

TOM. Yeah, me too.

BILL. (*Violently, almost hissing.*) Shut up! Here come Mom and Dad.

(MOTHER *and* FATHER *enter, sit down, and begin to eat breakfast.*)

MOTHER. Hi, boys. How did it go last night? Did you get a lot of candy?

TOM *and* BILL. (*At the same time.*) We sure did!

MOTHER. Well, that's nice. (*She turns to* FATHER.) I was so glad last night when I saw so many people participating in the UNICEF drive.

(TOM *and* BILL *glance at each other.*)

FATHER. So was I. I am sure that our school drive will earn a lot of money for UNICEF. I'm glad so many children are taking an active interest in other children around the world. UNICEF is such a worthy cause because it helps so many people.

(*When the conversation began,* TOM *and* BILL *had been sitting up tall and proud of themselves. As the conversation goes on, their shoulders begin to droop more and more.*)

MOTHER. Yes, I know. (*She looks at the boys.*) Boys, did you know that UNICEF buys food for starving children?

You are really lucky. You have so much food while other children around the world hardly have any.

FATHER. UNICEF also buys clothing for very poor families around the world. Every day we sit here and take clothes and food for granted, while other children feel lucky they even have any at all. I feel UNICEF has to be one of the greatest organizations in the world, and I'm glad to be a part of it.

MOTHER. I agree. (*Turning back to the boys.*) Would either of you like some more oatmeal?

BILL. (*Very low and sort of hoarse.*) N-no, thank you.

(*The boys sit silently with their heads drooped. After a few moments,* TOM *speaks.*)

TOM. (*Very softly.*) May we please be excused?

MOTHER. Of course, boys.

(*The boys rise and leave as the curtain closes.*)

SCENE 3

NARRATOR. The third scene takes place in Gibson's Sporting Goods Store that evening.

(*The curtain opens. The scene is that of a sporting goods store. A cashier's stand is at one end of the stage. A cashier is standing behind the stand doodling around doing something. There is a bright, shiny, new sled hanging on the wall. There are also other sporting goods items here and there. There is a UNICEF receptacle on the cashier's stand. The two boys enter from one side of the stage, talking with each other. Neither sees the sled.*)

BILL. But do you really think we should go ahead and get the sled? After what Mom and Dad said this morning. I—

TOM. (*Interrupting.*) I know! I know. I feel kind of lousy, too. I just can't make up my mind. Should we get the sled or not? We've got all the money for it, but—

(*Both boys raise their heads and see the shining sled on the wall at the same time. Their reasons for not getting the sled are forgotten. They both run to the sled and start examining it.*)

BILL. (*Really excited.*) Wow, just look at it! Isn't it a beaut?

TOM. (*Excited.*) Yeah! It's even got a steering device on it.

BILL. I bet it could even beat Randy Bowman's streamlined sled.

(*The* CASHIER *approaches the boys.*)

CASHIER. Can I help you, boys?

TOM. Yes. We'd like to buy this sled.

c. *Initial situation:* Yo is confused as to whether or not he is wearing shoes. His confusion is the result of taking drugs.

(MAD HADDER *comes out walking on his knees, carrying a head under his arms. He has a huge hat on. He runs right into* YO.)

MAD HADDER. (*Very angry.*) Why don't you watch where you're going? Can't you see I'm taking this head to the Wicked Which?

YO. (*Drawing back.*) Why—that's my head! (*Frightened, feeling his own head.*) Where did you get it?

MAD HADDER. When you've spaced out on acid as many times as I have . . . (*He makes a grotesque face and laughs hideously.*) you'll be a Mad Hadder, too! (*Looking at* YO's *feet.*) I like your shoes.

YO. (*Looking down.*) I don't have any on. I mean . . . I didn't think I had any on . . . until now. . . .

MAD HADDER. (*Doubling up with laughter.*) I'm a Hadder and you're a Had-Any. Oh, the Which will love it—love it!

YO. (*Frightened, but angry.*) Shut up! Shut up and go away! (*Shakes his head in an effort to clear it.*) I wish this whole thing would go away.

(MAD HADDER *exits.* YO *continues to walk to the opposite side of the stage. A roar is heard off stage.* YO *pulls back.* LYIN *enters, roaring.*)

LYIN. Where do you think you're going? And get some shoes on!

YO. But I was just told I had some on.

LYIN. (*Roaring.*) The Mad Hadder told you that . . . (*Coming up face-to-face with* YO.) didn't he? Didn't he?

YO. (*Pulling back.*) Well . . .

LYIN. Come on, don't lie to me. Who are you going to believe, a Mad Hadder . . . or me, Lyin? (YO *doesn't respond.*) It's a cinch you're having trouble believing yourself, though, isn't it? (YO *nods.*) Well, shape up or the Wizard of Is won't talk to you.

YO. The Wizard of Is?

LYIN. Yes. He should be here any minute. (*Looking back over his shoulder.*) I just hope he gets here before the Wicked Which.

YO. The Wicked Which?

LYIN. Of course. . . . Which escape, Which trip, Which narcotic . . .

YO. You, too?

LYIN. No! (*Pointing at* YO.) *Yo,* too! (YO *looks away guiltily.*) Oh, come on. *Yo* knows it. *Yo* just wants to have somebody else solve his problems for *Yo.* Just needs somebody to answer his which Which. Am I right? (*No response from* YO.) Of course, I am. You're trying to find the Wizard of Is before it's too late. Well, good luck. But the answer you get won't be what you think. (LYIN *exits.*)

YO. (*Calling.*) Wait a minute! What do you mean by that?

(YO *starts walking off the way he came, hopping and feeling his feet as he goes.* WICKED WHICH *enters, cackling.*)

WICKED WHICH. Hello, young man. What a beautiful shoe you have on.

YO. But, I have two shoes on. . . . I mean, I don't have any shoes on. . . . I mean . . . do I only have one shoe on? For my sake, which is it?

WICKED WHICH. It's always which! It's never one or two or three. It's always *which!*

YO. What are you talking about?

WICKED WHICH. You know very well what which—LSD, cocaine, mescaline, heroin, speed—which Which is all that's left to you now.

YO. But I'm not hooked on anything yet!

WICKED WHICH. (*Rubbing her hands.*) Oh, Yo and I know . . . Yo can tell me which Which. . . . Yo . . . which Which? YO. But I'm not, honest.

WICKED WHICH. (*Getting angry.*) Look at your feet! (YO *looks.*) Which has the shoe?

YO. I'm not sure.

WICKED WHICH. Neither does, stupid.

YO. (*Confused.*) But you said . . .

WICKED WHICH. Both do, stupid!

YO. But . . .

WICKED WHICH. Only your right foot. Feel it. Tell me. (YO *feels his right foot.*) That's your left. I said right. Which is it? (*Coming up to* YO *like a lawyer cross-examining.*) Which—which—which?

2. Review the beginning for the dramatic idea given in Chapter 2, and write a middle part.

3. The general concept to keep in mind when working on the middle section is that this presents the rising action of the play. Emotions become most intense, actions become most severe, and consequently the suspense builds to its height. With this in mind, write a middle for the play you began in Chapter 5.

~~~~~~

Accomplices
by James H. Norton

Characters

JUDGE	MANKIND
PROSECUTOR	LAWYER
AIR	POLICEMEN
WATER	POWER
FUTURE	COMFORT

MANKIND'S CHILDREN *and* GRANDCHILDREN

SCENE: *A courtroom. There is a judge behind his bench. Next to the judge's bench is a witness chair. In front of the bench are two tables. At one table sit* PROSECUTOR *and the plaintiffs,* AIR *and* WATER. *At the other table sit* LAWYER *and* MANKIND.

JUDGE. (*Pounding gavel.*) Order. Order in the court. The case of

Mankind versus Air and Water will begin. Prosecution, bring
up your first witness, please.

PROSECUTOR. Thank you. Will Air please take the stand? (AIR *gets
up and sits in the witness chair*.) Air, will you please tell us
in your own words what Mankind did on the 27th of October,
1601, through the present?

AIR. At first I wasn't worried
By the little puffs of smoke,
But then his puffs got bigger,
Quite more than just a joke.
Then Mr. Ford got going
With engines and with fumes,
And the world wars added greatly—
I'm almost totally consumed.

LAWYER. (*Jumping up*.) Objection. "Almost totally" is a generali-
zation which offers no definite evidence to the case.

JUDGE. Objection sustained. Proceed.

PROSECUTOR. Try to be more specific in your answers, Air.

AIR. Yes, sir.

PROSECUTOR. Now, Mankind needs you to exist. Why would he be
so ravaging on something that he *should* respect?

AIR. Man's mind can only see so far.
He thinks that I am endless,
But give each just one motor car,
And he'll pollute me to excess.

PROSECUTOR. Thank you. Your witness.

LAWYER. (*Stepping up*.) Hasn't my client manufactured many
things that, when put into Air, sweeten it?

AIR. I wouldn't need sweetness
If he wouldn't pollute me.

LAWYER. Just answer the question, please.

AIR. Oh, perfume's all right—
Just don't overshoot me.

LAWYER. Thank you. That will be all.

JUDGE. Will the Prosecutor bring in the next witness?

PROSECUTOR. Will Water take the stand, please? (WATER *steps
up*.) Will you tell the court in your own words what crimes
Mankind has committed against you in—say—just the last
fifty years?

WATER. I will try to make it brief.
For fifty years just no relief

Of garbage running in my streams,
Chemicals and bleach for jeans,
Factory and foundry waste
Have killed the fish and birds in haste,
And since Mankind has always drunk me
I think it's time he did un-junk me.

PROSECUTOR. Yes, I agree.

LAWYER. Objection. The prosecutor is here to elicit facts, not commiserate with the witness.

JUDGE. Objection overruled. I agree, too!

PROSECUTOR. Your witness.

LAWYER. (*Walking up.*) I have only one question, your honor. Water, isn't most of you salty and undrinkable? And isn't that a bigger crime against Mankind than Mankind's small abuse of you?

WATER. My salt has always served to clean—
A job that used to be routine;
So much filth now floods the ocean
My salt is not so strong a potion.

LAWYER. (*Shrugging.*) Oh, well. No more questions.

JUDGE. Will the prosecution call the next witness?

PROSECUTOR. That's all for now, your honor.

JUDGE. Will the defense call the first witness?

LAWYER. I have only one witness, your honor—the defendant, Mankind. Will Mankind take the stand, please? (MANKIND *sits in the witness chair.*) What is your defense? In your own words, tell us about these so-called horrible crimes that have been laid at your feet.

MANKIND. I can only say that . . . (*He jumps to his feet and points into the audience.*) Power and Comfort are the real perpetrators of these crimes!

(POWER *and* COMFORT *jump up from their seats in the audience and run down the aisle.*)

JUDGE. Stop them!

(*Two* POLICEMEN *at the back door come down the aisle and stop* POWER *and* COMFORT.)

JUDGE. Bring them up here.

(*The four mount the stage.* POWER *and* COMFORT *go to stand on either side of* MANKIND, *who is still seated in the witness chair.*)

MANKIND. All right, you guys. Tell them the facts.

POWER *and* COMFORT. (*Together.*) We told him to think of himself,
Put the Future of Man on the shelf.
So he smoked up the skies
Building Comfort king-size
In a push-button home did he dwell.

MANKIND. There! You see? *They made* me do it!

POWER *and* COMFORT. Don't put the blame all on us,
Or we'll cause a considerable fuss—
It was your lazy craze
And shortsighted ways
That did make us both dangerous.

(*There is a jarring note on a trumpet, and* FUTURE *comes down the aisle.*)

JUDGE. Who's this?

PROSECUTOR. (*To* FUTURE.) Am I glad to see you! (*To* JUDGE.) Your honor, at this time I would like to call on my star witness.

JUDGE. This is highly irregular . . . but considering the circumstances, proceed.

LAWYER. Objection!

JUDGE. Overruled!

PROSECUTOR. Will Future please take the stand? (FUTURE *sits in the witness chair.*) Future, what can you bring to us that may shed new light on this case?

FUTURE. I don't like to talk;
I don't like to squawk.
Just look and you'll see
Exhibit A, Exhibit B.

(*Enter down the aisles* MANKIND's CHILDREN *and* MANKIND's GRANDCHILDREN, *wearing gas masks.*)

MANKIND. (*Jumping up, horrified.*) Oh, no! Not my kids! My grandchildren! (*He sits down and buries his head in his hands.*)

LAWYER. Objection! This treatment is cruel and inhuman and . . .

FUTURE. (*Breaking in and going to the front of the stage.*) *And necessary!*
I am their only emissary.
Those still unborn

Cannot voice their scorn
Of the ways of Mankind,
Whose world's in a bind.
You must stop pollution;
They need a solution
So their Air will be pure
And their Water secure.
So Mankind, take heed
And fulfill their need.
Their present's tomorrow!
Don't let it be sorrow
They inherit from you.

(*Turning back to* MANKIND.)

What you've done, now undo!

(FUTURE *sits down at the* PROSECUTOR'*s table, as do all the* CHILDREN *and* GRANDCHILDREN.)

JUDGE. Will the defendants please step forward and approach the bench. (MANKIND, POWER, *and* COMFORT *step up to the bench.*) Mankind, Power, Comfort . . . you have been responsible for getting our world into a position where you might kill us all—forever! I now sentence you to fifty years of hard labor in laboratories, homes, factories, and schools, working day and night to discover solutions to your shortsighted and selfish ways. And after that fifty years, you will be retried; and if you have labored well and hard, perhaps your children and grandchildren who will be sitting in my place will be able to judge you less harshly. (*To the* POLICE-MEN.) Take them away.

(POLICEMEN *take away the three as the curtain closes.*)

7

The responsible resolution

WRITING AN ENDING TO A PLAY is not as difficult as writing a responsible resolution. The resolution is the final section of a play. However, using the term *resolution* rather than *ending* emphasizes that this is the place to resolve the conflict, not simply to end it. A responsible resolution answers all questions aroused in the beginning part of the play and resolves the basic conflict with something directly related to that basic conflict. Irresponsibly ending a play makes an audience feel they have been cheated. For example, in the dramatic idea presented on page 14, the assumption will be that the individual decided to cut school and go with the group to the party. Several times in the middle of the play, other conflicts and obstacles appeared, and the audience was afraid that the person would be caught. But each time, the person escaped, although each time it was a closer call. Now it is only 1:00 P.M., and the group decides to walk to the local market to buy food. The main character protests, but to no avail. On the way to the store, they are seen by one of their teachers. The group knows that the school authorities will learn they skipped school. You could now *end* the play by having the teacher killed in an auto accident, and thus save the group from discovery. But, can you see how this is cheating the audience and is not a responsible resolution? You simply ended it conveniently without much imagination, and the audience is angry because you solved the conflict with a quirk of fate. This type of resolution is similar to the stories that place a character in an extremely precarious situation and evade any real solution by having the ending be "And then I woke up."

Of course, the question, then, is How do you go about responsibly resolving a play? Perhaps your first thoughts should be in terms of what you are trying to accomplish with the play. Basically, a play is to entertain. Your overall goals should include the creation of an interesting plot with fast-moving action, dynamic characters, and significant conflict and its consequences that rise in intensity. The resolution of a comedy might be merely to entertain and amuse the audience. However, the resolution of a serious play will say something to the audience that goes beyond the primary purpose of simple entertainment. Two playwrights could take identical beginning and middle parts and illustrate two entirely different philosophies, depending on how they resolve the play. In the play *The Wizard of Is* (p. 32) another author could have let Yo remain in a state of confusion and crumple to the ground, unable to understand what the Wizard had meant. This would be a tragic or pessimistic ending, which implies that when a person gets as far into drugs as Yo has, it is too late for any kind of help. The ending in this text, on the other hand, implies that once a person discovers that he is the one who has to make his decisions, he can make a meaningful distinction between right and wrong, or good and evil, and overcome his problem.

Moreover, your resolution might be one that projects some specific kind of morality, such as "Honesty is the best policy." (See *Treat or Trick,* p. 9.) Here the purpose of your play is to teach a lesson. Whereas the resolution of *The Wizard of Is* attempts to make an overall comment about the nature of life (optimistic or pessimistic), this type of resolution is primarily and specifically didactic.

Another turn your play might take through the kind of resolution you adopt is to become some kind of protest. In the resolution of *The Wizard of Is,* you might put the blame for Yo's failure to meet his responsibility to make his own decisions on his parents, on his education, or on the values of the culture. Whatever resolution is selected, it should follow logically from the action that has preceded it.

There are several possible ways to resolve the problem of the person who, while cutting school, was recognized by a teacher. If you believe that a person who places social prestige above the honor and responsibility of having a lead in the school play should be brought to justice, perhaps your next scene will take place in the principal's office where the person will be properly punished. On the other hand, if you feel that this person was taken advantage of by the group and should be allowed to escape unpunished, perhaps your next scene will be in the teacher's home where the teacher will be convinced by the group not to tell the authorities. Then, too, you might feel that life usually works out to be a compromise. In this case, you might allow the person to perform in the current play, but later have him suspended from school as well as barred from ever acting in any other school plays. There are many other possibilities: the person might use superb acting ability to fool everyone; the person might confess and disavow deceitful ways, receiving some mild punishment; the person might protest by trying to sue the school for keeping him out of the play on the grounds that moral behavior should not be related to a student's extra-curricular activities, and so on. The point is to work within the basic conflict, being aware that how you resolve the problem will imply a philosophical perspective, a lesson of life, or a protest against something.

ACTIVITY

Read the following plays and evaluate their resolutions. Does the resolution follow from the previous action of the play? or is it artificial?

They Do Exist
by Reda Hansen

Characters

DOUG MARSHALL	NURSE TRAPP
CATHARINE SIMMS	DOCTOR MORSE

The curtain rises on a hospital room. DOUG MARSHALL *is in the bed, and a* NURSE *is leaning over him, shaking him gently. She is prim and neat, and not the least bit pretty. She's tall and her legs are stringy.* DOUG's *face is scratched slightly.*

NURSE. Mr. Marshall, Mr. Marshall, are you awake?

DOUG. (*Stirs as he awakens.*) Huh, what?

NURSE. (*Leans back.*) Ah, you're awake. (*Calls.*) Doctor! He's come out of it.

DOUG. Wha—what happened?

NURSE. (*Properly.*) Now *you* be quiet. (DOCTOR MORSE *enters.*) He seems to be OK, Dr. Morse.

DOCTOR. (*Cheerfully.*) Fine, let me examine him. You may leave, Miss Trapp.

NURSE. Thank you, Doctor. (*Exit.*)

DOCTOR. Now, let's see. (*Takes out tongue depressor.*) Open wide. Well, looks fine in there. (*Produces pocket flashlight.*) Now, let's look in your eyes. Good, good. (*Puts thumbs in front pockets and leans back.*) Well, you seem to be fine.

DOUG. What happened?

DOCTOR. (*Still cheerfully.*) You were in an auto accident.

DOUG. Yes, yes, I know. Did anyone die?

DOCTOR. There was a man in the car you hit. He was dead on arrival.

DOUG. How's Cathy?

DOCTOR. Cathy? Oh! Miss Simms. Fine, fine. She regained consciousness this morning. She'll be fine, just fine.

DOUG. When can I see her?

DOCTOR. Well, she's in the women's ward. When you're discharged probably.

DOUG. Probably?

DOCTOR. In all likelihood. Well, really must go now. You'll be fine.

DOUG. Thank you, Doctor, for everything.

ACT II

The scene is a park. There is a bench in the center of the stage. CATHARINE *sits there, looking constantly to her right. She is beautiful. She's small and slender, with long flowing hair. She wears a stylish dress.* DOUG *enters. They embrace.*

DOUG. Cathy! I worried so much about you! Are you all right?

CATHY. (*Nods.*) Uh-huh. Just a few bruises, but nothing that shows. (*She touches a scratch on his face, he winces.*) Oh, does it hurt, darling? (*They sit on bench.*)

DOUG. No, not much. We were lucky, you know. We could have been killed like—like . . .

CATHY. Like that man in the other car.

DOUG. You know?

CATHY. Yes, they told me.

DOUG. Didn't that hospital strike you as strange? I mean, well, different.

CATHY. (*Nods.*) Yeah, it really was. Did you notice that all the nurses were old. There wasn't one young one. And all the doctors in my ward were female. Not one man.

DOUG. Everything seemed so regimented. Suppose a man and woman both had heart trouble. Wouldn't they ordinarily put them in the same ward?

CATHY. Right. But there they had it separated into male and female.

DOUG. It's strange, really strange. I just have this eerie feeling that something has happened that we don't know about. Maybe when we were both unconscious.

CATHY. (*Shudders.*) Oooh, don't say that. It makes chills run up my spine.

DOUG. I'm sorry. Let's change the subject.

CATHY. You know, I can't help wondering what that man was like.

DOUG. What man?

CATHY. The man who—who died. Don't you ever wonder what people are like, people you don't know, like maybe someone you pass on the street? I just can't help wondering who that man was and whether he had a wife and kids and all that.

DOUG. Yeah, I know what you mean. But I guess it's too late now to find out.

CATHY. I guess so. Doug, how long were we unconscious?

DOUG. I don't know. I never thought to ask.

ACT III

The scene is a dress shop. Racks of women's uniforms are scattered about. There is a full-length mirror. DOUG *and* CATHY *enter. A matronly woman in a uniform comes out.*

WOMAN. May I help you? (CATHY *and* DOUG *are glancing around.*)

DOUG. (*To* CATHY.) Are you sure this is the place?

CATHY. (*Shrugs.*) Well, it says "Dress Shop."

WOMAN. May I help you?

CATHY. Yes, we're looking for a wedding dress.

WOMAN. A wedding dress?

CATHY. Yes. We plan to be married. (CATHY *and* DOUG *clasp hands and smile at each other.*)

WOMAN. I'm not sure I heard you right. You say you want a wedding dress?

DOUG. (*Loudly.*) Yes, a wedding dress.

WOMAN. (*Quickly.*) Hush! Keep your voice down. There are spies everywhere. You don't want to get arrested, do you?

DOUG. Arrested?

WOMAN. Well, you don't think they'd allow you to get married, do you?

CATHY. They?

WOMAN. (*Hastily.*) You'd better leave. If they come, I'll pretend I never saw you. Now go, scat!

(CATHY *and* DOUG *look at each other and then leave slowly. Their voices are heard from backstage.*)

CATHY. I just don't understand what's going on. Why can't a couple be married?

DOUG. I don't know. Something is going on that we don't know about. . . .

ACT IV

The scene is the park bench. It's fall now. Leaves are scattered about the ground. DOUG *is sitting on the bench, his head in his hands.* CATHY *enters.*

DOUG. Cathy! How are you? Why, you've been crying.

CATHY. (*Sadly.*) Yes.

DOUG. Why?

CATHY. (*A wild look in her eyes.*) They killed me.

DOUG. What?

CATHY. *They.* They kidnapped me and took me to this room. They had a man dressed up to look like you. He had a knife. They wanted me to think that you were going to kill me. (*Sobs.*) Oh, Doug, it was terrible!

DOUG. Cathy, are you all right? It's all in your mind.

CATHY. No! It was real.

DOUG. No, you just imagined it. Here, lean your head on my shoulder. Try to sleep.

CATHY. You think I'm crazy, don't you? Admit it! You do think I've gone crazy.

DOUG. Well . . .

CATHY. I'll tell you this—you're the one who's crazy, not me! You!

DOUG. What?

CATHY. You! You're crazy!

DOUG. So that's it. You're one of *them* now. You're on their side.

CATHY. No, no, you don't understand.

DOUG. You traitor. So you're one of them now. What's it like, Benedict Arnold?

CATHY. No, no, I'm not one of them. Oh, Doug, I'm scared. I'm frightened. All this, this change is frightening me. I don't know where to turn!

Resolution

DOUG. Oh, Cathy, I love you!

CATHY. I love you, too. You don't think I'm crazy, do you?

DOUG. No. (*They embrace.*)

CATHY. Who are they?

DOUG. (*Thoughtfully.*) I'm not sure. But *they do* exist.

CATHY. Where?

DOUG. In us. In our minds.

CATHY. Will they ever go away.

DOUG. (*Slowly.*) I don't know.

(*Curtain.*)

A Christmas Miracle
by Sharon Cook

Characters

MRS. DAVIS	JAKE
MR. DAVIS	MRS. ARNOLD
JEFF DAVIS	THREE MOVERS

SCENE 1: *It is early in the day and the room is cluttered with moving boxes and assorted articles of furniture.* MR. *and* MRS. DAVIS *are sitting on boxes talking.* JEFF *sits on the window sill with tears in his eyes, watching the snow fall. Outside there is a deep blanket of snow on the ground.*

MOTHER. (*Glancing at her watch.*) Where could those movers be? They said they would be here at nine sharp.

FATHER. They're probably being delayed by the storm. You know the news report said there've already been two accidents since it started yesterday.

MOTHER. I sure will be glad to get out of this year-round blizzard, and no more delays on account of the weather.

(*The teakettle starts whistling, and* FATHER *gets up to get it.* MOTHER *notices her son and sits beside him on the window sill.*)

JEFF. (*Looking up at his* MOTHER *after a long pause.*) Doesn't it ever snow in Florida?

MOTHER. Yes, it does, but not very often. I think their last snow was eight years ago.

JEFF. How come we have to move somewhere where it *never* snows? Christmas just isn't Christmas without snow.

MOTHER. You know we must go where your father can get a job.

JEFF. But you can't have Christmas without snow.

MOTHER. We'll still have Christmas, and I tell you what, we can get some of that fake snow and spray all over the windows and it will be just as though we were here at home.

JEFF. It just won't be the same, Mom.

(*The doorbell rings, and* MOTHER *goes to answer it.*)

FIRST MOVER. Hello. We're from the Acme Moving Company. We're terribly sorry about the delay, but the roads are completely iced over.

SCENE 2: *It is the living room of their new house. The same furniture is placed around and there are still several boxes that haven't been unpacked. It's the day before Christmas and a half-decorated tree stands in the corner.* MOTHER *and* FATHER *are digging into boxes in search of something.* JEFF *sits pouting in a chair by the window.*

FATHER. (*To* MOTHER.) Have you seen the boxes of outdoor lights?

MOTHER. I think I put them over there by the door.

FATHER. It sure is a hassle moving into a new house at Christmas.

MOTHER. (*To* JEFF.) You know it's always a lot more fun when we work together.

JEFF. It just doesn't seem right decorating the house for Christmas with no snow on the ground.

MOTHER. Come on, cheer up, it's almost Christmas. (*Pause.*) Well, why don't you go down to the corner and get yourself an ice-cream cone! Here's a quarter, get a double dip.

JEFF. Oh, I don't wanna.

MOTHER. Come on, the fresh air will do you good.

JEFF. Oh, all right.

(*His* MOTHER *hands him a quarter, and he trudges out the door. He walks down the street and steps into the ice-cream parlor and soon comes out with a double-dipper cone. He meets another boy about his age slowly walking down the street in ragged clothes, and he timidly walks along beside him.*)

JEFF. Hi.

JAKE. Hi, what's your name?

JEFF. Jeff Davis.

JAKE. I'm Jake. Say, you're new here in town, aren't you?

JEFF. (*Sadly.*) Yeah, we just moved here from Vermont.

JAKE. What's the matter? Don't ya like it here?

JEFF. (*After a pause.*) Well ... it's just that ... it just won't seem like Christmas without snow.

JAKE. Oh, I'm used to it. . . . Say, do you get presents?

JEFF. Oh, yeah! Lots of 'em.

JAKE. (*Sadly.*) Gee, (*Choking up.*) whud ya get last year?

JEFF. Oh, gee, I can't remember everything. Let's see. I got a new electric train, a baseball bat, a football, a toy rifle, a robot, a transistor radio, a pair of teddy-bear toys, a race car, a stuffed pig, a new bike with training wheels, (JAKE's *eyes start growing bigger.*) a two-hundred piece set of building blocks, a pair of ice skates, and there's lots more—I can't think of everything.

JAKE. Gee! You got all that?

JEFF. Yeah.

JAKE. (*Sadly.*) Golly, I'd be happy if I just got one present a year.

JEFF. Ya mean you don't get *any* presents?

JAKE. (*Sadly*) No . . . (*They round the corner and cross the lawn of the orphanage. They go up to a large window where inside they can see many other children in ragged clothes, dancing around and singing Christmas carols. They are making popcorn to hang on their bare cardboard tree with no presents under it, and they're having the fun of a lifetime.*) Ya see, I live in this orphanage with all these other kids.

JEFF. Ya mean all those guys, and nobody gets any presents?

JAKE. Yeah, our parents are gone, and the lady that runs this place can't afford to buy us presents.

JEFF. Golly!

JAKE. But that doesn't matter, we have so much fun together we don't need presents. It's the spirit of Christmas that counts.

JEFF. They sure are having a lot of fun in there. Ya mean it doesn't matter to you that you never have a white Christmas?

JAKE. No, don't you know what Christmas is all about?

JEFF. Sure, I know the story, but . . . doesn't it bug you not to have any snow?

JAKE. Not really. I just think of the true meaning of Christmas and be thankful for what I've got. (*They hear a bell ring from within the building.* JAKE *says excitedly.*) Oh, that's the dinner bell. I gotta go.

JEFF. Okay, see ya 'round.

JAKE. (*Opening the door.*) Okay, bye, Merry Christmas.

JEFF. Merry Christmas.

Resolution

> (JEFF *slowly walks off in a dream, thinking hard; suddenly an idea comes to him, and he runs the rest of the way home. He sneaks in through the basement window and soon reappears with an armload of toys. He runs down to the orphanage and knocks on the office door.*)

MRS. ARNOLD. (*Opening the door.*) Good evening, could I help you?

JEFF. (*Smiling and peering out from under the toys.*) I brought these toys for Jake and the other guys.

MRS. ARNOLD. What are you talking about?

JEFF. I was talking to Jake before, and he told me they never get any presents, so I brought these for 'em for Christmas.

MRS. ARNOLD. You mean you are just going to give these to the kids?

JEFF. (*Cheerfully.*) Yeah.

MRS. ARNOLD. This is very kind of you. Who should I say brought them?

JEFF. (*Excitedly.*) Oh! Don't say anyone! Just put them under the tree tonight, and don't let them know I brought them.

MRS. ARNOLD. (*Not really understanding.*) If you say so.

JEFF. (*Happily handing her the toys.*) Well, I gotta go now and get my Mom and Dad a present.

MRS. ARNOLD. Okay, bye. I know the kids will have a lot of fun with these.

JEFF. Bye. Merry Christmas.

MRS. ARNOLD. Merry Christmas.

(JEFF *walks rapidly down the street smiling all over, with his hands in his pockets. He steps into a department store and soon steps out with a very large package. He runs home and sneaks into the house. The lights go out.*)

SCENE 3: *It's about midnight on Christmas Eve. The house is dark, and no one is awake. The tree stands shining and all decorated in the corner of the room with a large pile of presents beneath it. Soon Jeff comes tiptoeing down the stairs with a huge wrapped box. He quietly places it under the tree and starts walking toward the stairs, when from behind the half-open curtain he sees a beautiful sight: snow. He runs to the window, full of happiness and flings open the curtain and just stands there looking up at the beautiful white flakes as they fall to the ground.*

JEFF. Now I know what Christmas is all about.

(*Curtain.*)

Which Way Is Up?
by James H. Norton

Characters

FISH ONE
FISH TWO

SCENE: *This play takes place in an ocean, at a point equidistant from the top and bottom.*

FISH ONE. I sure would like to sit down somewhere and rest.

FISH TWO. Yeah, me too.

FISH ONE. Well, let's swim down to the bottom to some comfortable rocks.

FISH TWO. OK. (*He starts moving stage left.*)

FISH ONE. That's toward the surface, stupid! Follow me! (*He starts moving stage right.*)

FISH TWO. Now you're the one that's going toward the top.

(*They both turn around and look at each other. They return stage center.*)

FISH ONE *and* FISH TWO. (*Together.*) Are you sure? (*They both laugh nervously.*)

FISH ONE. When was the last time you were down there?

FISH TWO. I don't remember.

FISH ONE. You have been there, haven't you?

FISH TWO. (*Unconvincingly.*) Of course, I've been there.

FISH ONE. Well, let's go then.

FISH TWO. OK, let's go.

Resolution

(*They both hesitate. This time* FISH ONE *moves stage left and* FISH TWO *stage right.*)

FISH ONE *and* FISH TWO. (*Together.*) Hey, where are you going? (*They both laugh nervously again.*)

FISH ONE. You know, I'm not really that tired. I mean, all that way to the bottom. Know what I mean?

FISH TWO. Yeah. I gotcha. I mean, it's really too hot today for a long swim like that.

FISH ONE. Yeah.

FISH TWO. Yeah.

(*Pause.*)

FISH ONE. It sure makes you feel better though.

FISH TWO. What's that?

FISH ONE. To know which way is up.

FISH TWO. Yeah.

(*Curtain.*)

ACTIVITIES

1. Write a responsible resolution to the play idea given on page 14.

2. Write a resolution for your own play.

8

Production notes

A GOOD PLAY CAN FALL FLAT if not properly blocked. Blocking is the organization of the action on stage. No matter how well your characters are developed and no matter how well they say their lines, if they stand in a straight line facing the audience—disaster!

In Figure 1, the characters are too far back on the stage. Unless the actors have powerful voices, many of their lines will be lost. Furthermore, all the attention is centered on one point,

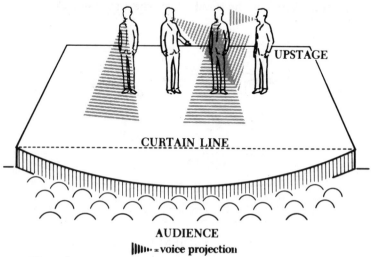

AUDIENCE

‖‖ᴵᴵᴵᴵ = voice projection

Figure 1

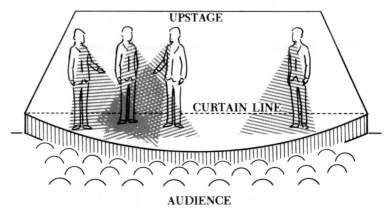

AUDIENCE

||||‧‧ = voice projection

Figure 2

and the rest of the stage is wasted. The audience will quickly lose interest because the play looks more like a police lineup than a dramatic production. Notice the difference between the blocking pattern here and that in Figure 2. In Figure 2, the placement of the actors allows their voices to carry into the audience. The blocking pattern uses the entire stage, not just one section of it.

Some blocking is spelled out in stage directions. But what about the rest of the action? When does a character sit down? When and where does he stand while others are talking?

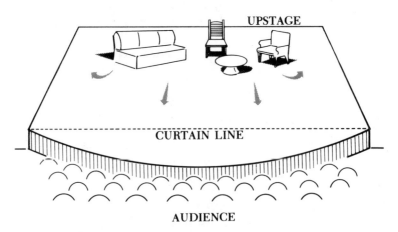

AUDIENCE

Figure 3

90   WRITING SHORT PLAYS

The most important aspect in blocking is to keep each character in view of the audience as much of the time as possible and keep him in view to as much of the audience as possible. As you block, have your director or some member of the cast go to different parts of the auditorium to establish the best blocking for a situation.

Since many people your age have not developed substantial voice projection, block as much action as possible downstage (see p. 38 for picture of stage locations). For the sake of symmetry, inexperienced directors tend to place the action in the middle of the stage area (see Figure 3). Usually, this is too far from the audience. Then, too, there is something boring about having everything going on equidistant from stage left and stage right. One way to avoid having all the action take place at center stage is to place the props so that the focus of the action will be downstage left or right (see Figure 4).

After you have established the basic focus of the action, let the characters move freely. Your audience would tire of characters glued to the same spot. As they move about, make most of their movement from one side to the other so they don't get lost upstage. It is important to consider the movements of the characters who aren't speaking as well as the one who is. All the people on the stage should have some specified movements. Nothing could be duller than having one person speak to several others who are sitting or standing motionless. Movement, of course, does

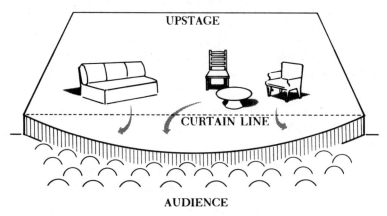

Figure 4

not only mean going from one point to another. Picking up a book, passing a cup, even squirming in a chair is movement.

Be sure to note your blocking on your individual scripts and keep it pretty much that way during rehearsals. Since you are not professionals, sometimes a slight change in position during performance will throw you and the rest of the cast off base so that they forget lines. So decide on definite blocking and stick to it.

Following is a manuscript page from *I'm Cold, Aren't You?* blocked to show you how to note the blocking for your play.

> SETTING: *Scene 1 takes place at an exclusive Eastern private school for the mentally disturbed.* SUZANNE *is seated alone in the recreation room.* JEFF PATTERSON *walks in.*

JEFF. S*walks up 2 steps*zanne? (*She looks up at* JEFF.) That's your name, isn't it? When did you arrive? I'm Jeff Patterson. I've been here almost two years. (*goes to window — back to Suzanne*)

SUZANNE. Oh, I guess I arrived about three yesterday, but I'm just guessing.

JEFF. We usually don't have such a small number in the recreation room, but tonight's the Liberty Dance in the counselors' hall. (*walking back to Suzanne*)

SUZANNE. Oh. That's very nice.

JEFF. Weren't you invited?

(SUZANNE *moves in her seat.*)

SUZANNE. No.

JEFF. That's too bad. I suppose you want to know why I didn't go? (*pulls up a chair & sits opposite Suzanne*)

SUZANNE. Well, I really can't say. . . .

JEFF. Well, you see—those counselors say I need a lot more therapy! (*gets up quickly and goes to window again*)

SUZANNE. Oh, that's too bad.

~~~~~~

ACTIVITY

According to your teacher's directions, block one of the plays given in the text. Work in small groups, and then compare different blockings for the same play at the end of the period.

~~~~~~

You can't perform a play until you know your lines. Generally, you must know your lines word for word. Poor memorization will confuse the other actors and ruin the play for everyone.

After the blocking has been done, begin to work through the play on stage, reading the lines from scripts. Then decide on a day when the scripts will not be allowed on stage, designate a prompter, and move through the play. When an actor doesn't know a line, he should call out "Line." Only then should the prompter read the line. The prompter is not to decide you need a line. Sometimes a pause is very important, and if the prompter jumps in with a line, he may ruin the scene.

One aid to memorization is having someone take the script from you and begin reading the play. When he comes to your line, he stops and looks at you. Try to respond with what seems to fit your situation at that time; many times it will be exactly the right line. If it isn't, have the person read the line exactly as it is written; then you repeat that line. If you spend an hour or so doing this, chances are you will know your lines very well.

This also might be the time to change a line. Your response might be better than the one in the script. Write down your line and present it to the entire cast at the next rehearsal. If you all agree to change the line to fit your interpretation of the character, this should make the line easier for you to handle. Likewise, if a line seems out of place or out of character, revise it now.

It is very important not to change lines deliberately during rehearsal unless you warn the cast. If you don't have this as a ground rule, you could cause a catastrophe the day of the performance. Variations in wording are not allowable, especially in cues—lines that signal the start of another action or speech. The other actor's mind is waiting for certain key phrases. If you decide to say, "Do you think this will help him?" instead of the proper line, "Do you think this will do him any good?" you might get a blank stare from the actor you are talking to and upset the entire scene.

The point is that you should be free to change lines up to a certain point in time, depending on the length of the play and the agreement of the cast. Then the lines should be memorized perfectly to avoid confusing other actors and spoiling situations that depend on specific line delivery.

Lines, no matter how well thought out, are useless if no one can hear them. Generally, you should shout, and when you do your voice will usually be at a perfect volume level. Get used to shouting, because the larger the audience and the theater are, the more sound is absorbed. You have worked hard to get to the point of putting on the play, so be sure the audience hears your lines.

Lines should be said with feeling. There is nothing worse than an actor saying "I'm so happy" in the same way a person would say "I just brushed my teeth." How can you get feeling into a play? One answer might be to exaggerate. In a comedy, try poking fun at your part by overdoing it, by hamming it up. Let yourself go in terms of putting emotion into your part.

Serious plays present greater difficulties: Note the stage directions provided for the play. Then project yourself into the role —become the character. If the play calls for you to be angry, think of something that makes you angry.

A technique that is as difficult as putting feeling into your part is learning to pause. Jack Benny gets some of his greatest laughs by pausing. Dramatic tension can be built to great heights through pauses. Authors usually indicate pauses that are essential, but there are many other places to pause. At first you will have a hard time seeing these places because the tendency is to read straight through the lines as you do when reading a book. Remember that these are spoken words. Try pausing at different places: in the middle of sentences, before new sentences, even before you start a line. Start listening for pauses in real conversation. Then see if you can make your lines more lifelike with pauses. Be sure to note successful pauses in your script.

Feeling and timing are correlated with word emphasis. Emphasis can change the entire meaning of a line. Take the line "It sure looks like rain." If you emphasize "sure," you are talking about the possibility of rain. If you emphasize "looks," you could be indicating that you can't understand why it isn't raining right now. If you emphasize "rain," you might be trying to decide whether the precipitation is not snow or sleet. So, after you think you know your part quite well, go through it and underline words you want to emphasize. Then, when you recite your lines to someone, make sure that person understands that the pauses and underlinings are part of the line and that he sees you execute them properly.

ACTIVITY

Take lines from plays in the text or from those you have written and practice saying them to someone. Try pausing and emphasizing in places you think wouldn't work. Your goal is to say the lines so that they appear natural in the context of the play.

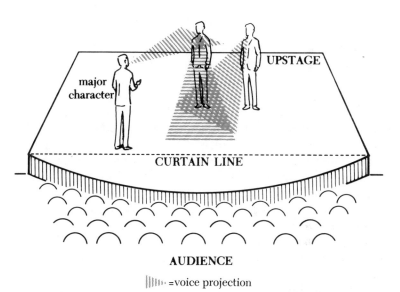

Figure 5

One major problem students have in acting is that they forget there is an audience out there and talk only to each other. There are a number of things to remember and work on to help correct this problem. First, watch out for upstaging. Upstaging is standing upstage from another actor, usually the main character (see Figure 5). The actor will then turn from the audience to say his line to the character behind him. The speaker's voice is projected toward the side or back of the stage and not to the audience. To avoid this,

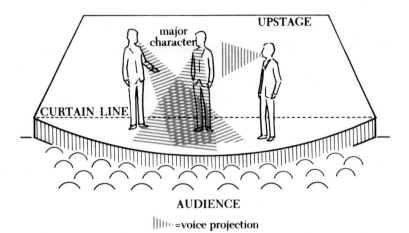

UPSTAGE

major character

CURTAIN LINE

AUDIENCE

||||⋯=voice projection

Figure 6

block so that all actors are parallel or in front of the main character. This will keep his lines from being lost (see Figure 6).

A second problem, even when the actors don't upstage, is that they tend to speak only to each other. They turn their backs directly to stage right or left, and much of the dialogue becomes lost in the wings. A basic rule to follow is to always keep at least three-quarter face to the audience. Then your voice will have a good chance of missing the side curtains and going out into the crowd. Although this three-quarter face will feel awkward at first, the audience will still have the illusion that real conversation is going on.

Yet another problem is learning to move while speaking. Although professionals do this with ease, you will have trouble. Because you are concentrating on so many things at one time, your lines will probably be missed by the audience. Therefore, another good rule is to say your lines either before or after an action. This is especially true of exits. Many a good exit line is missed as the actor turns to the side, or worse, to the back of the stage, and marches off to the exit. Say your last line clearly and strongly, then exit after delivering your line. Of course, this applies to entrances as well. Remember, your audience is seeing you on stage for the first time, wondering what part you have in the play or what new action you are going to bring. Come in, pause, then speak your line.

There are some tricks to make a minimum amount of time offer a maximum amount of scenery. First, there is the use of a scrim. A scrim is any sheetlike piece of cloth hung or draped so that it is translucent to a light bulb of any sort. To use the scrim, fashion crude cardboard figures, place them behind the scrim on the floor or attached to scrim and set a floodlight or a 100-watt bulb behind the object and you have convincing scenery. When an object is placed some distance behind the scrim, you will find that the size of the object has to be no more than 2-feet tall to cast a larger-than-life shadow on the scrim. Of course, a colored light will add another effect if desired. Furthermore, whole plays can be performed behind scrims. Because the audience can only see silhouettes, the actors can appear to have a lot of impossible things happen. A classic example is the operating-room scene in which the audience sees an interminable number of excruciating things being drawn from the stomach of the unfortunate patient. Further scenery can be provided by a roll of 4-foot wide butcher paper. Then black paint is all you need to make a quick fence, factory, or skyline. You need nothing more elaborate, as you are doing this for effect rather than for realism. You can then pin or tape the paper up to the back of whatever you are calling your stage.

Props are always a problem. Much of the time, instead of using real props, pantomiming them is better, as there is nothing to get lost. Any props can be pantomimed, but many times props are fun to make.

In conclusion, optimum conditions are not necessary for an enjoyable performance. As a matter of fact, it is the crude situation that inspires the imagination. Simple items, such as Christmas-tree spotlights, large pieces of cardboard, and taped sound effects, are only a few of the readily available things that can transform any area into a place of production. All you need is an imagination.

ACTIVITY

Select a character from a play given in the text or elsewhere, and describe how you would play this role. Remember to include the voice, body movements, and costume. Also, describe the set or sets for this play.

WRITING
SHORT
POEMS

1

Poetry:
private and public

POETRY WOULD NOT WIN many popularity contests in America. If Mr. Harris or Mr. Gallup were to conduct a poll asking "the average American" how much time he spends reading or writing poetry, it would probably not amount to the time spent signing checks, tying shoelaces, or waiting for buses. But, fortunately, there is one form in which serious poetry has been revived on a large scale, probably without the public even knowing it—through popular music. The best composers of rock are thoughtful, well-read, and poetically creative. And their words are familiar to the large number of people who listen to rock music. The Beatles, Bob Dylan, and others have continued a tradition that is as old as our civilization: singing about things that matter. Things that matter have always been the subjects of poetry.

One advantage of this new form of poetry is that it is destroying, once and for all, the old notion that poetry uses restricted language to talk about restricted subjects. This is nonsense. Any

word that can be used in other writing may also be used in poetry.
A poet has the same freedom as a prose writer in choosing subjects to write about. All the poet must do is bring honesty and
imagination to his topic, as in the following poem:

Fork

This strange thing must have crept
Right out of hell.
It resembles a bird's foot
Worn around the cannibal's neck.

As you hold it in your hand,
As you stab with it into a piece of meat,
It is possible to imagine the rest of the bird:
Its head which like your fist
Is large, bald, beakless and blind.

Charles Simic's fork was probably no different from the fork
you last used, but he saw something else in it. And that something
suddenly mattered, took on a new significance through his imagination.

Compare "The Fork" with a poem that makes a statement in
a different way:

This Is Just to Say

I have eaten
the plums
that were in
the icebox

and which
you were probably
saving
for breakfast

Forgive me
they were delicious
so sweet
and so cold
WILLIAM CARLOS WILLIAMS

A household fork, plums—what next? A fly, of course:

> Don't swat it!
>   the fly is wringing his hands
>   he's wringing his feet.
>
> ISSA

To discover something special in a fork, some plums, or a common fly is the function of a poet. Poetry, says the poet Marianne Moore, is "imaginary gardens with real toads in them."

The word "gardens" suggests or connotes something beautiful that has been planned. "Imaginary" tells us that poetry is created by the mind yet it is based on what is found in the world ("real"). To most persons, "toads" have negative associations—toads are thought of as ugly or perhaps as creatures that give warts. What Miss Moore is saying, then, is that the form of poetry is beautiful but that it can be written and is written about real things. And the subject matter of the poem becomes "beautiful" because of the poetic form.

Another way of putting this is: the aim of poetry is to catch experiences exactly as they happen. That is difficult because so many mixed elements can go into a single experience. Here is an example:

> You feel moody one evening during summer. Perhaps you have had a fight at home, or you feel shut in, bored, or stifled. So you set out from your house. You take a road that you have not taken before. Suddenly you are walking down some dingy streets. The people look menacing and unfamiliar. It is hot; the skin seems to be sewn onto the back of your neck. Uncollected garbage is ankle-deep in the gutter. The air smells of garbage. The houses seem to totter on their bases. The road signs read "No Waiting," "Keep Right," "No Loitering," "Private—Keep Out." Doorways seem to lead to stifling, drab interiors. A sickening depression settles onto you. Then, from behind an old frayed curtain, comes some music. A group is practicing, and the sound is good— rich, mellow, deep. It wails through the gathering darkness, and for a few moments you are transfixed. You

feel a strange set of emotions, not quite like anything you have felt before. There is the shadow of your earlier mood, the dirty streets, the heavy, sticky air; now there is this sound, sweet and long and cool. This, and much more.

There is only one medium that could catch these complexities and contradictions of experience. Perhaps a musician could suggest them through jazz, or a blues singer could touch on them. Perhaps a novelist like Salinger could hint at them. Certainly a sociologist could never reach them with his statistics and diagrams. A politician would never recognize such a thing—no votes there. A doctor could chart your pulse and blood pressure, but not the experience. A psychologist might find the right scientific terms to describe it but could never recall it as it was. None of the sciences could catch it. Yet, to you, this moment is all-important. It might lead to something else—an important decision or insight—or it might simply exist in and for itself. But it has a unique value. Only poetry can catch this moment, perhaps to portray it to someone else who was not with you, perhaps to keep it for you to relive in the future. This is the function poetry can perform on a personal level. It can catch experience as it is; not as the thermometers and barometers record it, but as it happened to you.

But poetry has another function, less personal, more public. In its private function it can be like music: intimate, fragile, subtle, evocative. In its public function it can be like a dance. It moves beyond logic, appealing to people with phrases they only dimly understand but that they feel inside. A Kennedy or a King, a Paul McCartney or a Bob Dylan, the Constitution or the marriage ceremony, a nickname or a word of greeting, a coach's last words or a defense attorney's final plea, a headline about a great game, an ad about a cold drink or the name of a place you want to visit— all these, in varying degrees of seriousness, may have the essence of poetry: they may communicate below the surface level of the words, filling the hearers' minds with a rhythm and a music that evoke an almost physical response. Given the right situation, the words are more than what they say: they are a style, a form, a gesture, a dance. They represent a sense of common humanity that runs deeper than the intellect can grasp. There is a life in the phrasing that defies analysis. There is a magic about the form of the words that cannot be explained. It is just *there,* and it is immediately recognizable to those who are open to its appeal.

Here are just a few examples:

"Ask not what your country can do for you—ask what you can do for your country." (John F. Kennedy)

"I have a dream . . ." "Free at last! free at last! thank God Almighty, we are free at last!" (Martin Luther King)

". . . that government of the people, by the people, for the people, shall not perish from the earth." (Abraham Lincoln)

Many of these pieces of public poetry depend to an extent on the situation for their effect, or on the imagination of the hearer. Think, for example, of the poetry in the name *Omaha.* Or of the kind of situation which would give the simple words "I do" an electrifying effect.

These, then, are the qualities of poetry. Not whether it rhymes or has the correct number of beats, or whether it contains phrases like "verdant meadows" or "tinkling streams." Poetry speaks immediately, with a voice that is contemporary and relevant, whether it was written in ancient Rome or modern America. As the poet and critic Ezra Pound said, poetry is "news that remains news."

In this section you will be asked to read and write poetry. To this end, you will be asked to make two contributions: (1) a patient study of the techniques that are necessary for putting your experiences on paper, and (2) much more important, sincerely felt and honestly recorded experiences that are entirely yours and that may be captured in a poetic form in a manner that is uniquely your own.

One suggestion: It is enormously helpful for any writer, but especially for a would-be poet, to keep a notebook of his or her experiences. What kind of experiences? As the book develops, you will find more and more experiences that are useful. For the moment, think about and write down the types of experiences, both public or private, that you have had. You might include any of the following: your dreams, the lyrics of an appealing song, mixed feelings at a particular moment, interesting names you notice, snatches of conversation overheard in the street, sudden sights (a truckdriver's face in a mirror as you drive past him), the sound a pigeon makes when it calls, a single gesture that caught your eye, an oddly shaped manhole in the street, impressions from the zoo (both animal and human), shades of light on the town clock, the feel of some new material as you touch it, reflections in a pool of water. In other words, anything that might be useful to you when you take up your pen to write poetry. Try recapturing in words the experience exactly as it happened.

~~~~~~~~~~~~~~~~~~~~~~~~~~~~~~~~~~~~~~~

ACTIVITIES

1. From history books, books of quotations, or other sources, find five sentences or phrases that have had a powerful effect on people, and describe the situation that made the words come to life. Look for combinations of words that have that quality of poetry. For example, if during the annual cat show somebody called out "Oh, no, it's my dog Rover!" this might well have a powerful effect. But it is not the poetry in the words that would cause the commotion; it is Rover's prowess as a cat-chaser. On the other hand, it was at Britain's darkest hour, when all hope seemed lost, that Winston Churchill assumed office, and instead of promising glory, freedom, safety, said, "I have nothing to offer but blood, toil, tears, and sweat." To his anxious listeners, huddled over their radios with the sound of air-raid sirens in their ears, these words came as a battle cry, bringing more hope than a thousand empty promises.

2. List five names that seem to you to possess the qualities of poetry.

3. On the way home from school this evening, look for poetry that is not based on language. Perhaps you will find a leaf of unusual shape or color or you will happen upon an unusual pattern in the railings and fire escapes. Or maybe an old magazine will supply a picture that catches your eye. Whatever it is, it will take an imaginative mind to find it. If you can, bring the object or a picture of it to class. If not, write about it, so that the class can hear and see exactly what you heard and saw.

4. In your opinion, what can poetry do that science cannot?

For example, what does science investigate? What does poetry investigate? Which is broader in scope?

5. Choose a single experience that you have had; make a list of some of the various elements that went into making that experience. For example, you might choose the first day back at school and compile a list like this:

Having to get up early in the morning again.
New teachers—confusion but excitement. Will I like them?
Meeting old friends again, having experiences to share.
Oh, no, back to the old routine.
New books that smell new and crackle when you open them.
Good resolutions—kept all but one, the first day, that is.
School food again!
Tired out—limp as a wet sock by the end of the day.
Perhaps this year will be better than last.

6. What elements are needed in a good school song? Try your hand at writing one, using your school's as a model. Remember, this is just a trial effort.

7. Imagine a situation that calls for an emotionally charged speech—say, just before the big game of the season, with the team gathered in the locker room. Write the speech aimed at rallying the listeners to a particular cause. This is not an exercise in argument or logical thinking; it is a test of whether you can make phrases that will excite your audience to action in this particular situation. Keep it short—a high pitch of emotion is hard to sustain. Build up to a climax.

8. Read "My Grandmother" by Jill Hoffman:

The subject came up about talent—I was wolfing down
The generous portions served in your house—
And you said, "If I could only write them
The way they happened, I have stories to tell . . ."
—Your hands like silk that took away my headaches,
You, the best cook in the world and more
Beautiful than anyone you played poker with—
But none of your stories ended; not one so much as
Hinted that my grandmother could die
In the middle of her own life, scarcely knowing mine.

The poem presents a sketch of the poet's grandmother. Notice how the poet used her grandmother's desire to write stories to unite the poem and to illustrate her character. Write a character sketch, either in prose or in verse, of a real or an imaginary person. Try to illustrate the person's character by showing the person in action.

9. Here is another Charles Simic poem. This time it's about a spoon! Choose a common object and try writing a Simic poem about it.

The Spoon

An old spoon
Bent, gouged
Polished to an evil
Glitter.

It has bitten
Into my life—
This kennel-bone
Sucked thin.

Now, it is a living
Thing: ready
To scratch a name
On a prison wall—

Ready to be passed on
To the little one
Just barely
Beginning to walk.

10. Read Richard Brautigan's "It's Raining in Love." One goal of his poetry is to achieve honesty and sincerity. Try your hand at a similar poem, telling in a relaxed way about how you feel on a particular subject. Don't worry about poetic form—begin and end the lines whenever you feel like it.

It's Raining in Love

I don't know what it is,
but I distrust myself
when I start to like a girl
a lot

It makes me nervous.
I don't say the right things
or perhaps I start
    to examine,
                evaluate,
                        compute
    what I am saying.

If I say, "Do you think it's going to rain?"
and she says, "I don't know,"
I start thinking: "Does she really like me?"

In other words
I get a little creepy.

A friend of mine once said,
"It's twenty times better to be friends
        with someone
than it is to be in love with them."

I think he's right and besides
it's raining somewhere, programing flowers
and keeping snails happy.
    That's all taken care of.

        BUT
if a girl likes me a lot
and starts getting real nervous
and suddenly begins asking me funny questions
and looks sad if I give the wrong answers
and she says things like,
"Do you think it's going to rain?"
and I say, "It beats me,"
and she says, "Oh,"
and looks a little sad
at the clear blue California sky,
I think, Thank God, it's you, baby, this time,
    instead of me.

Meet Richard Brautigan

Besides being a poet, Richard Brautigan is an Aquarian who
loves Chaos and Nature. He began selling his poetry on a street
corner in Haight-Ashbury (San Francisco) to earn the price of a

movie for himself and his friends. Today he is celebrated all the way from Greenwich Village to his out-of-the-way home in a little-known suburb of San Francisco—chiefly as a result of his second novel, *Trout Fishing in America*. Despite his success, his life-style has not changed: When he is not writing, he still likes to spend his time rapping with friends, seeing nature, and riding buses around the city. He prefers an unacclaimed, isolated existence and dreads encounters with viewers, reviewers, and interviewers. Yet he has given poetry readings at high school graduations and at San Quentin Prison.

Brautigan's wild imagination, coupled with his honest observation, makes him distinctive as a writer: To him, a floating beer bottle becomes a glass-backed trout just below the surface. Inspired by a piece of celery floating in a stream, he imagines that soon a whole cocktail party will be floating down that crazy stream. His message seems to be that everything around us is precious. He uses his imaginative vision of nature to praise what God gave and man is fast consuming. Yet he is optimistic about the future: He cannot believe that man has come this far only to poison himself with his own pollution.

Besides *Trout Fishing* (which, incidentally, is the name of the hero, not his hobby), Brautigan's works include *Please Plant This Book,* which is a collection of eight packets of real seeds, each with a poem attached; and a number of short stories collected in *A Confederate General from Big Sur* and *In Watermelon Sugar.*

2

Etch and sketch

POETRY USES THE IMAGINATION to express real experiences exactly as they happen. No word or idea that is open to other writing is closed to poetry. But if poetry is not set apart from prose because of ideas or vocabulary, what, then, is the difference between poetry and other writing?

The boundaries between poetry and prose are not final or definite. No one can say for sure just where the shore ends and the sea begins, where prose ends and poetry begins. The difference between them is a matter of degree: poetry *tends* to be more compressed, to suggest and imply more than does prose; it *tends* to place more emphasis on *how* something is said, and less on *what* is said; poetry *tends* to be more imaginative than prose, to use more comparisons, more surprises; poetry usually has a more regular rhythm than does prose, and an especially interesting shape or form.

Focus for a moment on the last of these distinctive qualities of poetry—the shape or form. Usually a poem is divided into lines. Some poems have lines of a set length while others have lines that vary greatly in length. What determines how long a line should be in a poem?

Take the following two sentences:

Star, if you are a love compassionate, you will walk with
us this year. We face a glacial distance, who are here
huddled at your feet.

These are pleasant sentences, but they do not attract the eye
particularly. On the other hand, by rearranging the lines thus:

Star,

If you are

A love compassionate,

You will walk with us this year.

We face a glacial distance, who are here

Huddld

At your feet.

WILLIAM BURFORD

All of a sudden, the shape or form explains what the poem is
about: "A Christmas Tree."

~~~~~~

ACTIVITIES

1. Why does the poet put the word "Star" on top and the
words "At your feet" at the bottom? What does the poetic form
add to the meaning of the words?

2. Suggest reasons why the word "huddled" is spelled differently in the poem than in the prose version.

3. Using "A Christmas Tree" as a model, write one of your
own in the shape of:

    a. A church   d. A lit candle
    b. A doorway   e. Some object of your choice
    c. A bottle

Be sure to relate the form to the meaning.

~~~~~~

Several modern poets have experimented in writing poetry that joins form and meaning. This is called concrete poetry. In this type of poetry, the meaning is based on a relationship of the shape of the poem to the words. "Au pair girl" is an example of concrete poetry.

```
          pair g
         rl au pair
        )air girl au
         au pair girl
        ıu pair girl a
       ırl au pair girl a
      ,air girl au pair gir
     ɟirl au pair girl au pair
    )air girl au pair girl au pa
   air girl au pair girl au pair
   pair girl au pair girl au pa
   ıu pair girl au pair girl aı
     ʼirl au pair girl au paiʼ
       ʼirl au pair girl ˗
```

IAN HAMILTON FINLAY

~~~~~~

ACTIVITIES

1. In the preceding poem, what is the relationship between the shape of the poem and the sound of the words? The phrase "au pair girl" means a young girl, usually from another country, who takes care of children and does light housework in return for spending money. Does the meaning of the phrase add to the meaning of the poem? Why or why not?

2. "Car," on the facing page, is another example of concrete poetry.

Create a concrete poem of your own. Use an idea of your own or one of the following possibilities:

a. A tall story   c. Infinity
b. Upside down   d. Square root

~~~~~~

In William Burford's "A Christmas Tree," it is obvious why each line has a certain length, and a little thought will show how each part of the poem relates to the whole. But not every poem is shaped like an object. What decides line-length in those cases?

Basically there are two ways: by meaning and by syllable count. By and large, it is easier to break lines up by syllables than by meaning. Once you have decided how many syllables you will have in a line, you can stick to that pattern, with perhaps one or two exceptions for variety or to make special points. But if you are breaking a poem into lines by meaning, you must continually surprise everybody by your inventiveness. You are freer in the sense that you avoid set rules—but you are less free in that you must create your own form as you go. Following are two examples of poems that break lines by meaning rather than by syllable count:

The Universe

What
is it about
the universe
about
us stretching out? We within our brains within it think
we must unspin the laws that spin it. We think
why because
we think
because.
Because
we think
we think
the universe
about
us.

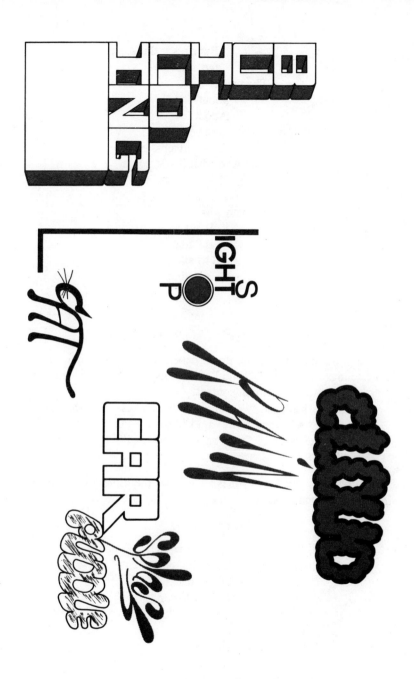

But does it think,
the universe?
Then what
about?
About
us? If not, must there be cause
in the universe:
Must it have laws? And what
if the universe
is *not about*
us? Then what?
What
is it about
and what
about
us?

MAY SWENSON

Analysis of "The Universe"

1. The meaning of the poem depends on the multiple meanings of "about," "spin," and "unspin." What do each of these words mean in context?
2. In the sentence "We think/ *why* because/ we think/ *because*," why are "why" and "because" in italics?
3. How does Miss Swenson use line breaks to achieve emphasis?

"The Pressures" by Leroi Jones also shows the difficulty in achieving free-verse patterns:

The pressures

(Love twists
the young man. Having seen it
only once. He expected it
to be, as the orange flower
leather of the poet's book.   5
He expected
less hurt, a lyric. And not
the slow effortless pain
as a new dripping sun pushes
up out of our river.)   10

And

having seen it, refuses
to inhale. "It was a
green mist, seemed
to lift and choke   15
the town."

Analysis of "The pressures"

1. Suggest reasons why the poem starts in the middle of the line and with a parenthesis.
2. Why is there a break after "expected it" (line 3) and then again after "expected" (line 6)?
3. Why is the line "less hurt, a lyric. And not" broken into short sections while the next three lines run smoothly, without a break?
4. Why is the word "And" singled out to make line 11?
5. Why is there a break after " 'It was a"? Shouldn't the article "a" go with its noun clause "green mist"?

These two poems illustrate some of the difficulties involved in writing free verse. The poet should use the line breaks to suggest new significance for the words.

The second method of determining the length of your line is by counting the syllables. One method is to establish a pattern for the number of syllables in each line. Adelaide Crapsey invented a form called the cinquain, with lines of, respectively, 2, 4, 6, 8, and 2 syllables.

Triad

These be
Three silent things:
The falling snow . . . the hour
Before the dawn . . . the mouth of one
Just dead.

The difficulty is in presenting an experience in only twenty-two syllables. As a poet, you must compress your ideas into a few brief words. Miss Crapsey gives three illustrations of silent things. She arranges her examples so that the words "Just dead" appear as the final line. This arrangement gives the words more emphasis. Much of the effect would be lost if she had rearranged the images so that "The dawn" was the final line.

Writing lines in which the pattern emphasizes certain key words requires thought and frequent revision. It is unlikely that the pattern will appear in the first draft. You will have to redo your original lines many times before the structure of the lines complements the meaning.

ACTIVITIES

1. Rewrite the poem, changing "silent" to some other adjective. Add three "things" that illustrate the adjective you have selected. Keep the same syllabic pattern.

2. Another form of cinquain is the word cinquain. It follows these rules:

Line 1—A word for an object—"Boots"

Line 2—Two words that define or describe the object—"Shiny, heavy"

Line 3—Three words that describe an action related to the object—"Marching on stone"

Line 4—Four words that express an attitude toward or an emotional feeling about the object—"I wish they'd stop," or "Establishment on our minds"

Line 5—One word that sums up lines 1–4—"Crushing" or "Madness"

Try writing a word cinquain.

3. Write an original cinquain using the 2, 4, 6, 8, and 2 syllabic pattern.

The Japanese haiku is a three-lined poem that is divided into lines by syllable count. The syllabic pattern is 5–7–5.

> Winter-evening snow . . .
> The uncompleted bridge is all
> An arch of whiteness
> **BASHO**

A summer shower
Along all the street, servants
Slapping shut shutters
SHIKI

See the red berries . . .
Fallen like little footprints
On the garden snow
SHIKI

In addition to having three lines of 5–7–5 syllables, the haiku usually follows four other rules:

1. Every haiku contains a reference to nature—in the three poems above, respectively, "winter . . . snow," "summer shower," and "berries . . . snow."

2. The subject is a particular event; there is no generalizing. The experience is caught and presented objectively.

3. The time is *now*, the present, and not the past or the future. The effect is immediate.

4. The poem has a mystical quality. This particular moment is special, the poet seems to be saying.

Here are two more haiku. Which of the two cheats a little on the above rules? How?

Little silver fish
Pointing upstream moving downstream
In clear quick water
SOSEKI

Energetic ant
Silhouetted on the still
Snow-flake peony
BUSON

~~~~~~

ACTIVITIES

1. Write your name down the page. Try to find adjectives that describe you that also begin with each of the letters. For example, *Francis* might appear as:

F un-loving
R estless
A ffectionate
N ervous
C areful
I maginative
S erious

Add a second verse, based on your last name. But, if you do, make the distinction between your personal and your family self. Your first name is your private self; your surname is your public image, together with your responsibilities. If you can, use full sentences instead of simple adjectives. Be inventive.

2. Compose a sequence of associated thoughts that begin with and end on the same object. Thus, you will progress by free association through a circle of thoughts back to where you started. Here's an example:

> This spot of ink on my desk shaped like a question mark
> How will the game come out this afternoon; we're first and
>   they're second
> After last week's game Mary put her arm 'round me
> Should I take Alice or Susan to the dance Saturday?
> They'll be playing the new record "Sunflower Weary"
> I'm tired; should have gone to bed earlier; must start a fitness
>   campaign
> I'll go on a diet, too
> Diet of Worms, oh, no, history test next period
> This spot of ink on my desk shaped like a question mark

Or, keep thoughts out of it and just associate sensations and objects:

> curtain moving slowly / dance / Alice / brown eyes / sun-
> burn / Nantucket / job this summer / ice-cream salesman /
> shortchanged me, did you? Take that—and vanilla topping,
> too / slapstick / Charlie Chaplin / boots and stick / stick at
> nothing / zero / night / curtain moving slowly

Having completed the circle of your meditations, find the best way to arrange them on a page.

3. Write a poem to the telephone book, using one of the forms described in the chapter. If possible, use names as your material.

4. Create an advertisement for a product of your choice (real or imaginary). Emphasize your ideas by giving them an overall shape.

5. E. E. Cummings, or, as he spelled it—e. e. cummings, created surprising typographical layouts for his poems. He used capital letters only when he needed them for effect, not to begin poetic lines, sentences, or names. Here (written as prose) are three of his poems. How would you shape the following into lines?

a. a grin without a face(a look without an i) be careful (touch nothing)or it'll disappear banglessly(into sweet the earth)& nobody (including ourselves) will remember (for 1 fraction of a moment)where what how when who why which (or anything)

b. nite) thatthis crouched moangrowl-&-thing stirs(mid)a life whats wh (un)ich(curling) silently are(midnite also conceals 2 phantoms clutched in a writhewho room) as hows of whine climbscreAM exploding aRe(n't

c. old age sticks up Keep Off signs)& youth yanks them down(old age cries No Tres)&(pas)youth laughs (sing old age scolds Forbidden Stop Mustn't Don't &)youth goes right on growing old

Remember, you are completely free to break the lines wherever you wish, to capitalize whatever you want, even to break up words if that makes a point.*

6. Write a description of a scene, one with which you are familiar or one that you can imagine. Revise your original prose (1) to make it impersonal, that is, to remove the I's, and (2) to tighten and clarify the writing by using concrete nouns, adjectives, and verbs. When you have completed your revision, divide the prose description into lines by one of the following methods:

a. Establishing a pattern with a fixed number of syllables per line.
b. Ending the line whenever you have a comma or other punctuation mark.
c. Beginning or ending a line with a word that you want to emphasize.

* The correct layout for each poem appears in the Teacher's Manual.

d. Creating a pattern of your own that relates to the meaning of the poem.

7. The poet W. H. Auden said poets enjoy "hanging around words listening to what they say." In the following poems, the poets are playing with words. Read both to help you to open your imagination to the various forms of poetic line.

Adrian Henri's Talking after Christmas Blues

Well I woke up this mornin' it was Christmas Day
And the birds were singing the night away
I saw my stocking lying on the chair
Looked right to the bottom but you weren't there
    there was
        apples
            oranges
                chocolates
                    . . . aftershave
—but no you.

So I went downstairs and the dinner was fine
There was pudding and turkey and lots of wine
And I pulled those crackers with a laughing face
Till I saw there was no one in your place
    there was
        mincepies
            brandy
                nuts and raisins
                    . . . mashed potato
—but no you.

Now it's New Year and it's Auld Lang Syne
And it's 12 o'clock and I'm feeling fine
Should Auld Acquaintance be Forgot?
I don't know, girl, but it hurts a lot
    there was
        whisky
            vodka
                dry Martini (stirred
                  but not shaken)
                    . . . and 12 New Year resolutions
—all of them about you.

So it's all the best for the year ahead
As I stagger upstairs and into bed
Then I looked at the pillow by my side
I tell you baby I almost cried
   there'll be
     autumn
      summer
       spring
        . . . and winter
—all of them without you

ADRIAN HENRI

Rhapsody on a Rusty Trypewriter

"$ #-*&%@ ¢ is a heck of a lot of money!"
Remarked dOQN3G   (pronounced Barcleigh).

"likeitainteasyjustsittingthereallldaybeingpunchedbysecretaries"
Said the Trypewriter.

"@¢¼." "and a QUARTER?!?"
Cried dOQN3G   (pronounced Ducesne).

"whenigrowupiwanttobeacomputor"
Said the Trypewriter.

"Scarlet ribbons for her reels."

"helpihaveswallowedaninkyreeltwocapitalN'sandarubberband"

?
Commented dOQN3G   (pronounced Vittraielli).

"Two million words, that's how many the average trypewriter
   types—
I means trypes—
In a lifetime. And I've tryped 1,999,997, and
mmmm
     ffff (gasp)
         llll
        . . . .
            sqquuirru phmp
      ⁋K   p   . . .

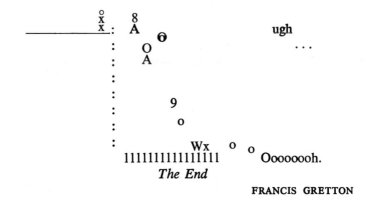

The End

FRANCIS GRETTON

3

A language
of your own

HAVE YOU EVER TRIED INVENTING a language of your own? Sometimes you need words that are entirely your own to express what you want to say to a friend or just for yourself. The English language changes because people invent new words or add new meanings to old words. Americans are constantly inventing or adopting new words. Many recent additions to the language have come from the black culture:

1. *Do your own thing:* do what you want, without giving in to group pressure.

2. *Stoned:* feeling good.

3. *Go through changes:* have anxieties, self-doubts.

4. *A together person:* one who is happy with himself.

Others from the same source, like "fox," "jive," "burn," and "wail," are coming into general use at this very moment.

Here is a poem that is largely made up of imaginary words.

Jabberwocky

'Twas brillig, and the slithy toves
   Did gyre and gimble in the wabe;
All mimsy were the borogoves,
   And the mome raths outgrabe.

"Beware the Jabberwock, my son!
   The jaws that bite, the claws that catch!
Beware the Jubjub bird, and shun
   The frumious Bandersnatch!"

He took his vorpal sword in hand;
   Long time the manxome foe he sought—
So rested he by the Tumtum tree,
   And stood awhile in thought.

And, as in uffish thought he stood,
   The Jabberwock, with eyes of flame,
Came whiffling through the tulgey wood,
   And burbled as it came!

One, two! One, two! And through and through
   The vorpal blade went snicker-snack!
He left it dead, and with its head
   He went galumphing back.

"And hast thou slain the Jabberwock?
   Come to my arms, my beamish boy!
O frabjous day! Callooh! Callay!"
   He chortled in his joy.

'Twas brillig, and the slithy toves
   Did gyre and gimble in the wabe;
All mimsy were the borogoves,
   And the mome raths outgrabe.

LEWIS CARROLL

Did you follow the story? A young man's father warns him
about a monster, but the son goes out anyway, kills it, and returns
in triumph. Don't worry if you don't recognize many of the words
—Lewis Carroll invented them. They mean whatever makes sense
to you.

ACTIVITIES

In most of the exercises in this chapter, there are no "right" and "wrong" answers. So be creative and forget any anxiety that you may have felt about making mistakes.

1. Give the following a name:

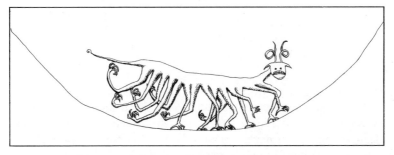

2. Which of the following words best covers the given meaning?

a. Stomp home, self-satisfied and triumphant.
   (1) Gimble   (2) Whiffle   (3) Galumph
b. Indescribably horrible, violently salivating.
   (1) Vorpal   (2) Frumious   (3) Uffish
c. Slimy and weak.
   (1) Mimsy   (2) Tulgey   (3) Frabjous

3. Select the definition that seems to you to fit the italicized word from the poem:

a. *Frabjous*   (1) Dreary, rainy
                 (2) Suitable for washing
                 (3) Perfect
                 (4) Cold and wintry
b. *Gyre*   (1) Trudge
             (2) Progress in spiral motions
             (3) Go shopping
             (4) Lift heavy weights
c. *Manxome*   (1) Friendly
                (2) Doglike
                (3) Aged
                (4) Elusive, hard to find

d. *Vorpal*   (1) Rusty and bent
          (2) Automatic
          (3) Trusted and true
          (4) Cheap

4. Write a complete sentence in a language of your own. The reader should be able to understand generally what it means without translating it.

~~~~~~

Onomatopoeia

In inventing words, the challenge is to find sounds that convey your meaning directly and do not need definitions. Comics regularly coin such words; *splatt, zoink, blam* and *fweeee* might describe, respectively, an egg hitting the pavement, a rubberoid death ray finding its mark, a man walking into a tree, and a nuclear-powered disintegrator at work. But these soon become tiresome, since they are so crude and obvious.

Consider, instead, words that have already been minted. But approach them as if you were seeing them for the first time. Get the "sound" and "feel" of them: *bombard, choke, yawn,* and *echo.*

> *Bombard* has heavy, explosive sounds; the *b* and *d* together with the long, slow *om* and *ar* give the word both weight and violence (power). It is a slow, relentless word.

> *Choke* sticks in the throat with its *k* sounds, which come from the back of the gullet.

> *Yawn* has an open, rubbery sound: just saying the word brings on the urge to do it.

> *Echo* has a light double sound. It evokes the mocking double note that it refers to.

When words sound like what they mean, the effect is called *onomatopoeia*. Note, however, that it is not just the sound that creates this effect; the meaning has to combine with the word-music before onomatopoeia is achieved. For example, the words *murmur* and *manner* sound alike, but only the first is *onomatopoetic*. This term applies not only to words that imitate natural sounds, such as *hiss,* but also to lines and sentences in which the sound blends with the meaning.

In "Pretty Words," Eleanor Wylie both describes and uses this technique:

Pretty Words

Poets make pets of pretty, docile words:
I love smooth words, like gold-enameled fish
Which circle slowly with a silken swish,
And tender ones, like downy-feathered birds:
Words shy and dappled, deep-eyed deer in herds,
Come to my hand, and playful if I wish,
Or purring softly at a silver dish,
Blue Persian kittens, fed on cream and curds.

I love bright words, words up and singing early;
Words that are luminous in the dark, and sing;
Warm, lazy words, white cattle under trees;
I love words opalescent, cool and pearly,
Like midsummer moths, and honeyed words like bees,
Gilded and sticky, with a little sting.

~~~~~~~~~~~~~~~~~~~~~~~~~~~~~~~~~~~~

ACTIVITIES

1. Which of the numbered words best suits the phrase quoted from Eleanor Wylie's poem?

    a. "smooth words, like gold-enameled fish/ Which circle slowly with a silken swish"
        (1) Alabaster   (2) Muffler   (3) Chip   (4) Fiend
    b. "playful [words] . . . purring softly"
        (1) Batter   (2) Serpent   (3) Feast   (4) Prickle
    c. "tender ones, like downy-feathered birds"
        (1) Fat   (2) Dangerous   (3) Timid   (4) Competition
    d. "bright words, words up and singing early"
        (1) Sparkle   (2) Murmurs   (3) Mammoth   (4) Weary
    e. "Words that are luminous in the dark"
        (1) Dull   (2) Dead   (3) Fantasy   (4) Drain
    f. "Warm, lazy words"
        (1) Snake   (2) Drowse   (3) Clap   (4) Spatter

g. "opalescent, cool and pearly [words],"
   (1) Swarm   (2) Sweet   (3) Stillness   (4) Smart
h. "honeyed words . . . / Gilded and sticky, with a little sting"
   (1) Silver   (2) Melt   (3) Bleat   (4) Moon

2. Invent words of your own to mean the following:

a. Swallow with relish.
b. Make an angry motion with the arms.
c. Irritate in a small way.
d. Boring, empty, listless (adjective to describe a *day*).
e. A new name for yourself.

3. Squint your eyes and look at a light. Describe the images (pictures, patterns) that you see. This is how the poet Gerard Manley Hopkins described them:

> tender trambeams truckle at the eye.

4. Explain how the sound imitates the meaning in the following words. (Example: *scratch*—the word contains hard, tearing sounds; the *s* hisses, the hard *c* (k), *t,* and *ch* assault the ear; the *r* delays the word, drawing it out.)

a. water	c. blunt	e. chuckle	g. batter	i. lull
b. kick	d. crooked	f. mummy	h. hiss	j. cold

~~~~~~

The language of poetry is the language of compression, of saying as much as you can as quickly and cleanly as possible. The best way to achieve compression is to choose your words carefully. The following poems illustrate this idea:

The Written Word

A	B
The spoken or written word	The written word
Should be as clean as a bone,	Should be clean as a bone,
As clear as is the light,	Clear as light,
As firm as is a stone.	Firm as stone.
Two words will never serve	Two words are not
As well as one alone.	As good as one.

The basic rule of good writing is "Show, don't tell." A good writer presents his experiences through his nouns and verbs, rather than through his adjectives and adverbs. Nouns and verbs are the core of any sentence; adjectives and adverbs only qualify, trim, and adjust the words they modify. Modifiers are secondary elements in a sentence, and they should be used only when the nouns and verbs cannot clearly re-create the experience.

Use concrete, exact nouns and strong, active verbs. Whenever possible, avoid using abstract nouns, passive verbs, and the verb "to be."

Assonance and alliteration

Consider the following lines:

Beat an empty barrel with the handle of a broom.
VACHEL LINDSAY, "The Congo"

The day of his death was a dark cold day.
W. H. AUDEN, "In Memory of W. B. Yeats"

The moan of doves in immemorial elms,
And murmuring of innumerable bees
ALFRED TENNYSON, "The Princess"

Each of these lines creates its own sound effects. How? Did you notice that in each excerpt an initial consonant sound was repeated and that this repetition was the main technique for orchestrating the language? There is a word to describe this, *alliteration*. Alliteration is the repetition of initial sounds, usually consonant sounds but sometimes vowel sounds.

In the first line, the sound that is repeated is the *b* of *beat, barrel,* and *broom*. *B* is an explosive, bouncing sound, made by pushing the breath through the lips abruptly; it is a suitable echo for a drum beat. A line that uses words beginning with only *b*'s would be noisy and bouncy: balloons, breaking, banging, bouncing, black and blue. In the line by Auden, the *d*'s set the sound tone. The *d* sound tends to be dull, dark, dreary, drab.

In Tennyson's lines, there is only one example of alliteration: the *m* of *moan* and *murmur*. However, Tennyson underscores the alliteration by repeating the *m* sound within several words: *immemorial, murmuring,* and *innumerable*. The *m*'s are mellow, intimate, calm, and melting, and they imitate the moan of the doves and the humming of the bees.

But notice that it is the sound, not the letter, that must be repeated to make alliteration; in *write* and *real, knob* and *nail,* there is alliteration; in *write* and *willow, knee* and *kick,* there is none.

Now consider these lines:

> Tyger, tyger, burning bright
> In the forests of the night.
> WILLIAM BLAKE, "The Tyger"

> Hungry the owlet shall seek out the mouse.
> DONALD JUSTICE, "Another Song"

Did you notice the devices used in these lines to gain sound effects? In the first quotation, Blake repeated the *i* sounds to comb the flow of his words. In the second, it is the *ou* sound that is repeated. This technique of repeating vowel sounds is called *assonance.*

When poetry was written (and sung) in England, before the Norman Conquest, the land was inhabited by Angles and Saxons. Their poetry was based on alliteration, just as much later poetry was based on rhyme. Here is Burton Raffel's translation of an Old English poem that retains much of the word music of the original. The poem takes the form of a riddle. Can you guess what it is about?

Riddle 32

> Our world is lovely in different ways,
> Hung with beauty and works of hands.
> I saw a strange machine, made
> For motion, slide against the sand,
> Shrieking as it went. It walked swiftly
> On its only foot, this odd-shaped monster,
> Traveled in an open country without
> Seeing, without arms, or hands,
> With many ribs, and its mouth in its middle.
> Its work is useful, and welcome, for it loads
> Its belly with food, and brings abundance
> To men, to poor and to rich, paying
> Its tribute year after year. Solve
> This riddle, if you can, and unravel its name.

ACTIVITIES

1. Indicate where the poet has used alliteration in the riddle.

2. List five sayings that make use of alliteration and five that make use of assonance. Examples include "safe and sound," "last chance."

3. List any five advertising slogans that make use of alliteration and/or assonance. Examples: "perspiration problem solved," "fruit of the loom."

4. Compose a sentence of which the first word begins with *a*, the second with *b*, the third with *c*, the fourth with *d*, and so on as far as you can go into the alphabet. Example: "A beautiful cat doggedly examined, feeling glad, her icky jello, knowingly left moldering near. . . ."

5. Compose a poem in which every word in the first line begins with *a*, every word in the second line with *b*, the third *c*, the fourth *d*, and so on through the whole alphabet. Example:

An Austrian army awfully arrayed
Boldly by battery besieged Belgrade.
Cossack commanders cannonading come,
Dealing destruction's devastating doom. . . .
ALARIC WATTS

Working in groups will help to create individual lines. Use a dictionary, a thesaurus, or a dictionary of synonyms.

6. Select the best words from those listed below to fill the blanks:

When the hounds of spring are on winter's traces,
   The ___a___ of months in meadow or plain
Fills the shadows and ___b___ places
   With ___c___ of leaves and ___d___ of rain.
ALGERNON SWINBURNE, "When the Hounds of Spring"

a. saddest   leader   coldest   mother
b. country   windy   secret   tiny
c. lisp   sound   green   beauty
d. patter   ripple   shower   wash

7. In the following poem, "Counting Out Rhyme," the words that have been omitted have a similarity in sound to those around them. Filling in the blanks is a bit like doing a crossword puzzle, but it is good practice in preparation for your own writing. In this case, there is a "correct answer," which consists of the words selected by the poet. But so long as your choice is similar in sound to the surrounding words, it will not be considered incorrect.

> Silver bark of beech, and sallow
> Bark of yellow _____ and yellow
>   Twig of _____.
>
> Stripe of green in moosewood maple,
> Color seen in _____ of apple,
>   Bark of popple.
>
> Wood of popple _____ as moonbeam,
> Wood of _____ for yoke and barnbeam,
>   Wood of hornbeam.
>
> Silver _____ of beech, and hollow
> _____ of elder, tall and yellow
>   _____ of _____.

> EDNA ST. VINCENT MILLAY

Advanced use of onomatopoeia

The use of alliteration and assonance are, in effect, extending onomatopoeia to cover whole lines or whole poems. But language can echo meaning without the repetition of vowel and consonant sounds. Take the following line, in which Siegfried Sassoon describes a house at midnight:

> Everyone yawning. Only the clocks are alert.
>   "Falling Asleep"

The first half of this line contrasts with the second half. The first half speaks about the tired people, the second about the sleepless clocks. But can you also detect a contrast in sound, as well as in sense, within this line? The first half contains rubbery, slow, open sounds; the second half contains quick ticking noises, quiet but clear. The sounds of the words echo the meaning. In the first half, the *v, y,* and *n* sounds, coupled with the long, stretching vowels, provide the effect; in the second half, the hard *c* and *t* sounds are mixed with quick vowels.

We will now stretch the concept of onomatopoeia to its limits. In what way does the form of the following poem echo its meaning?

> There was a young man from Sudan,
> Whose verses just wouldn't scan; *
> When they asked him why,
> He answered, "Well, I
> Always try to fit as many words into the last line as I
>   possibly can."

Here the writer has done what he described: he has fitted as many words into the last line as he possibly could, thus preventing the last line from scanning. This is still rather crude and obvious, of course. Here is a subtler example of the same technique:

> And ten low words oft creep in one dull line.

Alexander Pope is describing the poetic ability of some of the dreary poets of his day. How many words are there in this line? What adjective best describes them? What do all the words have in common?

Here is a different way of gaining onomatopoeia. In "Dulce et Decorum Est," Wilfred Owen describes a man being asphyxiated by gas:

> He plunges at me, guttering, choking, drowning.

The reader almost gags as he says the words. How has Owen gained this effect? Answering the following questions should help you to discover how Owen achieved the effect of gagging.

1. Why has Owen broken up the smoothness of the line with three disjointed words at the end?
2. What sounds are dominant in the three participles that end the line?
3. Where in your mouth do you make these sounds?

---

* **scan:** sound right rhythmically.

You should constantly be listening or looking for words or phrases that appeal to you, especially if their sound imitates their meaning. When you hear or see a particularly interesting word or phrase, write it in your notebook.

Here is a final example of onomatopoeia. This time you must listen very carefully indeed to pick up the effect:

> pity this busy monster,manunkind.
>
> not. Progress is a comfortable disease:
> your victim(death and life safely beyond)
>
> plays with the bigness of his littleness
> —electrons deify one razorblade
> into a mountainrange;lenses extend
>
> unwish through curving wherewhen till unwish
> returns on its unself.
>   A world of made
> is not a world of born—pity poor flesh
>
> and trees,poor stars and stones,but never this
> fine specimen of hypermagical
>
> ultraomnipotence. We doctors know
>
> a hopeless case if—listen:there's a hell
> of a good universe next door;let's go
>
>   E. E. CUMMINGS

We will ignore, for the purposes of this analysis, the obvious difficulties, such as the lack of capital letters and the unfamiliar word, "manunkind." Concentrate instead on the word "not," which ends the first sentence but begins the second line. Why didn't Cummings fit the word into the first line, so that each sentence might have a line to itself? That would have been neater.

What goes on in the reader's mind as he reads the first line? He is first lulled into a feeling of security: He, together with the rest of mankind (or "manunkind"), is going to be pitied. It is a very comfortable feeling to know that the poet is sympathetic to his situation. Then comes the "not." All of a sudden the security blanket is snatched away. He is not to be pitied at all; instead he is to be treated as a diseased object that enjoys its disease. The reader is startled into awareness, and now he is ready to ask "Why?" Why should he not be pitied? The answer is in the rest of the poem. Man(un)kind is a stupid, boastful, vicious monster, who has turned nature into a plastic world. Here, the poet's aim was not harmony, but shock. Cummings used the form of the poem to enhance the meaning.

ACTIVITIES

1. Indicate the sound patterns in the following two paragraphs, pointing out any vowel or consonant sounds that are repeated often enough to have an effect on the reader's ear:

> I sought, and soon discovered, the three headstones on the slope next the moor—the middle one, gray, and half buried in heath—Edgar Linton's only harmonized by the turf and moss creeping up its foot—Heathcliff's still bare.
>
> I lingered round them, under that benign sky; watched the moths fluttering among the heath and harebells; listened to the soft wind breathing through the grass; and wondered how anyone could ever imagine unquiet slumbers for the sleepers in that quiet earth.
>
> EMILY BRONTË, *Wuthering Heights*

2. Change the italicized words in "Pied Beauty" so as to create a description of your own, as was done in the following example:

Streets that *follow* like a *tedious argument*
Of insidious intent . . .

   T. S. ELIOT, "The Love Song of J. Alfred Prufrock"

to

Streets that *dance* like a *May morning*
Of youthful promise . . .

or

Alleys that *twist* like an *injured snake*
Of parched dust . . .

Pied Beauty

Glory be to God for *dappled things*—
    For *skies* of *couple-color* as a *brinded* * *cow;*
      For rose-moles all in stipple * upon trout that swim;
Fresh-firecoal chestnut-falls;* *finches' wings;**
    Landscape plotted and *pieced—fold, fallow,* and *plow;**   5
      And *áll trádes, their gear* and *tackle* and *trim.*

All thing *counter,** *original, spare,** *strange;*
    Whatever is *fickle, freckled* (who knows how?)
      With *swift, slow; sweet, sour; adazzle, dim;*
He fathers-forth * *whose beauty is past change:*   10
      Praise him.

               GERARD MANLEY HOPKINS

3. Write a paragraph in which you describe a scene, choosing words with sounds that evoke feelings of softness and mellow beauty. Then write another paragraph describing the same scene, except that it has a mood of violence and fear, again suggested by the sounds of the words you choose. The following examples show the same scene from two different perspectives.

  a. The muted lamp gave off a mellow light, which made for a mood of harmony.

  b. The blinding light blazed garishly with a blood-red glow.

4. Find language to portray the following:

  a. An elephant lying down.
  b. A man walking along briskly, then slipping and falling.
  c. A long, slow, hot afternoon.
  d. A diver diving gracefully from a high-diving board and entering the water perfectly.
  e. Two trains in a head-on collision.
  f. A line that imitates the progress of (1) a dinosaur (2) a kangaroo (3) a flea (4) a horse (5) a centipede.

---

2. brinded: an archaic form of *bridled,* which means "irregularly streaked." **3. stipple:** in painting, a method of reproducing effects of light and shade by use of dots rather than lines. **4. Fresh-firecoal chestnut-falls:** Chestnuts when they fall from the tree are encased in green husks. These break open to reveal the nut, that is red and brown and that, according to Hopkins, looks as bright as burning coal. **finches' wings:** Goldfinches, for example, have yellow and black wings. **5. fold, fallow, and plow:** respectively, an enclosure, usually for sheep; unused land; land being farmed. **7. counter:** going in an opposite or opposing direction, as in *counterclockwise.* **spare:** scarce. **10. fathers-forth:** begets.

5. Find single words or compose lines that use alliteration and assonance to portray the following:

a. Crunching up a piece of paper.
b. A skater stopping by dragging his skates sideways on the ice.
c. Honking of cars at rush hour.
d. A cat walking through leaves.
e. A small stone dropped into water.
f. The audience showing their appreciation after a Beatles concert.
g. A ping-pong ball bouncing on a table.
h. Padding of bare feet on a polished floor.
i. Seagulls screaming.
j. A drumbeat.

6. Here is another riddle poem.

Riddle 11

> I wear gray, woven over
> With bright and gleaming gems. I bring
> The stupid to folly's paths, fool
> The ignorant with sin, urge all useless
> Roads and ruin the rest. I can't
> Explain their madness, for I push them to error
> And pick their brains, yet they praise me more
> For each seduction. Their dullness will be sorrow,
> When they lead their souls on high, unless
> They learn to walk wisely, and without my help.

> Translated by Burton Raffel

Try your hand at imitating it with a poem of your own. Try repeating a consonant or vowel sound two or three times per line.

4

Imagery

IMAGINE YOU ARE SWIMMING in fresh, clear, cold water and someone from the bank calls out, "How does it feel?" Or you are digging into a three-layered, nut-and-cream–covered hot fudge sundae when someone asks, "What's it like?" Perhaps someone asks, "What's her latest record like?" when you've heard it, and it's indescribably good.

How do you set about communicating these experiences? First, forget all the adjectives you had lined up at first: *fantastic, monumental, incredible,* and so on. They don't describe anything. There is only one way really to approach making such a communication: by assembling a number of sharp, clear experiences that resemble the experience you are trying to describe, and saying that this experience is a combination of those.

The earliest forms of poetry that we know of were simple chants or hymns in honor of the sun or the moon or the fertility of the earth. In the early myths of each nation or tribe, there were fundamental ideas and pictures that have been the nucleus of poetry ever since. Some of these objects that have kept their fascination for people in all ages include the sun's rising and setting, the moon, the stars, the sea, the wind, ice, fire, trees, the heart, the stomach, sickness and health, cats, eagles, swallows; also: wandering, dreams, the sword, mirrors, a rod of gold, and a golden bowl. These basic experiences are burned into the human mind, known and felt by people everywhere. So, too, are the common processes of life that never lose their mystery or their immediacy: birth, love, death, home, family life, mother and father, sisters and brothers, growing up, widening awareness of the world, and coming of age. They are experiences common to all poetry. It is from these and similar experiences that the poet creates his poetry. When he depicts an experience so clearly that the reader can see it, smell it, hear it, touch it, or taste it in his imagination, this word is called an image.

A. E. Housman described imagery as "something sacred, ugly or beautiful, but it must arouse awe. A swan or an octopus, a toothless hag or a fair young child, Beatrice * or La Belle Dame Sans Merci.* Our dreams are full of sacred beings, but we cannot distinguish between the beautiful and the ugly." Another way of defining imagery is to say imagery is the verbal representation of sense experience.

Here, then, is your answer to the original question, "How does it feel?" You answer in images, in concrete experiences, that vividly communicate how it feels, tastes, looks, and so on.

Modern poetry is still concerned with the basic elements of nature, but there is a new dimension. Contemporary poets are often city centered. Their images are of streets, chromium, neon lights, parks and roller coasters, bridges, supermarkets, traffic, garbage, the faces of the people on the sidewalk or in line waiting for buses. Notice how, in the following excerpt, T. S. Eliot re-creates an early twentieth-century city:

> The winter evening settles down
> With smell of steaks in passageways.
> Six o'clock.
> The burnt-out ends of smoky days.
> And now a gusty shower wraps
> The grimy scraps
> Of withered leaves about your feet
> And newspapers from vacant lots;
> The showers beat
> On broken blinds and chimney-pots,

* Two perfectly beautiful women in poetry.

And at the corner of the street
A lonely cab-horse steams and stamps.
"Preludes"

In order to re-create the experience, Eliot uses images appealing to the senses of smell, sight, and sound. Through the imagery he selects, he indicates his attitude toward the scene: the day is "burnt-out," the leaves are "grimy scraps" as are the newspapers that come from "vacant lots." The scene is a series of impressions that stimulate unfavorable ideas in your mind. (Eliot had an acute sense of smell, and steak was, at this time, associated with tenement living. And so for Eliot, the picture was even more unfavorable than it might be for you.)

Perhaps another way to emphasize the need for imagery is by saying a poem should show, not tell. Instead of stating "winter is cold," Shakespeare writes that winter is a time

When icicles hang by the wall,
And Dick the shepherd blows his nail.
And Tom bears logs into the hall,
And milk comes frozen home in pail.

Each picture illustrates the coldness of winter.

Poets will re-create an experience that the readers may not have experienced, by using images that are within the experience of most people. Robert Hayden describes a diver sinking into the ocean by suggesting he

Swiftly descended
Into canyon of cold
Nightgreen emptiness.

Each word, taken individually, is within the experience of most readers. We know what a canyon is; we have all felt cold, have seen the night. Perhaps we can recall the night as having a green color. Even if we can't, we can visualize the green ocean and the night, and by putting the two together can imagine the diver moving in the dark, greenish water. By mentioning familiar images, Hayden communicates an experience that most persons have not had.

ACTIVITIES

1. Make a list of the images in the following:

a. The window contained photographs of more or less undressed dancing girls; nondescript packages in wrappers like patent medicines; closed yellow paper envelopes, very flimsy, and marked two-and-six in heavy black figures; a few numbers of ancient French comic publications hung across a string as if to dry; a dingy blue china bowl, a casket of black wood, bottles of marking ink, and rubber stamps; a few books, with titles hinting at impropriety; a few apparently old copies of obscure newspapers, badly printed, with titles like *The Torch, The Gong*—rousing titles. And the two gas-jets inside the panes were always turned low, either for economy's sake or for the sake of the customers.

JOSEPH CONRAD, *The Secret Agent*

b. Season of mists and mellow fruitfulness,
　　Close bosom friend of the maturing sun;
Conspiring with him how to load and bless
　　With fruit the vines that round the thatch-eves run;
To bend with apples the moss'd cottage trees,
　　And fill all fruit with ripeness to the core;
　　To swell the gourd, and plump the hazel shells
With a sweet kernel; to set budding more,
And still more, later flowers for the bees,
Until they think warm days will never cease,
　　　For summer has o'er-brimm'd their clammy cells.

JOHN KEATS, "Ode to Autumn"

2. Replace the images that have been italicized with alternative ones that create a different picture or a different mood:

In the evening they had a *fire of cones* in the *airtight stove.* The *flames growled* in the *chimney.* Danny and Pilon, *well-fed, warm,* and *happy,* sat *in the rocking chairs* and *gently teetered back and forth. At dinner* they had *used* a *piece of candle,* but now only the *light from the stove cracks dispelled* the *darkness of the room.* To make it *perfect, rain* began to *patter on the roof. Only a little leaked through,* and that *in places where no one wanted to sit anyway.*

JOHN STEINBECK, *Tortilla Flat*

3. Describe some ordinary object—a coin or a piece of fruit. Note the shape, color, smell, and other of its characteristics. Avoid using generalizations, such as "small," "tall," or "heavy"; instead, use concrete language to create your description.

4. Choose several images that would depict your classroom at a typical moment, for example, during morning roll call, or during a particular lesson, on a hot or cold day, a Monday morning or a Friday. Make the images describe a single overall feeling such as morning bleariness, excitement, nervousness, or boredom.

5. Play some music (without lyrics) that interests you particularly. Answer the question "What am I?" while the music is playing. For this exercise, it is not absolutely essential that you have music, but it does help enrich your imagination. Here are some examples of images that came to students in similar circumstances:

   a. What am I? I am a mirror, a spectator to people's egotism. Even as I watch others display themselves vainly, using every ounce of talent, I can only observe the finery of those, wishing I could be like them, knowing it is forever out of my reach.
   b. What am I? I am a snowflake, falling silently to earth. One in a million or a billion more. Yet I am different from all the others. From the time that I was born, I have had my own pattern, set my own ways.
   c. What am I? I am a mockingbird, picking up another's song in an effort to make new friends.
   d. What am I? I am a window mannequin. People are not interested in the real me, but in what I look like or seem to be. In me they see an image or themselves or another.
   e. I become a coat which protects my internal organs from the cold.
   f. I become the seed of a tree. I slowly emerge from my outer shell to start the gradual process of growing. I work my way slowly up to my life-giving source, the sun. Always growing, never ceasing, I grow onward toward the limitless beauty of the vast expanse of the sky.

6. Play some music, without lyrics, that means a great deal to you. Jot down the images that come into your mind. Here are some examples from students:

Crashing waves against a cliff, always fading. In a cavern with different shades of light on the stalagmites, different rock formations. Canoeing down a foamy, bubbling river. The path of a piece of wood going downstream, foaming rapids and quiet pools. Dogs snapping at fallen leaves. Like a person falling down a long, winding stairway. A train speeding through a dark forest, destroying the peace of the morning. Butterflies spread out and fall down like snowflakes. Feels very dull, is in a slump, has nothing to do. The hush of a crowd waiting to hear the verdict, guilty or not guilty.

7. Starting tonight, record your dreams as exactly as you can remember them. If you can remember a dream from the past, write it out now. List the images contained in the dream. Are they different from the images you create when you are awake?

If you can't remember a dream, try this technique: Relax completely; try to exclude all conscious thoughts. Let images come to you from inside, from behind your conscious mind. For example, imagine you are on a road and describe what you see. (The difficulty will be to erase the conscious thoughts from your mind. Your conscious mind must be completely empty, or the unconscious images will not come.)

8. Here are two selections that emphasize the freshness of imagery. Both are lists honoring life.

I've known rivers:
I've known rivers ancient as the world and older than the flow
 of human blood in human veins.

My soul has grown deep like the rivers.

I bathed in the Euphrates when dawns were young.
I built my hut near the Congo and it lulled me to sleep.
I looked upon the Nile and raised the pyramids above it.
I heard the singing of the Mississippi when Abe Lincoln went
 down to New Orleans, and I've seen its muddy bosom
 turn all golden in the sunset.

I've known rivers:
Ancient, dusky rivers.

My soul has grown deep like the rivers.
LANGSTON HUGHES, "The Negro Speaks of Rivers"

These I have loved:
                White plates and cups, clean-gleaming,
Ringed with blue lines; and feathery, faëry dust;
Wet roofs, beneath the lamp light; the strong crust
Of friendly bread; and many-tasting food;
Rainbows; and the blue bitter smoke of wood;
And radiant raindrops couching in cool flowers;
And flowers themselves, that sway through summer hours,
Dreaming of moths that drink them under the moon;
Then, the cool kindliness of sheets, that soon
Smooth away trouble; and the rough male kiss
Of blankets; grainy wood; live hair that is
Shining and free; blue-massing clouds; the keen
Unpassioned beauty of a great machine;
The benison of hot water; furs to touch;
The good smell of old clothes; and other such—
The comfortable smell of friendly fingers,
Hair's fragrance and the musty reek that lingers
About dead leaves and last year's ferns. . . .
                     Dear names,
And thousand others throng to me! Royal flames;
Sweet water's dimpling laugh from tap or spring;
Holes in the ground; and voices that do sing;
Voices in laughter, too; and body's pain,
Soon turned to peace; and the deep-panting train;
Firm sands; the little dulling edge of foam
That browns and dwindles as the wave goes home;
And washen stones, gay for an hour; the cold
Graveness of iron; moist black earthen mold;
Sleep; and high places; footprints in the dew;
And oaks; and brown horse chestnuts, glossy-new;
And new-peeled sticks; and shining pools on grass;
All these have been my loves.
           RUPERT BROOKE, "The Great Lover"

Using one or the other of these two poems as a mode, create your own tribute to life or to an area of life—your school, your home town, America, sports, music, etc. Neither poet uses a very difficult verse form; you should not worry about your meter or line length. Your images may not be gentle and soft like Hughes's, or objects that you love like Brooke's. They may be terrifying, mysterious, noisy, angry, silent, or they may be objects of hate, boredom, desire, fear.

~~~~~~

It is possible to tell a lie and tell the truth at the same time. Consider this sentence: It turned out that our English teacher was a tiger on the tennis court. Now, it is clear that their English teacher was not striped, did not have a four-foot tail, and was not a beast of prey (in the usual sense, at least). Therefore, the sentence is a lie *literally*—that is, if you take it at face value. But in another sense, it is true and a more effective way of saying what was intended than any *literal* statement. For this English teacher has many (though not all) the qualities of a tiger, once he steps onto the tennis court. His forehand drives are merciless, his speed is uncanny, he stalks his opponent relentlessly.

This way of telling the truth (by lying) is called using *figurative language*. It involves using language imaginatively, as opposed to literally, where one interprets the meaning "to the letter," or according to its surface meaning.

If you think for a moment, you will see that you use figurative language every day. If you refer to a person as being "rather bright," for instance, you are comparing his mind to a light; if you describe him as "somewhat dim," you are again talking as if intellect could be measured in terms of light and dark, as if light meant intelligent, and dark meant less intelligent. In this case, you are using the comparison without knowing it. This is a dangerous business, since you are transmitting equivalencies and values (intelligent = light, stupid = dark) without realizing it. Words are full of traps of just this kind. As you use words, make a habit of asking yourself: What am I implying with these words? Am I making an implied comparison, and, if so, what am I comparing to what?

Poets make more frequent use of figurative language than most people. They make comparisons between one idea and another that is apparently quite different. In fact, their aim is frequently to produce a *fusion* or a *complex* of images. It is their way of catching the complicated experience. Ezra Pound described an image as "a cluster of fused ideas which is endowed with energy." He was thinking of the double-barreled type of image.

There are four degrees or stages of subtlety in putting double-images together:

1. Simple comparisons, in which the point of likeness or difference is made clear and explicit. This can be written as "*A* is as . . . as *B*": "the ball was as flat as a pancake"; "she stood as stately as a flag"; "he was as tall as a lamppost." These comparisons are called *similes.*

2. Comparisons in which the writer states that two things are like one another, but the reader is left to discover for himself how they are alike. The equation for this is "*A* is like *B*": "The pool at evening is like a darkened mirror"; "smoke is like a vague memory"; "the night comes like a nun." These also are *similes.*

3. Comparisons that drop the word that indicates that the two are only *like* each other, not the *same* as each other. The equation for this is "*A* is *B*"—not "*A* is like *B*": "death is a smiling crocodile" (not, "death is *as treacherous as*," or "death is *like*," or "death *may be compared* to a smiling crocodile"). Other examples include: "love is a dark forest"; "words are boxes with thoughts in them." This technique is called *metaphor.* It leaves the reader to work out for himself that the writer does not intend the two halves of the comparison to be considered *literally* the same.

4. The subtlest but most effective comparisons, where the equation is not *"A is B,"* but *"A has some qualities* or *does some things* that *B* has or does, *but you never mention B."* In short, *A* does what (*B*) does, but you do not see (*B*). Notice how the comparison works in the following examples:

a. When I am pinned and wriggling on the wall
         T. S. ELIOT, "The Love Song of J. Alfred Prufrock"

["I" is compared to an insect, but the insect is not mentioned.]

b. . . . in the mist of tears
  I hid from Him, and under running laughter
      FRANCIS THOMPSON, "The Hound of Heaven"

[In the first half, "tears" are compared to "mist," a "third degree" comparison, but in the second half, "laughter" is simply made to do *what water does,* without ever making the direct statement that *laughter* is like *water*.]

c.   I have no spur
To prick the sides of my intent, but only
Vaulting ambition, which o'erleaps itself
And falls on the other [side].
      WILLIAM SHAKESPEARE, *Macbeth*

[Here "ambition" acts like a horse, and Macbeth is the rider.]

d. The yellow fog that rubs its back upon the window-panes,
The yellow smoke that rubs its muzzle on the window-
          panes,
Licked its tongue into the corners of the evening,
Lingered upon the pools that stand in drains,
Let fall upon its back the soot that falls from chimneys,
Slipped by the terrace, made a sudden leap,
And seeing that it was a soft October night,
Curled once about the house, and fell asleep.
      T. S. ELIOT, "The Love Song of J. Alfred Prufrock"

[To what is the "fog" compared?]

One more type of comparison belongs here—*personification*. This is a technique whereby inhuman or inanimate creatures are given the characteristics of, and are treated as if they were, human or animate. "Laughing skies," "gurgling streams," "weeping rain" are three often used examples of personification. It is a dangerous device because it has been misused and overused in the past. Be sparing with it.

~~~~~~

ACTIVITIES

1. Give four examples of simple images and four of complex images (double-barreled images).

2. Without looking back, write out the four degrees of image making in terms of *A* and *B*.

3. Fill in the blanks:

a. He was as crafty as a _____.

b. He fought like a _____.

c. When in a good mood, Uncle George was a _____.

d. Caught in his own trap, the villain _____ed and _____ed [verbs] at the Caped Crusader. [Show the villain doing the same thing as a beast of prey.]

4. In the following, *what* is being compared to *what?*

a. Death, will you shake off all my leaves?

b. Time dropped in decay, and the wax ran down its side.

c. With a cold-blooded smile, Mr. Sinister stretched out a tentacle.

d. Peace comes dropping slowly from morning to night.

e. Pity . . . Shall blow the horrid deed in every eye,/ That tears shall drown the wind. [This is extremely difficult: the "horrid deed" is murder; what is it being compared to, by implication?]

f. We are such stuff/ As dreams are made on and our life/ Is rounded with a sleep.

5. Assign the following comparisons to its category, *one* through *four*:

a. Her nose looks like a little white onion.

b. You knew it was time to be careful when Nancy's voice became velvet.

c. Before the car had gone fifty feet, it was swallowed up in the fog.

d. He knew as much about navigation as a fly in a milk pan.

e. There in the west was the new moon, a tiny grin in the sky.

f. The wind is exhausted.

g. What is this thing called age, tied to me as to a dog's tail?

h. Restless thoughts, like a deadly swarm of hornets, rush upon me.

i. I'm feeling blue.

~~~~~~

Before you are ready to make comparisons of your own, read these seven fundamental guidelines for creating effective comparisons:

1. All likenesses must be new. An overused comparison is much less effective than a fresh one. In the same way, a new coin is sharper to the thumb than an old one that is worn. Likewise, you cannot expect to evoke an emotion with a worn-out image. Metaphors like "bright" and "dim" have been so often used that they no longer register as metaphors. They are called dead metaphors, or sometimes fossilized metaphors. Comparing love to a rose, kisses to wine, or tears to rain shows little imagination. Overused comparisons are referred to as clichés. Other examples of clichés: "My heart is singing like a bird" and "he was as good as gold."

2. The two halves of the comparison must be taken from separate areas of life. The parts should not be too close, or the comparison will lack energy. Two examples of poor images might be "smoke like fog" and "ice like frozen milk."

3. On the other hand, comparisons should not be strained or too far-fetched. There must be some degree of similarity between the two areas. In the comparison "In the dark, the cat's eyes were like luminous peas," there is no similarity between the two objects being compared.

4. The two halves of the comparison must match grammatically. Cracks on the floor of an ancient mansion are not like an old man's palm: the cracks are like the wrinkles; the floor is like the palm.

5. Avoid vague or general comparisons: to compare a clown's face to a duck waddling home is not clear enough. The comparisons should be specific and concrete.

6. Do not compare something to what is lesser in stature or importance. Keep a sense of proportion. Do not compare clouds to cotton candy (or anything in nature to what is man-made) or compare rocket officials waving their blueprints after a successful blast off to students emerging from an examination. The effect is anticlimactic and often produces unintentional humor. But to compare an evil king who does not belong on the throne to a dwarf in giant's robes illustrates the idea that an evil man does not belong in a position requiring a man of character. In this case, the comparison is intended to show a lack of proportion.

7. Make your comparisons uniform in tone. Decide at the start what effect you are aiming to create, and stick to it. Do not write "a silver wind, clouds like ghosts, and a moon like bubble gum." This image creates unintentional humor.

ACTIVITIES

1. Are the following comparisons successful or not? Give your reasons.

a. As fresh as the dew.
b. Like a small gray/ coffee-pot/ sits the squirrel.
c. The skull was picked clean as a surgeon's scalpel.
d. Mornings as fresh as washed parsley.
e. Her voice was like the sound of blended flutes/ Blown by black players upon a picnic day.
f. The ape swung through the trees like a monkey.
g. The ship, a clumsy ghost/ In the enveloping mist.
h. Brown as owls.
i. The scars on the moon's face/ Were like a wreck'd galleon.
j. Clocks ruling like overseers.
k. The flag moved/ With royal grace, like a colored handkerchief.
l. At my back I always hear/ Time's wingèd chariot hurrying near.
m. Memory like a juggler tosses its plates into the air.
n. Great mammoths . . ./ Like palaces of patience, in the gray/ And changeless lands of ice.
o. I shall put my foot down with a firm hand.
p. Now then, team, I want you to keep your ear to the ground, your nose to the grindstone, your shoulder to the wheel, your eyes skinned and pull your finger out.
q. Shake/ The late leaves down, which frozen where they fell/ And held in ice as dancers in a spell.
r. To take arms against a sea of troubles.
s. Thou [the West Wind], from whose unseen presence the leaves dead/ Are driven, like ghosts from an enchanter fleeing.

2. List and analyze the images in the following poems. How effective are they? Do they conform to the guidelines for imagery presented in this chapter? Give reasons to support your opinion.

a. Strong Men, riding horses. In the West
   On a range five hundred miles. A Thousand. Reaching

From dawn to sunset. Rested blue to orange.
From hope to crying. Except that Strong Men are
Desert-eyed. Except that Strong Men are
Pasted to stars already. Have their cars
Beneath them. Rentless, too. Too broad of chest
To shrink when the Rough Man hails. Too flailing
To redirect the Challenger, when the challenge
.Nicks; slams; buttonholes. Too saddled.

I am not like that. I pay rent, am addled
By illegible landlords, run, if robbers call.

What mannerisms I present, employ,
Are camouflage, and what my mouths remark
To word-wall off that broadness of the dark
Is pitiful.
I am not brave at all.

b. Oh, dark as ink was the fateful day;
It is burned like mist into my memory.
I'll never forget the foxy way
Fate barred the door and took the key.

Like a football was his face,
As he told me that I'd lost the race.
I was like a man in pain,
Or a statue left out in the rain.

c. That time of year thou mayst in me behold
When yellow leaves, or none, or few, do hang
Upon these boughs which shake against the cold,
Bare ruined choirs, where late the sweet birds sang.
In me thou see'st the twilight of such day
As after sunset fadeth in the west,
Which by and by black night doth take away,
Death's second self, that seals up all in rest.
In me thou see'st the glowing of such fire,
That on the ashes of his youth doth lie
As the deathbed whereon it must expire,
Consumed with that which it was nourished by.
     This, thou perceivest, which makes thy love more
          strong,
     To love that well, which thou must leave ere long.

3. Choose two activities or scenes about which you have different feelings. You may like one, detest the other; or you may laugh at one, be angry at the other. Show how you feel about them simply by the comparisons you make, as is done in this example:

A lesson I like and one I dislike: Contrasting images

Like: Work as challenging as a maze; charts as intriguing as a code; wisecracks as funny as a clown's; knowledge as useful as my shoes.

Dislike: Wisecracks as sour as crab apples; discussions like sermons; homework as frustrating as a cake to a woman on a diet; knowledge as useful as a saw to a scuba-diver.

4. In this excerpt, notice how the abstract idea of "Time" is made clear and concrete through a series of images.

There was a smell of Time in the air tonight. He [Tomás] smiled and turned the fancy in his mind. There was a thought. What did Time smell like? Like dust and clocks and people. And if you wondered what Time sounded like it sounded like water running in a dark cave and voices crying and dirt dropping down upon hollow box lids, and rain. And, going further, what did Time *look* like? Time looked like snow dropping silently into a black room or it looked like a silent film in an ancient theater, one hundred billion faces falling like those New Year balloons, down and down into nothing. That was how Time smelled and looked and sounded. And tonight—Tomás shoved a hand into the wind outside the truck —tonight you could almost *touch* Time.

RAY BRADBURY, *The Martian Chronicles*

Write a paragraph describing clearly and concretely how one of the following feels. Develop the paragraph through a series of images, not by telling a story.

a. Boredom   c. Fear   e. Loneliness
b. Coldness   d. Frustration   f. A subject of your own

5. Read the following and apply the techniques to topics suggested below:

The tree is a book and can tell stories of years past.
The tree is human, for its moods change with the seasons.

The tree is an old man wrinkled with age.
The tree is a listener to which you can tell all.
The tree is a scholar with much knowledge.
The tree is an elder with much experience in living.

Write a similar series based on one of the following, portraying aspects of your subject by means of images:

a. A cat on the wall   c. A river   e. School
b. A scarecrow   d. An ice-cream man   f. A book

6. Here is an image poem written by Walt Whitman:

A Noiseless Patient Spider

A noiseless patient spider,
I mark'd where on a little promontory it stood isolated,
Mark'd how to explore the vacant vast surrounding,
It launch'd forth filament, filament, filament, out of itself,
Ever unreeling them, ever tirelessly speeding them.

And you O my soul where you stand,
Surrounded, detached, in measureless oceans of space,
Ceaselessly musing, venturing, throwing, seeking the spheres
    to connect them,
Till the bridge you will need be form'd, till the ductile anchor
    hold,
Till the gossamer thread you fling catch somewhere, O my
    soul.

The poem relies on a single, extended comparison. Write a similar poem based on a single, extended simile or metaphor.

5

Blood rhythms

PUT YOUR FINGER TO YOUR PULSE. What do you feel? It probably feels to you something like: bump BUMP, bump BUMP, bump BUMP. In fact, it is more like this: bump BUMP, *bump BUMP*, bump BUMP, *bump BUMP*. (soft LOUD, *less-soft VERY LOUD*, etc.)

When a pattern repeats itself regularly, like your blood-beat, it becomes a rhythm. Thus, day-night, day-night, day-night is a kind of rhythm. And spring-summer-fall-winter, spring-summer-fall-winter is a form of rhythm. Work and eat, work and play; work and eat, work and play is a kind of rhythm. So, too, birth-love-death, birth-love-death has its own rhythm.

Words also have rhythms, based on their sounds: alternating *loud* and *soft; stressed* and *unstressed; fast, slow*. The unit of word rhythm is the syllable. Thus, *colossal* goes soft-loud-soft: co-LOS-al. *Handyman* goes *loud-soft-loud:* HAN-dy-MAN. If you speak the words naturally, they fall into a natural sound pattern, once there is sufficient repetition to be noticeable. Without repetition, of course, the rhythm is unable to establish itself. The sentence "I swung the thing and let it go" repeats a pattern sufficiently for a rhythm to form: the pattern is soft-loud-soft-loud-soft-loud-soft-loud, or I SWUNG the THING and LET it GO.

As you speak a word in a sentence, certain syllables naturally become loud, others soft. If you had a machine that recorded the voice level, the dial would leap every time you used a stressed syllable. Some syllables would, of course, be less loud than some, yet louder than others or, in other words, in-between in their stress. These in-between syllables became loud or soft according to the stresses around them, just as a man of average height would be seen as short or tall depending on whether the man beside him was a giant or a midget.

The meaning of the words affects the sound values. In the sentence *I told you the door was green,* the emphasis changes the *meaning,* as well as the *sound:*

A: George told me the door was green.
B: *I* told you the door was green.
    [loud-loud-soft-soft-loud-soft-loud]

A: Yes, you wrote it to me last May.
B: I *told* you the door was green.
    [soft-loud-soft-soft-loud-soft-loud]

A: No, it must have been Henry you told.
B: I told *you* the door was green.
    [soft-loud-loud-soft-loud-soft-loud]

A: Perhaps you were referring to some other door.
B: I told you *the* door was green.
    [soft-loud-soft-loud-loud-soft-loud]

A: Or perhaps you meant the window.
B: I told you the *door* was green.
    [soft-loud-soft-soft-loud-soft-loud]

A: But the door's red now, not green. They've repainted it.
B: I told you the door *was* green.
    [soft-loud-soft-soft-loud-loud-loud]

A: Oh, so it wasn't red *then?*
B: I told you the door was *green.*
    [soft-loud-soft-soft-loud-soft-loud]

The point of this somewhat repetitive conversation is that the stress depends on the meaning, and so, therefore, does the rhythm.

Similarly, a syllable is loud or soft according to the syllables around it. Note that the syllable *be* is stressed or unstressed according to the surrounding syllables:

1. THAT HE should BE the ONE to JUDGE.
2. He doesn't want to know or do,
   he SIMPly WANTS to BE.
3. It SHOULD be JOHN, you KNOW.
4. beLIEVE the WORDS we SPEAK.

So it is up to your ear to judge if a syllable carries a stress or not, guided by (1) the meaning and (2) the natural sound value of the syllables as they emerge from the context.

~~~~~~

ACTIVITIES

1. Mark the following lines with their natural stresses, placing a "/" over syllables that are stressed, and a "." over those that are unstressed. Check your dictionary if you are not sure which syllables are stressed.

a. The tiger waved a friendly paw.
b. The call of the drums was strong.
c. "Never, never!" said the Count.
d. "Merrily, merrily shall I live now."
e. When the mother of months in meadow and plain.

2. Remembering the two guides—stress what follows the sense and stress what is natural—create lines that run as follows:

a. / . / . / . /
b. . . / . . /
c. / . . / . . /
d. . / . . / . . / . /
e. / . . / . . / /

3. Write a dialogue using the sentence *"Find your hat if you lost it"* seven times, each time emphasizing a different word.

~~~~~~

A rhythm, then, is a repeated pattern. There is a need in man to find a rhythm in everything he does: his music and his habits, his work, his walk, his worship, and his words. Whether he is typing or skipping, dancing or eating, he tends to fall into a rhythm.

Children, when they experience grief, often cry or chant rhythmically for comfort. When speakers are faced with the stares of an audience, they often rock backward and forward to steady themselves.

In poetry, rhythm is especially important, and it is both more regular and more prominent than in prose. In poetry, a basic pattern of sound is usually repeated over and over, with minor variations. The name of the basic unit of this pattern is a *foot*. In general, a foot is made up of one stressed syllable, together with either one or two unstressed syllables. Occasionally, a foot will be made up of two loud beats. Other feet are possible, but a poem that contains all stressed syllables or all unstressed syllables would not have much variety. It would be all plod, or a fussy skitter of syllables. The four most common feet in English are

iamb (adj., *iambic*) = soft-LOUD (. /)
troche (adj., *trochaic*) = LOUD-soft (/ .)
anapest (adj., *anapestic*) = soft-soft-LOUD (. . /)
dactyl (adj., *dactylic*) = LOUD-soft-soft (/ . .)

The names may sound unfamiliar at first, because they are the ancient Greek names. But they are worth learning, so that one may refer conveniently to the different patterns.

How often is this pattern repeated in one line? That depends. Usually the poet makes the decision before starting to write, and then maintains that count. Again there are the names (Greek again):

A *monometer* is a line with one foot.
A *dimeter* is a line with two feet.
A *trimeter* is a line with three feet.
A *tetrameter* is a line with four feet.
A *pentameter* is a line with five feet.
A *hexameter* is a line with six feet.
A *heptameter* is . . . well, that should be enough for most
   poems.

By combining the number of feet with the name of the foot, you can describe any kind of rhythm. An iambic tetrameter has four iambs:

> To kiss the girls and make them cry.

A dactylic trimeter has three dactyls:

> Seventy years as a mariner.

A trochaic hexameter has six troches:

> "Trust me, tell me, risk it, tell me," pleaded Tommy.

And so on. If you reverse the process and mark the beats on a line that has already been composed, that is called scanning the line or poem.

Looking at poems using each of the major types of natural feet will make the patterns clearer. The first is the iambic foot:

> . / . / . / . / . /
> That time of year thou mayst in me behold
> . / . / . / . / . /
> When yellow leaves, or none, or few, do hang
> . / . / . / . / . /
> Upon those boughs which shake against the cold

> WILLIAM SHAKESPEARE, Sonnet 73

The trochaic reverses the iambic pattern.

> / . / . / . / .
> Searching once I found a flower
> / . / . /
> By a sluggish stream.
> / . / . / . / .
> Waxy white, a stealthy tower
> / . / . /
> To an Indian's dream
> / . / . /
> This its life supreme.

Blood red winds the sallow creek
  Draining as it flows.
Left the flower all white and sleek,
  Fainting in repose.
  Gentler than a rose.

Red man's pipe is now a ghost
  Whispering to beware.
Hinting of the savage host
  Once that traveled there.
  Perfume frail as air.

RICHARD EBERHART, "Indian Pipe"

Notice that the last syllable in lines 2, 4, and 5 is missing. This is a common variation of the foot. Poets try to end lines on stressed syllables because the last syllable in a line is emphasized just by being last. They try to add to the emphasis by stressing the syllable as well.

The first syllable in a line also is a point of special emphasis. Poets writing iambic feet frequently will make the first foot of the line trochaic, in order to reinforce the emphasis.

The third basic foot is the anapest:

```
 . .  /  . .  /  . .   /    . .   /
As a friend to the children commended me this Yak;
 .  .  /  . .  /  . .  /
You will find it exactly the thing;
 .  .  /  . .  /  . .  /  . .  /
It will carry and fetch, you can ride on its back,
 .  /  .. /  . . /
Or lead it about with a string.
```

HILAIRE BELLOC, "The Yak"

The last basic foot is the dactyl:

```
 /  . .  /  . .  /  .
This was the year of the blackbird.
 /  . .  /  . .  /  .
That was the year of the swallow.
 /  . . /  . . /
Time is a bird on the wing
 . /  . . /  . . /  .
Today is an owl in a hollow.
```

MAXINE CASSIN, "Annals"

One or both of the final unstressed syllables are often dropped from the last foot in a line.

From the poems presented so far you can see that every poem is not made up of regular rhythms. Within each pattern there is room for variations. Go back and scan the last two stanzas of "Indian Pipe." Are they regular?

Although many poems have been written with metrical rhythm, many have been written with looser patterns. A common pattern of a looser kind is one that maintains a certain number of stressed syllables per line (say, 3, 4, or 5), but uses as many unstressed as are needed. In "A Pact," Ezra Pound asserts his poetic independence from Walt Whitman. Whitman would often write poems with no set number of beats per line, insisting on total rhythmical freedom. Pound also demanded freedom, but there was a structure: four stressed syllables per line.

A Pact

I make a pact with you, Walt Whitman—
I have detested you long enough.
I come to you as a grown child
Who has had a pig-headed father;
I am old enough now to make friends.
It was you that broke the new wood,
Now is a time for carving.
We have one sap and one root—
Let there be commerce between us.

The stressed syllables are sometimes linked by means of alliteration, continuing a tradition that comes from Old English poetry.

ACTIVITIES

1. Create lines in the following meters:

a. Iambic pentameter.
b. Dactylic trimeter.
c. Anapestic tetrameter.
d. Trochaic hexameter.
e. Iambic dimeter.
f. Trochaic heptameter with the first foot a dactyl.

2. Scan "She Dwelt among the Untrodden Ways." Use a "/"
to mark the stressed syllables and a "." to mark the unstressed
syllables.

> She dwelt among the untrodden ways *
>> Beside the springs of Dove,
> A maid whom there were none to praise
>> And very few to love:
>
> A violet by a mossy stone *
>> Half hidden from the eye!
> Fair as a star, when only one
>> Is shining in the sky.
>
> She lived unknown, and few could know
>> When Lucy ceased to be;
> But she is in her grave, and, oh,
>> The difference to me!

WILLIAM WORDSWORTH

3. Bounce a ping-pong ball on a hard surface. Write a line
of poetry that imitates the rhythm of the bounce.

4. Write a line that imitates the following:

a. A horse galloping.
b. A bottle-making machine.
c. The scamper of mice.
d. Falling rain.
e. You walking.

~~~~~~

So far so good. Syllables make up feet, feet make up lines, and
lines make up poems. At that rate, you could invent a poetry
machine, a kind of metronome with a pen stuck in it, and you
would put Shakespeare out of business. But, as you may have
guessed, there is a snag. Anything that is completely regular and
that never varies also becomes dull quickly, as in work and
eat, work and sleep, work and eat, work and sleep. That is
fine for five, or even six days of the week. But then you do want

* Note: In line 1, count *the untrodden* as three syllables, omitting the *e* of *the;* in
line 5, consider *violet* as having two syllables.

to vary the routine. Hence Sunday's rhythm, which is more like: sleep and eat, sleep and play, sleep and eat, sleep and play. Even within Sunday, the rhythm may be varied to avoid boredom. The same goes for poetry: A rhythm that runs with relentless regularity—tum-ti, tum-ti, tum-ti—soon begins to resemble a toothache or the Chinese water torture (whereby a drop of water would fall on the victim's head with absolute regularity in exactly the same spot hour after hour: the water drops soon began to have the same effect on the victim as blows with a sledge hammer).

So a poet will no more write a whole poem with the same rhythm than he will write one with no rhythm. And it is at this point that we must make a distinction between rhythm and meter. The meter of a poem is its regular underlying pulse that never varies, once it has been set up at the beginning of the poem. The rhythm is the varied pattern that keeps the reader on his toes waiting for the next variation. Usually, the poet will establish a meter in the first two lines and then vary it subtly thereafter: change a foot here, put in an extra syllable there, include a syllable that is neither loud nor soft but in-between, or leave out a syllable altogether.

Once poets have established the meter, they vary the rhythm freely, realizing as they do so that they are throwing stress onto the variation. And they use this stress to emphasize important words or ideas. An example of how breaking a pattern emphasizes the variation may be seen in the following sequence:

> He took a new-laid egg and passed it to a friend,
> Who took the new-laid egg and passed it to a friend,
> Who took the new-laid egg and passed it to a friend,
> Who took the new-laid egg and passed it to a friend,
> Who dropped it.

The regularity of the pattern before the change threw emphasis onto the variation when it did occur. When things are placed side by side, their differences tend to appear.

In free verse, the line acts as the basic rhythmic unit. There is no pattern of either accents or syllables in free verse. The rhythm of free verse approximates the sound of natural speech. And it avoids having to twist language to fit metrical constructions. Lines break to emphasize specific words or to create tension, that is, a strain between the normal patterns of speech and the patterns imposed by the poem.

Examine the lines in "The Red Wheelbarrow" by William Carlos Williams:

> so much depends
> upon
>
> a red wheel
> barrow
>
> glazed with rain
> water
>
> beside the white
> chickens.

The lines force the reader to look closely at each word. All free verse should, through its lines, focus special attention on words or on relations between words, ideas, or images.

The last variation that we will consider here is that between slow and fast. You probably know that your pulse varies according to your state of excitement: The more excited you are, the more energy you use, the faster your blood beats. The calmer you are, the more tranquil, the slower is your pulse. A long-distance runner should have a comparatively slow pulse, because it is better suited to such sustained activity. It is significant that the first sign that a doctor looks for to indicate how well a body is functioning is the pulse. Like the pulse, a poem will move quicker or slower as it describes more exciting or more thoughtful subject matter.

To make a line run slowly, you should use more stressed syllables and shorter words. This is suitable for funeral descriptions, slow-moving thoughtful passages or stately ceremonies. To speed up your rhythm, use fewer stressed syllables and longer words. This will make your poetry skip and dance.

ACTIVITIES

1. Alliteration and assonance were originally *rhythmical aids*. This means that poetry built its rhythm upon the repetition of stressed vowel or consonant sounds within the same line. The

sound would be repeated two or three times. Write a poem based on a personal experience of your own or on a story that you already are familiar with (perhaps a Greek legend, or a story you have taken from a newspaper or magazine). Use as your chief musical device alliteration on the stressed syllables. Aim at two or three repetitions per line.

2. The following stanza establishes the meter in the first line and then proceeds to vary it. What is the meter? Point out where and how the poet varies.

Last night, ah, yesternight, betwixt her lips and mine
There fell thy shadow, Cynara! thy breath was shed
Upon my soul between the kisses and the wine;
And I was desolate and sick of an old passion,
    Yea, I was desolate and bowed my head:
I have been faithful to thee, Cynara! in my fashion.
                    ERNEST DOWSON, "Cynara"

3. Write one line or more that imitates the following:

a. A diver doing a belly flop.
b. A man carrying a heavy weight.
c. A frog's progress.
d. A clock ticking—relentless time.
e. Many soldiers marching in step.

4. Write a poem to be recited against your favorite non-vocal record. Focus your composition on an interesting similarity or contrast of rhythms.

5. Read "Arithmetic" by Carl Sandburg.

ARITHMETIC is where numbers fly like pigeons in and out of
    your head.
Arithmetic tells you how many you lose or win if you know
    how many you had before you lost or won.
Arithmetic is seven eleven all good children go to heaven—
    or five six bundle of sticks.
Arithmetic is numbers you squeeze from your head to your
    hand to your pencil to your paper till you get the answer.
Arithmetic is where the answer is right and everything is nice
    and you can look out of the window and see the blue
    sky—or the answer is wrong and you have to start all
    over and try again and see how it comes out this time.

If you take a number and double it and double it again and
then double it a few more times, the number gets bigger
and bigger and goes higher and higher and only arithmetic can tell you what the number is when you decide
to quit doubling.

Arithmetic is where you have to multiply—and you carry the
multiplication table in your head and hope you won't
lose it.

If you have two animal crackers, one good and one bad, and
you eat one and a striped zebra with streaks all over
him eats the other, how many animal crackers will you
have if somebody offers you five six seven and you say
No no no and you say Nay nay nay and you say Nix
nix nix?

If you ask your mother for one fried egg for breakfast and
she gives you two fried eggs and you eat both of them,
who is better in arithmetic, you or your mother?

Write a free-verse poem in which you illustrate what something is. You might illustrate a subject you are taking in school, a
sporting event, or something abstract such as love. Each line of
your poem can give a specific point as Sandburg does, or you can
create your own line patterns.

6

Tone and mood

IF SOMEONE SAYS TO YOU, "Go on, just try it!" it is important
to know whether he is sincerely encouraging you to greater efforts
or whether he is spoiling for a fight. Usually, the tone of the
speaker's voice will indicate which interpretation is valid.

Like spoken language, poetry is a method of communication.
It is important that you clearly indicate your attitude toward the
subject of your poem. If you are seriously discussing something,
you don't want your readers to think you are being funny. And
to have the reader interpret a humorous poem as a serious
statement would be equally disastrous. In your writing, you must
convey, through words, the tone, that is, the attitude you have
toward the subject. As you read the following poem, try to determine the attitude of the poet Lucilius toward the girl Mycilla:

Mycilla Dyes Her Locks

Mycilla dyes her locks, 'tis said,
    But 'tis a foul aspersion;
She buys them black, they therefore need
    No subsequent immersion.

If you read only the first two lines, you would think that Lucilius was defending the girl. But the last two lines make it clear that he is not defending her at all.

The range of tones available to you is as wide as is the range of human emotions or attitudes. Your attitude may be affectionate, angry, humorous, or it might be a combination of attitudes, as in "The Lost Mistress" by Robert Browning:

> All's over then; does truth sound bitter
>   As one at first believes?
> Hark, 'tis the sparrow's good-night twitter
>   About your cottage eaves!
>
> And the leaf-buds on the vine are woolly,
>   I noticed that, today;
> One day more bursts them open fully—
>   You know the red turns gray.
>
> Tomorrow we meet the same then, dearest?
>   May I take your hand in mine?
> Mere friends are we,—well, friends the merest
>   Keep much that I resign:
>
> For each glance of the eye so bright and black
>   Though I keep with heart's endeavor—
> Your voice, when you wish the snowdrops back,
>   Though it stay in my soul forever!—
>
> Yet I will but say what mere friends say,
>   Or only a thought stronger;
> I will hold your hand but as long as all may,
>   Or so very little longer!

In Browning's poem, a man is breaking up with a girl he loves, and he is thinking about how he will have to act toward her now. Evidently the two will meet in public quite often, and he will have to conceal his true feelings.

What is the tone of voice of the speaker? Is he sincere, or is this just a show of emotion? Is he taking the situation coolly, or is he ranting and raving? Perhaps you agree that this poem has a bitter, passionate tone, underneath its surface voice of iron control.

ACTIVITY

Describe the tone of the following poems:

Love Song

Your little hands,
Your little feet,
Your little mouth—
Oh, God, how sweet!

Your little nose,
Your little ears,
Your little eyes, that shed
Such little tears!

Your little voice,
So soft and kind;
Your little soul,
Your little mind!

SAMUEL HOFFENSTEIN

Holy Thursday

Is this a holy thing to see
In a rich and fruitful land,
Babes reduced to misery,
Fed with cold and usurous hand?

Is that trembling cry a song?
Can it be a song of joy?
And so many children poor?
It is a land of poverty!

And their sun does never shine,
And their fields are bleak and bare,
And their ways are filled with thorns:
It is eternal winter there.

For where'er the sun does shine,
And where'er the rain does fall,
Babe can never hunger there,
Nor poverty the mind appal.

WILLIAM BLAKE

Little Rock Arkansas 1957
dedicated to the nine children

Clasping like bucklers to their bodies, books,
nine children move through blasts of killing looks.
Committed to this battle each child dares,
deliberately, the fusillades of jeers.
Their valor iron in their ironed clothes
they walk politely in their polished shoes
down ambushed halls to classrooms sown with mines
to learn their lesson. Obviously nine's
a carefully calculated number, odd
not even, a suave size than can be added to, discreetly, later, or culled now
should one child break not bend; or fail to bow
sufficiently his bloody head . . . a rule
to heed, child, be you black and going to school.

ISABELLA GARDNER

~~~~~~

When you write poetry, consider which is the best way to communicate the experience. Should you be passionate? detached? humorous? In many cases, the subject matter will suggest the appropriate tone. Remember, though, that just because the experience is important you don't have to be solemn. Many ideas can be put across effectively by an amusing anecdote with a light touch.

In communicating the tone, you must pay close attention to selection of words. The choice of one noun or verb over another is often all-important in suggesting your attitude. This suggestive factor in words is called *connotation.* It is opposed to the dictionary definition of the words which is called the *denotation.* You have probably had to supply a synonym for some word: Fat = buxom = broad-beamed = chubby = plump = stout = fleshy = full-bodied, etc. But, although they are equal in one sense, they do not all carry the same emotional force. Call a girl *fat,* and you will probably receive quite a different reaction from the one you'll receive if you call her *plump.* A similar reaction will occur if you call a man *scraggy* instead of *lean.* If you call a man *normal,* he will be much more pleased than if you call him *ordinary.* Refer to a person as being *middle-aged,* rather than *in the summer of his years,* and he may be rather rude. The difference is considerable, yet the denotation does not recognize the difference, any more than a computer can tell a great piece of music from one that is mathematically concocted by a technician. The difference lies in the human and emotional elements of the medium (which are exposed by the *connotation*). So it is in a poem: The value of the word lies in its emotional force, its aptness, its relation to a pattern of connotation. This is why a poem cannot be effectively paraphrased or summarized; in doing so the connotation of the words is lost.

Consider the connotations of the following poem:

Horse Latitudes *

When the still sea conspires an armor
And her sullen and aborted
Currents breed tiny monsters,
True sailing is dead.

Awkward instant
And the first animal is jettisoned,
Legs furiously pumping
Their stiff green gallop,
And heads bob up
Poise
Delicate
Pause
Consent
In mute nostril agony
Carefully refined
And sealed over.

JIM MORRISON

The words "conspire" and "armor" suggest a sinister hostility to human need; even the word "still" develops a morbid meaning in this context. The sinister note of inhumanity is picked up in the last two lines with the words "Carefully refined" and "sealed over." And these, in turn, give additional impact to

* On old Spanish ships, when the sea became calm and the vessel could not move, cargo, including livestock, had to be jettisoned.

words as "Poise," "Delicate," "Pause," and "Consent," which use the stiff language of politeness and tearoom conversation to describe horses in the desperate struggle for life. The words "sullen," "breed," and "aborted" convey the mood of suppressed anger that underlies the poem. Fitting into this pattern are such combinations as "stiff . . . gallop," "mute nostril agony," and "Awkward instant." This poem is not only an account of the jettisoning of living things, the sealing over of love-evoking energies by a cold, remorseless, inhuman expanse of nonfeeling. It is also an account of the repression of natural feelings in an oversophisticated, unnatural society. And it is the emotional values, the connotations of the words, that allow this wider meaning to emerge with latent power.

Words call up and are involved in the deepest forces of human life. They evoke body movements like a pumping, a battle lunge, a reaching out toward, a dance. They involve the earliest childhood recollections; they involve the deepest fears and needs. The pledge of allegiance and the marriage ceremony are not just formulas. They are living energies. Words such as *freedom* or *democracy* cannot be plumbed to their emotional depths. Men will die for them, not knowing exactly what the words mean. A poem uses such forces, or it becomes a mechanical concoction, not a living organism whose surface may be words but whose core is the dance of life itself.

From the discussion, you can see that the connotations of a word may be positive or negative, favorable or unfavorable. In many cases, the connotations of a word will vary—the word "hippie" will carry positive connotations to some, negative to others.

In writing your poems, you must be aware of

1. The denotation of the words—they should make sense.
2. The connotations or the emotional coloring of the words.

ACTIVITIES

1. What is the difference between a glass that is half full and one that is half empty? (We may assume that glass and contents remain constant.)

2. What are the connotations of the following words? How do they differ?

Example: *Childish* suggests immature, irresponsible, lacking seriousness.

Childlike suggests creative, full of wonder, spontaneous, fresh.

- a. Lubricated, oily
- b. Apartment, flat
- c. King, husband to the queen
- d. Meat, flesh
- e. Eager, greedy
- f. Enthusiastic, fanatical
- g. Father, papa
- h. Grasp, clutch
- i. Swing, lurch
- j. Impulsive, rash

3. Use each of the following words in two sentences. In one sentence, the word should have positive connotations; in the other, negative.

Example: (a) He had a *frank,* open face.
(b) They were selling the "*frank* and candid" memoirs of a notorious courtesan.

a. military	d. decent	g. choosy
b. accident	e. humble	h. farsighted
c. rigorous	f. single	

4. Find the correct word from those offered in each of the following contexts:

- a. _____ to one's parents is often considered a virtue.
  (1) Docility   (2) Servility   (3) Obedience   (4) Conformity
- b. The ballet dancer _____ gracefully across the room.
  (1) Slithered   (2) Glided   (3) Slipped   (4) Oozed
- c. His _____ progress suggested that he would prove reliable.
  (1) Slow   (2) Crawling   (3) Sluggish   (4) Measured
- d. "Oh, Miss Grace," he cried, "your diet has made you so delightfully _____."
  (1) Slender   (2) Thin   (3) Scraggy   (4) Lean

e. He has cut the story to half its original length, making it
_____ but not too much so.

(1) Abrupt   (2) Scrimpy   (3) Terse   (4) Concise

~~~~~~

Closely related to the idea of *tone* is that of a poem's *mood*. Whereas the tone of a poem derives from the poet's "voice," the *mood* is the atmosphere created by his attitude toward his subject. Compare three different restaurants:

In one you find shells, old wooden tables that squeak, sawdust on the floor, curiously carved candles, casual waiters, a touch of incense in the air, and enough rock music to drown the conversation. In the second, the table tops are plastic, there is a synthetic squirt bottle of ketchup for fiddling with, the menu is wrapped in transparent material that can be wiped off, there is a choice of sitting at the fountain or in a booth, and Lawrence Welk can just be heard from the radio through the kitchen door. In the third, everything is polished wood, silence, and deep red velvet; the waiters are smartly dressed in red uniforms, and the candles are behind tinted glass; the menu is written in a quaint script; and the walls are tastefully hung with prints of nineteenth-century England.

Each of these restaurants sets a mood, and each of the details contributes toward the mood. Similarly, a poem sets its mood with its details: its images, its word choices, with innumerable intangible hints all pointing in the same direction.

Consider the mood (or moods) of this poem:

Cargoes

Quinquireme of Nineveh from distant Ophir
Rowing home to haven in sunny Palestine,
With a cargo of ivory,
And apes and peacocks,
Sandalwood, cedarwood, and sweet white wine.

Stately Spanish galleon coming from the Isthmus,
Dipping through the Tropics by the palm-green shores,
With a cargo of diamonds,
Emeralds, amethysts,
Topazes, and cinnamon, and gold moidores.

Dirty British coaster with a salt-caked smoke stack
Butting through the Channel in the mad March days,
With a cargo of Tyne coal,
Road-rails, pig-lead,
Firewood, iron-ware, and cheap tin trays.

JOHN MASEFIELD

The poem has two distinct moods. Masefield creates a contrast between the first two stanzas and the last. The first two stanzas set a mood by careful choice of images. Here is a table of the chief differences:

Stanzas 1 and 2	Stanza 3
quinquireme, stately galleon	dirty coaster
Nineveh, distant Ophir, Palestine, Tropics	British Channel
rowing, dipping	butting
sunny, palm-green shores	mad March days
ivory, peacocks, sandalwood, cedarwood, wine, diamonds, emeralds, gold moidores	Tyne coal, road-rails, pig-lead, cheap tin trays

The contrast is obvious if the images are set side by side: The first two stanzas contain images of the exotic, distant, stately, ancient, rare; the third, images of the close, ugly, modern, common, cheap.

But it is not only in the meaning that the contrast is made, but also in the sound of the words: in the first two stanzas there are many long, graceful words; in the third stanza the words are blunt and stunted. The effect is also supported by the rhythm: the first two stanzas are flowing, with a leisurely sweep; the third stanza halts, stutters, rasps.

All these elements, and others less easily defined, point toward a single contrast: the mood of the first two stanzas with that of the third.

What point was the poet making with this contrast? That is for the reader to judge, based on the clues provided by the poet: perhaps that modern times lack the grace and romance of the past; or perhaps that the here-and-now is more practical, less romantic than the distant once upon a time. Or perhaps Masefield believed that modern times are really more ugly than times past; perhaps he believed that they only appear to be so. He has given us the contrasted moods. It is up to us to interpret what the contrast means.

There are several general guidelines as to techniques to be used in building a mood or a tone.

1. Having more stress sounds per line creates a slower, more dignified effect. Rhythms and meters having more unstressed sounds usually create a lighter, quicker effect.

2. Certain sounds have a harsh or a soft tone. Guttural sounds, such as *g* and *k,* have a harsher tone than do *l, m,* and *n.* The *b, t, p* sounds are explosive. Lines can use the effects of these sounds to underscore their meaning as in these examples, the first by John Donne, the second by Robert Herrick:

a. bend/ Your [God's] force to break, blow, burn, and make me new.
b. Melting melodious words to Lutes of Amber.

In Donne's line, the explosive *b* sound predominates, but it gives way to the softer *m* and *n* sounds as Donne prays God will transform his rebellious spirit. Herrick's softer tone reflects his subject, Julia's voice, which is "So smooth, so sweet, so silv'ry."

3. The images you use to convey the experience will suggest your attitude or create a mood. This is the most important technique. William Wordsworth's comparison of England to a "fen of stagnant water" clearly indicates his attitude toward his country.

ACTIVITIES

1. In Chapter 3 you were asked to write descriptions in which series of images built up a certain idea or mood such as fear, cold, or boredom. Write a description of a room or a scene in which a certain mood is dominant. Emphasize that mood by the way you portray the scene and by the details you select. Underline the mood wherever you can by the use of sounds. Here is Edgar Allan Poe doing something of the sort in the first stanza of his poem, "Ulalume":

The skies they were ashen and sober;
    The leaves they were crispèd and sere—
    The leaves they were withering and sere:
It was night, in the lonesome October
    Of my most immemorial year:
It was hard by the dim lake of Auber,
    In the misty mid region of Weir—
It was down by the dank tarn of Auber,
    In the ghoul-haunted woodland of Weir.

Notice how Poe uses a number of devices to support his overall mood:

  a. The rhythm is anapestic, a lighter meter.
  b. He uses *l, m,* and *n* sounds to create an effect of moaning and indefiniteness and loss.
  c. His use of repetition gives the effect of a ghost, or a memory, returning to haunt.

Imitate those devices that you think will be useful.

2. What is the situation of the speaker in the following poem? What is the overall mood of the poem? List some of the images that help to create this effect.

Spectator

From the high brick window
Way up here
I can see the street.
It fills with people
Dressed in black,
Quiet, neat.
They stare up.
In double-file, they cross
In my direction.
Now I can hear
Their leather feet
Clatter on the stairs.
Surely they are not
Coming here
With their brown paper,
Smell of incense, flowers.

The bolt turns in the door.
I cannot turn.
The walls tilt and lean.
The people prop them up.
In the black shadows
Whispers frame
A familiar, familiar name.

SUSAN SCHAEFFER

3. Write a poem similar to "Cargoes," describing three different automobiles, restaurants, dates, schools, summer camps, etc. Clearly indicate what your tone is throughout the description. Set your contrasting moods by your choice of detail primarily, but also by any other method that you find effective.

4. In your notebooks, practice

a. Writing descriptions in which you capture the mood through images. Focus on essential details.

b. Listing words related by sound or words in which sounds harmonize or in which sounds contrast.

c. Noting words and phrases in which the sound is related to meaning.

7

The shape of things

POETRY IS POETRY, some people believe, only to the extent
that the *how* dominates or is equal to the *what*. A poem invites
you to consider the form of its message as well as the ideas it contains. Over the centuries, poets have developed a number of commonly used forms or shapes. There are, of course, units of form
within the form: the line, the sentence, and the meter. But most
important is the overall form of a poem, the shape that holds it
all together. We have discussed a number of short forms in Chapter 2: the haiku, the concrete poem, and so on. There are other
short forms that have rhyme as a unifying element. And, of
course, traditional stanza forms have various patterns of rhyme.

Rhyme consists of an identity of sound in two or more
words; the identity consists of both vowel and consonant sounds:
name—game; applaud—defraud. Words with identical vowel
and consonant sounds are called perfect rhyme. One function of
rhyme is musical. In this it is like alliteration and assonance. Another function is metrical in that it binds together the ends of
lines. And it allows the poet to join lines in couplets, stanzas, or
complete poetic forms.

~~~~~~

ACTIVITIES

1. Find one or more rhymes for each of the following:

a. Mississippi   d. fountain
b. Vladivostok   e. astrolabe
c. Tipperary   f. onomatopoeia

2. A Clerihew, a poem named for its inventor, Edmund Clerihew Bentley, contains two couplets that paint a brief, humorous picture of a famous person. The poet must use the name as one of the rhymes, preferably as awkwardly as possible. For example:

> William Makepeace Thackeray
> Was often accused of quackery.
> He wrote *Vanity Fair*
> While inside of a bear.

Try your hand at one.

3. Besides perfect rhyme, there are other variations of rhyme:

a. near rhyme—the repetition in stressed syllables of the final consonant sound: name—lime.
b. eye rhyme—words in which the spelling gives the impression of perfect rhyme. The actual pronunciation of the words shows that they do not sound the same: over—cover.
c. multiple rhyme—rhymes involving more than two syllables: Timbuktu—hymnbook, too.

Compose examples of each of these forms of rhyme.

~~~~~~

Traditionally, poets have used rhyme as one method of organizing their stanzas or their poems. The Clerihew consists of two couplets; there is no definite meter or stress pattern. The limerick is more complex because it combines rhyme with a set number of stressed beats per line. See if you can discover the pattern of stressed sounds in the following limericks.

As a beauty, I am not a star;
There are others more handsome by far;
   But my face I don't mind it
   For I am behind it:
It's the people in front get the jar.

No matter how grouchy you're feeling,
A smile is always quite healing;
   It grows like a wreath
   All around your front teeth,
Thus preserving the face from congealing.

    The pattern is 3, 3, 2, 2, 3, which gives the form a singsong quality suited for light verse. In many limericks, the last line is a variation on the first line. Thus repetition accentuates the singsong quality of the form.

ACTIVITY

    Try writing a limerick about someone or something at school. The person or object can be real or imaginary.

    Modern folk singers have revitalized the ballad form. The original ballads grew up in a time before there were printing and books accessible to the public. In those days, troubadors, or traveling poets, would earn their living by moving from village to village, castle to castle, telling stories to musical accompaniment. These wandering minstrels were often the chief conveyors of news from place to place, and they were responsible not only for inventing new stories but also for not letting the best of the old ones be forgotten. These stories grew into slightly varying shapes, with slightly different events and emphases in different areas. But despite these minor variations, many thousands of them remained intact and traveled the length and breadth of Europe, across the Atlantic, and even down to Australia and South Africa.
    The ballad form was the product of this situation. It was

built around short units that the minstrel could easily remember. And if his memory failed, he could quickly compose new lyrics based on what had gone before. The action tended to be simple and quick, progressing in leaps and bounds, with some filler material that varied from version to version. Four-line stanzas became the rule; the rhyme scheme was either abcb or abab. The metrical scheme was four beats per line or four beats alternating with three.

> There dwelt a man in faire Westmerland,
> Johnie Armstrong men did him call,
> He had neither lands nor rents coming in,
> Yet he kept eight score men in his hall.

In "Edward, Edward," note the characteristics of the form, especially the use of repetition, that builds the suspense to a climax.

Edward, Edward

> "Why does your blade so drop with blood,
> Edward, Edward?
> Why does your blade so drop with blood?
> And why do you walk so sad, O?"
> "O I have killed my hawk so good,
> Mother, Mother
> O I have killed my hawk so good,
> And I had no more but he, O."
>
> "Your hawk's blood was never so red,
> Edward, Edward,
> Your hawk's blood was never so red,
> My dear son I tell you, O."
> "O I have killed my red-roan steed,
> Mother, Mother,
> O I have killed my red-roan steed,
> That was once so fair and free, O."
>
> "Your steed was old, and you have got more,
> Edward, Edward,
> Your steed was old, and you have got more,
> Some other woe you weep, O."
> "O I have killed my father dear,
> Mother, Mother,

O I have killed my father dear,
    Alas, and woe is me, O!"

"And what is the penance you'll do for that,
                    Edward, Edward?
And what is the penance you'll do for that?
    My dear son, now tell me, O."
"I'll set my foot in yonder boat,
                    Mother, Mother,
I'll set my foot in yonder boat,
    And I'll sail over the sea, O."

"And what will you do with your towers and hall,
                    Edward, Edward?
And what will you do with your towers and hall,
    That were so fair to see, O?"
"I'll let them stand till they down fall,
                    Mother, Mother,
I'll let them stand till they down fall,
    For here never more must I be, O."

"And what will you leave to your children and wife,
                    Edward, Edward,
And what will you leave to your children and wife,
    When you go over the sea, O?"
"The world's wide room, let them beg through life,
                    Mother, Mother,
The world's wide room, let them beg through life,
    For them never more will I see, O."

"And what will you leave to your own mother dear,
                    Edward, Edward,
And what will you leave to your own mother dear?
    My dear son, now tell me, O."
"The curse of hell from me shall you bear,
                    Mother, Mother,
The curse of hell from me shall you bear,
    Such counsels you gave to me, O."

Like most ballads, "Edward, Edward" tells a brief, dramatic
story in simple language. There is little or no background material
given.

Modern folk singers allow much more freedom in their bal-

lads. Although modern ballads still tell stories, the ballad stanza
has been abandoned. Today, a ballad may be written in couplets
or without rhyme. The narrative impulse remains the same—
modern writers of ballads want to tell stories, accompanied by
music.

ACTIVITY

Write a ballad, using either the ballad stanza or a modern
adaptation.

The four-line stanza is the most popular English stanza. It
suits a variety of metrical patterns and a variety of rhyme schemes.
As one critic has pointed out, if you group four lines of anything
on a page, it will look like a poem. However, effective stanzas have
an internal unity that should build to a climax. The climax comes,
of course, in the last line.

Each line, as well as each stanza, should build toward a
climax. As a rule, the middle is the least interesting part of the
line, the beginning more interesting, and the end most interesting.
The use of rhyme at the end of a line emphasizes the position
where the most interesting material comes. Likewise, using rhyme
at the climax of the stanza—that is, the last line—provides an
ending that musically blends with what has gone before.

The idea of climax in a stanza or a poem can best be illustrated in the sonnet, such as "Harlem Dancer."

> Applauding youths laughed with young prostitutes
> And watched her perfect, half-clothed body sway;
> Her voice was like the sound of blended flutes
> Blown by black players upon a picnic day.
> She sang and danced on gracefully and calm,
> The light gauze hanging loose about her form;
> To me she seemed a proudly swaying palm
> Grown lovelier for passing through a storm.
> Upon her swarthy neck black shiny curls

Luxuriant fell; and tossing coins in praise,
The wine-flushed, bold-eyed boys, and even the girls,
Devoured her shape with eager, passionate gaze;
But looking at her falsely smiling face,
I knew her self was not in that strange place.

CLAUDE MCKAY

The rhyme scheme is abab cdcd efef gg. But notice that the similarity of *palm* and *storm*, *gaze* and *face* create a closer harmony of sound. This form is known as the Shakespearean sonnet, after the poet who made it famous. Notice how the twelve lines all show the dancer's surroundings detracting from the grace of her dance. But the last two lines reverse this. Her real self is somewhere far away from the squalor which seeks to destroy her beauty—perhaps in Africa or a Caribbean Island, where the dance would derive a different meaning from the different setting.

The rhyme scheme parallels this thought pattern. The three four-line sections (quatrains) build up to the final couplet that reverses the poem. The couplet contains the climax of the poem, both emotionally and from the point of view of form. Notice how the first two quatrains end in periods; the end of one set of rhymes coincides with the end of a sentence. In your poems you should strive for a similar blending of idea and form.

Throughout the history of English poetry, rhyme has played an important role. Most fixed stanza forms are based on certain rhyme schemes coupled with a definite metrical pattern. Today, poets have turned away from fixed stanzaic forms and rhyme. They have adopted free verse as the dominant pattern of the age.

It is hard to determine exactly why modern poets have abandoned rhyme and fixed forms. Perhaps it reflects their general attitude toward authority and tradition. Or maybe the subjects of modern poems do not fit into strict rhyming and metrical patterns. If you are writing about the ugliness of modern cities or the breakdown of civilization, it seems out of place to beautify the poem with rhyme or to balance the lines in a strict metrical pattern.

Several specific objections have been raised against the use of rhyme. First, too many poets fall back onto clichés for their rhymes. Alexander Pope, writing in the eighteenth century, called attention to this perennial problem:

Where'er you find "the cooling western breeze,"
In the next line, it "whispers thro' the trees";
If crystal streams "with pleasing murmurs creep,"
The reader's threatened (not in vain) with "sleep."

Creative use of rhyme requires constantly employing unusual rhyme words. John Keats's rhyming "cinnamon" with "Lebanon" and "lavender'd" with "transferr'd" shows far more creativity than would rhyming "moon" with "June."

A second objection to using rhyme is that poets often inverted the normal word order to place a rhyme word at the end of a line. (The same objection is raised against using meter: poets invert word order or add unnecessary words in order to fill the metrical pattern of the line.) If you read older poems, you will notice that inverted word order often interferes with the clarity of the poem. To be effective, rhyme should not interfere with the natural sentence pattern or with the meaning of the line.

While it is true that rhyme is a convention, it is part of the conventions through which poetry works. It is not essential to poetic expression, yet because it is a historical literary convention, rhyme can help to achieve the "interdependence of expression and tradition."

8

The finished product

THE CHAPTERS OF THIS BOOK have discussed what kind of experiences may make material for a poem and have analyzed some of the devices that may be used to catch those experiences and transform them into poetry. This chapter is intended to lead you to the point of actually writing a finished poem.

With this thought looming over you, you may be asking "What can I say in a poem? Exactly what does one put into a poem?" There are no hard and fast rules about this. Some poets write to point out a moral, some to tell a story or relate an incident, some to sketch a scene or character, some to catch an experience, some to make a statement, some to feel the joy of the language and rhythms. You may write with any of these aims in mind, or some, or all, or none. You may write to set something straight in your thoughts, a memory that keeps nagging away at you and that you want to settle somehow. You may write out of sheer good spirits or because you can't help yourself. Some people even write because they have an assignment due at nine o'clock the next morning!

So, the immediate surge of panic you may have felt at the prospect of having to write a poem and of having to have something to say should be subsiding by now, as you realize that almost anything can be the subject of a poem.

The important thing is to write about what is important to you, to give something of yourself, and to write honestly. If you do not have a subject, a good way to get one is simply to list the ten things most precious to you. Remember you are your own best subject, your own best model.

Poetic inspiration is difficult to discuss in the abstract. Poets are inspired to write in a variety of ways. Melville Cane states that he often goes into a darkened room, clears his mind of conscious thought, and lets images come from his unconscious. Other poets have been inspired by a story, a theme, a phrase, a single line. The German poet Schiller, it is said, kept a rotten apple on his desk because the odor helped him to write.

The question of "how does one begin" must be put into perspective. What you start with and what you end up with are two entirely different things. Here is what one modern poet, Robert Lowell, says about his poems:

> INTERVIEWER. Do you revise a very great deal?
>
> LOWELL. Endlessly. . . . When I am writing in meter I find the simple lines never come right away. Nothing does. I don't believe I've ever written a poem in meter where I've kept a single one of the original lines. Usually when I was writing my old poems I'd write them out in blank [unrhymed] verse and then put in the rhymes. And of course I'd change the rhymes a lot. The most I could hope for at first was that the rhymed version wouldn't be much inferior to the blank verse. Then the real work would begin, to make it something much better than the original out of the difficulties of the meter.
>
> INTERVIEWER. Have you ever gone as far as Yeats [William Butler Yeats] and written out a prose argument and then set down the rhymes?
>
> LOWELL. With some of the later poems I've written out prose versions, then cut the prose down and abbreviated it. A rapidly written prose draft of the poem doesn't seem to do much good, too little pain has gone into it; but one really worked on is bound to have phrases that are invaluable. And it's a nice technical problem: how can you keep phrases and get them into meter?

So where or how you start is really not that important. What counts is where you go from there, and then from there, that counts. Dylan Thomas, another outstanding modern poet, used to write all his rhymes in first and then fit the poem to them. The opposite approach seems to be advocated by Marianne Moore, who says, "I am governed by the pull of the sentence as the pull of a fabric is governed by gravity. . . . I never plan a stanza. Words cluster like chromosomes, determining the procedure."

And here is what Robert Frost says on the subject of writing a poem:

> INTERVIEWER. Making couplets "offhand" is something like writing on schedule, isn't it? I know a young poet who claims he can write every morning from six to nine, presumably before class.
>
> FROST. Well, there's more than one way to skin a cat. I don't know what that would be like, myself. When I get going on something, I don't want to just—you know . . . Very first one I wrote I was walking home from school and I began to make it—a March day—and I was making it all afternoon and making it so I was late at my grandmother's for dinner. I finished it, but it burned right up,* just burned right up, you know. And what started that? What burned it? So many talk, I wonder how falsely, about what its costs them, what agony it is to write. I've often been quoted: "No tears in the writer, no tears in the reader. No surprise for the writer, no surprise for the reader." But another distinction I made is: however sad, no grievance, grief without grievance. How could I, how could anyone have a good time with what cost me too much agony, how could they? What do I want to communicate but what a *hell* of a good time I had writing it? The whole thing is performance and prowess and feats of association. Why don't critics talk about those things—what a feat it was to turn that that way, and what a feat it was to remember that, to be reminded of that by this? Why don't they talk about that? Scoring. You've got to *score*. They say not, but you've got to score, in all the realms—theology, politics, astronomy, history, and the country life around you.

* **burned right up:** perhaps meaning 'didn't solidify, didn't work out.'"

In any game, there are rules that define the game: You cannot pick the ball up, you must carry it only so far, you must move a certain way, there is a goal or net to put the ball over or into. To bring the best out of yourself physically, you set challenges for yourself: to run at a certain speed, climb a rock, walk a particular distance, jump a stipulated height, knit an unusual pattern, or cook an exotic meal. Poetry is no different. To bring the best out of yourself creatively, you will also need to set yourself rules. Poetry without restrictions is like high jumping without a bar, or, as Robert Frost put it, "playing tennis with the net down." Now you may be the sort of person who invents his own games, or you may be the sort of person who prefers to play a game that has clear rules already set down, the sort of person who likes a game that others have tried and excelled at, and who feels that half the fun of a sport is watching and imitating the great players. Well, if you are the first kind of person, one who prefers to make his own rules, you may want to try your hand at free verse. That has no set rules, and it demands that you set your own challenges, really no different from swimming a river, making a dress, climbing a tree, or taking a certain number of steps with your eyes closed. If you are the sort who prefers tennis, track, or tiddlywinks—all of which have accepted rules—you may prefer to try your hand at a form of poetry that has rules already laid out.

It would be wrong to write only free verse. Trying to write poems that have a specific meter and/or rhyme scheme will increase your technical proficiency. Learning the rules and playing the game according to the rules teaches the discipline that a good poet needs. Working with rhyme imparts an awareness of the sounds of words and a sense of form not available in free verse. The fixed form of the sonnet presents problems not found in any other verse form. Similarly, writing free verse allows you to experiment with rhythms not possible with rhyme.

Here is a poem in praise of freedom that makes use of the sonnet form. Because the poet Robert Hayden is writing within a tradition, he can break its rules and transcend the past. Without the tradition he would have been forced to create a new form, and he would have lost the energy that derives from his knowing what has been done before but his doing it differently because of a special occasion. Real poetic freedom is not formlessness but being able to use the rules that exist without getting tangled up in their restrictions.

Frederick Douglass

When it is finally ours, this freedom, this liberty, this beautiful
and terrible thing, needful to man as air,
usable as earth; when it belongs at last to all,
when it is truly instinct, brain matter, diastole, systole,
reflex action; when it is finally won; when it is more
than the gaudy mumbo jumbo of politicians:
this man, this Douglass, this former slave, this Negro
beaten to his knees, exiled, visioning a world
where none is lonely, none hunted, alien,
this man, superb in love and logic, this man
shall be remembered. Oh, not with statues' rhetoric,
not with legends and poems and wreaths of bronze alone,
but with the lives grown out of his life, the lives
fleshing his dream of the beautiful, needful thing.

ROBERT HAYDEN

Notice especially how Hayden has transcended the conventional iambic pentameter. He retains the five-beat line, but he
includes more than the usual number of unstressed syllables. The
effect of this is to get rid of the automatic stress that alternating
soft and loud tends to fall into, thus allowing the strong words to
thrust themselves into prominence on their own merit. No single
word carries more than one stress, so that each individual word
is encouraged to stand on its own. The exception to this is in line
6, which has a different tone. Notice the rhythmical energy of the
first line, which results from this technique:

When it is finally ours, this freedom, this liberty, this beautiful

Too many sonnets allow the stress to fall on words such as "when,"
or "this," that is, on naturally unstressed words. Throughout
Hayden's poem, the stresses fall on the naturally strong words,
strong in meaning as well as in sound.

Notice how Hayden has reshaped the traditional sonnet form,
which was often divided into the octet and the sestet. Here the
division is reversed—six and eight. It is the kind of reversal that
is used to celebrate special occasions, and it is effective because
there is a tradition to reverse. Notice how free the rhymes are: in
the conventional sense they are hardly rhymes at all; they are more
sympathies of sound.

It is important to see that this sonnet derives its freedom and power from acknowledging and transcending a tradition that is centuries old. This is the real meaning of poetic freedom.

In other words, experiment. Don't limit your method of poetic expression. Try writing a sonnet, or a short, rhymed poem with a basic anapestic meter, or a limerick, or a poem in free verse.

When you write, keep the following guidelines in mind:

1. Write of an experience *of your own,* or one that *you know well.* Keep it fresh in your mind and describe it honestly.

2. Feel free to be inventive with words. This may not be carried to the extent of inventing new words, which might be out of place in a traditional kind of poem. But an ear to the sound and an eye to the significance of your words will give the poem freshness.

3. Make your language imitate the effects and experiences you are describing. If there is a sea, make your words wash like the ocean; if there is a race, have your language gallop.

4. Use fresh images, not clichés. Describe your experience as far as possible with images that appeal to one or more of the senses, *objects* you can see, hear, touch, taste, smell. Be alive to the connotations of words.

5. Remember the options you have open for different ways of making comparisons. The fourth type is usually the subtlest, but it is also the hardest to get right.

6. Aim at a single mood throughout your poem, intensified toward the end.

7. Think of the dramatic situation in your poem: who is talking, where, to whom, under what circumstances?

8. Create a situation containing tension at the beginning of your poem and resolve it in the last two or three lines.

9. Set in your first line a situation that the reader can grasp and that will interest him. In the last line you should resolve that situation, having satisfied his interest.

There are several "don'ts" in creating poems:

1. Don't use unnatural-sounding language, inversions, old-fashioned words.

2. Don't be afraid to vary the meter, but be sure that you have established it before you vary it.

3. Don't let the reader predict what will happen next. Surprise him. But let him say after the surprise, as at the end of a detective story, "Yes, of course, that's how it was bound to work out!"

4. Don't expect to write a great line the first time. Work on it until it comes right. Don't be afraid to alter or scrap wording or ideas that don't fit.

5. Don't give up! The easier the poem was to write, the harder it will be to read.

WRITING
SHORT
STORIES

1

Introduction

BY THE TIME YOU HAVE conscientiously worked through this section, you will have written at least one example of almost every kind of short prose composition, culminating in a full-dress short story.

While you are working, two things will be asked of you: First, to study a number of literary techniques as they have been used by skilled writers and to use them creatively in your own work; second, and more important, to give something of yourself, to share with others your special vision of the world. You see the world in your own particular way, and how you see it—what you consider important, how you interpret what you see, what connections you see between things—is of great importance and worth recording.

The urge to create a lasting pattern from life's apparent disorder runs deep in man. Every tribe and nation has its legends, its imaginative tales of heroes and events, many of which have a basis in fact. All of them have an additional ingredient: they not only tell what happened but also use the imagination to transform, as if by magic, what *did* happen into what *is always* happening. In other words, the tales present an event as something universal, something that affects everyone and that is relevant to each person's life.

Literature grows out of the vision that an artist brings to his subject. He shows the object exactly as he sees it. Perhaps you have seen a painting by a modern artist that doesn't reproduce exactly the person who modeled for the picture. The painter Picasso painted a woman with a face that was moon-shaped, green, half-male, half-female. Is this how Picasso sees a woman? Yes, in a sense. He sees and records not only the face in front of him but also what lies behind the face: the dreams, the fears, the values, the ambitions, the personality, the character. These are just as much a part of the "real" person as the features of her face or the cut of her clothes. So, if Picasso's subject is a woman who is always dreaming about her perfect lover, he might paint half of her face as that of her lover—but not as she sees her lover, since Picasso cannot know that (nor does he need to). He records her lover's face as a circular moon-shape, to suggest that this is her ideal. Picasso is painting the reality that lies *underneath the face of reality,* transforming what he saw into what is always true.

And it is the same vision that will be demanded of you, as you prepare to write a short story. You will be asked to observe scenes, people, events, to form your own vision of them, and to record that vision faithfully by means of the techniques and forms that will be described in this section. Finally, you will be asked to organize your vision and to compress it within the limits of a short story.

The short story is defined as fiction that varies from 200 to 10,000 words in length. Most short stories are somewhere between 1,500 and 3,500 words in length. Anything shorter than 1,500 words is usually thought of as a short short story. If you look at the examples in this part, you will see that according to this definition they are almost all short short stories, rather than short stories. Once this is realized, it is quite safe, and much more convenient, to refer to the stories simply as short stories.

Length, however, is not the most important factor in characterizing a short story. What is? Primarily, it is the unity of the action, the singleness of the effect. This idea is hard to grasp in the abstract, so as an illustration here is a very short story, one that contains all the main elements:

Appointment in Samarra

Many years ago, there was a man in Bathsheba who asked his servant to go to market. His servant had known many years, and was faithful in service. Though his hair was white, he stood as tall as a young date tree in the autumn, whose leaves are beginning to fall, while the fruit of abundance draws to an end about it.

The servant went to market, and among the throng he saw Death, dressed in black and as pale as the moon that grows thin. Death made a gesture, and the servant grew frightened; for, although there were many people in the marketplace, who crowded to buy the things that would bring them joy while they lived, none of them heeded the lonely pair.

And he ran home to his master, and he said, "Master, today I saw Death in the market amid the throng. And he made a threatening gesture to me. Master, I shall make haste and I shall ride like the wind to Samarra, for Samarra is many miles from here, and Death will not find me there."

So the servant rode away to Samarra, and his master was sorely troubled, as is the traveler in the desert who is called to the side of his dying father and his long journey draws to an end. And he went to the market and he sought out Death, whose dress was dark as the sea at night when the fisherman is lost, and his face was as pale as a grave on a frosty night.

And the master said to Death, "Why did you make a threatening gesture at my servant? He has done me good service, and is old in years."

And Death replied, "I made no threatening gesture at your servant. That was a start of surprise. For I saw him this morning in Bathsheba, but this night I was to meet him many miles away in Samarra."

What do the terms "unity of action" and "singleness of effect" mean when applied to this short story? Simply, they mean that everything in the story is related to a single idea or situation. Every word is somehow a part of that single action or effect.

Everything in the story centers upon a situation that has the servant doing his best to avoid meeting Death, when, in fact, the old man is rushing to meet it.

Contained within that action or effect is a theme—not a moral, but a vision, perhaps, of what life is like. How is this vision of life communicated? First, there is a conflict, a state of tension: The servant is old and he sees Death in the marketplace. This conflict between Death and the servant is over something of value to the servant: his life! This conflict occurs in a setting that gives a location to the action. There is a certain mood, suggested perhaps by the comparisons. And the servant has personality—not a very deeply drawn one, to be sure, but a personality, nevertheless.

As the conflict develops, there is a seesawing action that moves toward settling the conflict in favor of one side or the other. Will Death win, or will the servant win? First one seems to have the upper hand, then the other. There are, it is true, hints that foreshadow the outcome. That is all part of the unity. The action becomes more suspenseful as the story approaches its conclusion. The servant will ride like the wind to Samarra, perhaps escaping Death after all. But Death's final remarks give us the verdict. It has been preordained all along.

Death will keep his appointment in Samarra. This information is a high point, a climax, that resolves the conflict generated in the beginning of the story. The stakes (the servant's life) have been played for and won. Everything in the story has led up to this revelation, which is a statement of a vision of life—or one aspect of it. Death is seen as inevitable, and the story seems to suggest that we accept it and make the best of it, thus avoiding a long ride when the time comes!

A short story, then, is a relatively short, unified composition having an initial conflict leading to a final climax that resolves it. It has a major character, with at most two or three minor characters, and a setting, all illustrating a view or vision of life. You will not be asked to present a comprehensive philosophy of life. You are asked to give your own vision of life as you know it and can honestly portray it.

The activities that follow this chapter and the material in the next chapter will further develop this crucial idea of your own personal vision by allowing you to explore yourself. Hopefully, it will help both to free your imagination and to furnish you with material for characters and a statement about how you see a part of life. Remember that you are your own best model; if you feel something, the chances are that others will feel the same. All you have to do is take hold of it and use your imagination to express it. Your personal vision of things is the most precious gift that you have.

~~~~~~

ACTIVITIES

1. Take the story of the following poem:

> Ding, dong, bell
> The cat's in the well.
>
> Who put her in?
> Little Johnny Green.
>
> Who pulled her out?
> Little Tommy Trout.

Let the class form four groups. Each group will write the story, in no more than a hundred words, as *one* of the following— the cat, Johnny Green, Tommy Trout, the cat's owner—would see it. Each should tell the story in *three* paragraphs. Writers should beware of avoiding the worst of all traps: ridiculing the character they are presenting. It is essential that all writers are serious in telling their version of the story.

Then one member from each group is selected for a communal reading. The four readers—*A, B, C, D*—should read their material in the following order:

a. *A* reads his paragraph 1.
b. *B* reads his paragraph 1.
c. *C* reads his paragraph 1.
d. *D* reads his paragraph 1.
e. *A* reads his paragraph 2.
f. *B* reads his paragraph 2, and so on.
g. Finally, all four read together, synchronizing the start of each paragraph.

How was the effect different from reading each story from beginning to end? What was the effect of breaking down the stories by paragraph? What was the effect of the communal reading?

2. Each student should take a large sheet of paper and write a first sentence to a short story, putting the last three words of the sentence on a separate line. Then he should fold the paper, so that only the last three words are showing, and pass the sheet to a neighbor. Now each student should write the next sentence of the story on the sheet in front of him, based on the three words of the previous sentence. Then the papers should be passed on again. No student should write on the same sheet twice during this exercise. After going around the class, the stories are brought to a conclusion. The stories may then be read.

3. Three students sit out in front of the class. Each decides to become a character of a specific age, sex, and walk of life, who has a specific purpose, such as waiting for a bus. He must assume that identity without giving visual or verbal clues beyond his general stance and demeanor. The idea is not to be stagy or to act out who is represented. Rather, they should become that person for a time in their imaginations. It is up to the class to guess what sort of person each has become by the way he holds his body and by his facial expressions.

4. *Switches:* This is a method of dramatic interaction, again impromptu. Two students are in front of the class. A member of the audience names a profession, such as barber. That is the starting point. The actors then use the profession to improvise an action—for example, one becomes the barber, the other the customer; or both are barbers working side by side, or they are together in a bar discussing haircuts. When one of the actors chooses, he takes an action of the other and uses that gesture to switch the situation into another situation involving an entirely different profession. For example, one actor may be showing the barber his bald spot. The "barber" suddenly becomes a surgeon examining a wound, or a matador fighting a bull, or a policeman dealing with a drunk, or a monarch conferring knighthood. The point is to find a sharp, clean switch and for the partner to follow what the change is as quickly as he can. Continue the activity until a series of transformations have been completed.

5. Another game, similar to Switches, is having two students in front of the class. Someone names a profession, an object to be dealt with, and a punch line—for example: salesman, an egg, and "there's a gorilla right behind you." The two must

incorporate all three into an action. The punch line concludes the action. The students should try to introduce the final line naturally.

6. *Press Conference:* Two students sit before the class. There has been an *incident,* the facts of which are determined before the game starts. The two are there to defend their conduct during the incident. Questions are fired at them by the "press," that is, the class. The two students have one restriction: in phrasing their answers they may not use the words "No," "Yes," or "I." If one does, his place is taken by the questioner who prompted the slip. The situation remains constant, however.

～～～～～～～～～～～～～～～～～～～～～～～～～～～～

2

Loosening up

YOUR MIND IS COMPOSED of two sections—your conscious and your unconscious. Somehow the two are connected but nobody knows for sure exactly how.

The conscious is the part of your mind that you are directly aware of; it reasons, judges, and verbalizes. But the unconscious part is just as important, though much harder to "tap." People have been studying it for years, but it remains largely a mystery. It may be man's animal brain, operating below the level of reason; it may be the permanent part of his soul; perhaps it is the part of him that most truly is himself.

There are a number of ways of knowing what is going on in your unconscious. One is through hypnosis. The unconscious also is revealed through psychosomatic effects. Have you ever wondered how some people are afflicted with the most authentic illnesses on days on which exams have been scheduled? The inflamed throat is unarguable; the high temperature is real enough. What is happening is that the body is unconsciously willing itself to be ill, in order to avoid what it conceives as a worse fate.

Dreams are the best way of determining what is happening in your unconscious mind. For a dream is a message from your unconscious to your conscious mind. But since, when you dream, your conscious mind is sleeping and should not be disturbed, the message is delivered in a kind of code. The meaning of the dream only becomes clear after some study and thought.

Poets and creative writers have long been aware that some of their best material is rooted in the unconscious mind. The reason for this link between literature and the unconscious is that the latter is involved with man's deepest emotions and needs. Moreover, it finds the most ingenious ways of communicating these emotions and needs—as in dreams. And creating ways of communicating man's deepest hopes and fears, anxieties and desires is at the core of all great literature.

All this is not to say that the conscious mind has no role to play in the creative process. Broadly speaking, it is with the conscious mind that the writer criticizes, deletes, plans, and organizes the material that comes from his unconscious. The purpose of this chapter and the questions that follow it is to put the emphasis, for a while, on the unconscious, so that you can write initially *without* the aid of the censor, the policeman, the judge— your conscious mind. Our task will be to release the creative energies of that midnight ocean, the unconscious.

As stated above, the unconscious has the most ingenious ways of communicating to the conscious its desires and anxieties, hopes and fears. A dream argues with its own kind of logic. It may seem ridiculous when you wake up: The tall, faceless man, who reminded you of someone you know, is going to take out your tooth. You sit up in terror with an acute sense of loss. Lo and behold, the someone you know is not in the least similar to the tall, faceless man, and what would he want with your tooth anyway? And why all this bother over a stolen molar? Yet, the terror and sense of loss were real enough, and all your actions seemed logical when you were dreaming. This kind of dream logic has been used by a number of great writers: Franz Kafka, James Joyce, Lewis Carroll, Edgar Allan Poe, and Hermann Hesse, to name but a few. Many of the best songs from the "rock" culture, especially by the Beatles, use dreamlike sequences.

Here is an example of "dream writing" from *Through the Looking-Glass*. As you read, look for elements of dream, but also for elements of reality. Ask yourself in what way Lewis Carroll has used his dreamlike material to throw light on reality.

From **Through the Looking-Glass**

"Tickets, please!" said the Guard, putting his head in at the window. In a moment everybody was holding out a ticket: they were about the same size as the people, and quite seemed to fill the carriage.

"Now then! Show your ticket, child!" the Guard went on, looking angrily at Alice. And a great many voices all said together ("like the chorus of a song," thought Alice) "Don't keep him waiting, child! Why, his time is worth a thousand pounds a minute!"

"I'm afraid I haven't got one," Alice said in a frightened tone: "there wasn't a ticket office where I came from." And again the chorus of voices went on. "There wasn't room for one where she came from. The land there is worth a thousand pounds an inch!"

"Don't make excuses," said the Guard: "you should have bought one from the engine-driver." And once more the chorus of voices went on with "The man that drives the engine. Why, the smoke alone is worth a thousand pounds a puff!"

Alice thought to herself "Then there's no use in speaking." The voices didn't join in, *this* time, as she hadn't spoken, but, to her great surprise, they all *thought* in chorus (I hope you understand what *thinking in chorus* means—for I must confess that *I* don't), "Better say nothing at all. Language is worth a thousand pounds a word."

"I shall dream about a thousand pounds tonight, I know I shall!" thought Alice.

All this time the Guard was looking at her, first through a telescope, then through a microscope, and then through an opera glass. At last he said "You're traveling the wrong way," and shut up the window, and went away.

Analysis of "Through the Looking-Glass"

1. Clearly, this passage is not a direct account of a dream by the author. On the other hand, it could easily have

been prompted by a dream. What situations seem as if they are from a dream?

2. Has Lewis Carroll gained anything by making this a dreamlike sequence, rather than reporting the event realistically? If so, what? If not, why? Would a realistic picture be more successful? Does the unreality of some of the action prevent him from making serious points?

3. What dream might have prompted this sequence?

ACTIVITIES

The following exercises are entirely for your own reference. You will be under no obligation to hand in assignments.

1. Close your eyes. Physically lower your breathing so that you are breathing in your stomach, behind your solar plexus. Focus your thoughts and feelings on that region. This is the center of your emotions. Let your emotions from that region come out through your breathing. Sigh, so that there is a little burr, of whatever emotion you have there, on your breath. Now, as you exhale, use that breath to say your name several times. What is your reaction? Is it pleasure, fear, relief, boredom, excitement, a mixture of two or more of these?

2. Close your eyes. Center your breathing, as in the previous exercise. Turn off your thoughts, letting only those come through that cannot help themselves. Imagine you are on a road, walking. Describe the landscape that you see around you.

3. Take a large sheet of paper, and, as honestly as you can, write the answers to the following questions. The purpose of this exercise is to allow you to explore yourself.

    a. What is the best and happiest situation you can imagine?

    b. What is the worst situation you can imagine?

    c. What would you wish for if your most fantastic dreams were to be realized?

    d. What is your most terrible fear?

    e. What do you most wish and fear according to what you tell your friends? When you are alone? Are they the same or different?

f. What were you afraid of in earlier years?

g. List one desire, one anxiety, one source of irritation, one of comfort.

h. Do you side with the conqueror or the underdog (1) in real life and (2) when you read about it?

4. All good writing is concerned in some way with values— the things the person considers important. This exercise and the one following are aimed at letting you think about your own value system. Mark the following either *1, 2,* or *3* according to their value to you. (*1* indicates that the item is of little value to you; *2,* that the item is of some value; *3,* that the item is important.)

a. Getting good grades.

b. Being feared.

c. Reading, listening to music, enjoying some art form.

d. Pleasing your fellow students.

e. Being like others, being normal.

f. Pleasing your parents.

g. Athletic competition.

h. Experiencing a sensual pleasure, such as eating or staying in bed.

i. Writing, painting, making something.

j. Being different, not being lost in the crowd, being individual.

5. Rank the following items starting with those you dislike most and ending with those you dislike least.

a. Loneliness.

b. Being ridiculed.

c. Causing pain in someone you like.

d. Death.

e. Disapproval from parents.

f. Loss of a limb or power.

g. Making a decision.

h. Boredom.

i. Being temporarily deprived of a need for things such as food or sleep.

j. Being shut up, confined in a narrow space.

6. Write continuously for ten, twenty, or thirty minutes, de-

pending on how much time you wish to spend. Set an alarm or some other reminder.

Write without pausing, without even thinking what you are saying. At first, nothing may come, in which case you should write "My mind is a blank" or "I don't know what to write." An alternative is to write your own name as often as you can, until thoughts start to come. And they will, soon enough. You should be recording at full speed for however long you decide to spend. But do not throw away the paper when you have finished your time span. Read it carefully, looking for trends, for ideas that are repeated. This is your unconscious mind speaking to you through the conscious controls. What is it telling you? You can usually discount the first page or two. After that your psyche will be in its stride.

7. Record an actual dream you have had. If you cannot remember an actual dream, this exercise will have to wait. But for future reference, a good way of remembering what you have dreamed is to ask yourself as soon as you wake up: What am I thinking about? What led me to think about this? What led to that? And soon you will have picked your way back to the dream thought-train that first occupied your thoughts when you awoke.

8. Write down the images evoked by the following. Perhaps your reaction will be a single word like "no" or "love"; or it may be a picture, like "sea and sky." You may wish to concentrate on a single keyword and develop your reactions to it in detail.

a. Terror	d. Satisfaction	g. Anxiety
b. Black	e. Red	h. White
c. Tall	f. I can't	i. Fat

9. Construct an imaginary dream, such as might come to one of the following:

a. A cat sleeping in the sun, with flies buzzing past.
b. A two-year old child, sleeping during a thunderstorm.
c. A very old man asleep in the cold. There is a tap dripping nearby.

~~~~~~

3

How does it feel?: the sketch

In LITERATURE, a sketch is a brief composition presenting a single scene, character, or incident. The sketch confronts the reader with something that the reader has not clearly perceived. It focuses on a specific person, place, or situation and presents it simply yet vividly.

Writing sketches is an essential step in your development as a writer. A sketch lays the groundwork for writing more developed work. Description and characterization play vital roles in writing effective short stories. And sketches provide an opportunity to practice the techniques used in description and characterization.

At the same time, as sketches prepare you for more advanced writing, they are in themselves finished products. Because they are short, they must be unified. Only one scene is described, one character portrayed, one incident presented. Thus, the sketch contains within it the principles of unity that a writer must master in order to develop.

Let us take an apple—we could take a place, a person, a mood, but a simple example is probably best. Now, suppose a writer "sees" this apple in his mind's eye. Can *you* see it? Not yet. All you can do is to imagine an apple of your own or to think in a general way of the fruit commonly known as "apple." Either of these might be sufficient for certain contexts, but for a sketch and often for a short story, it is necessary for a writer to make his subject distinctive.

How can a writer give his apple reality? First, he can say what the apple looks like: Is it red or green? large or small? smooth or wrinkled? Probably none of those entirely. So he must specify.

Once questions like these have been answered, you can "see" the apple. But that is not enough. There are other senses to be included in the description:

How does it feel? Cool or warm? plump or withered? firm or soft? bruised or intact?

What does it smell like? Aged, like cider or vinegar? sweet as a spring orchard? mellow or tart? fresh or stale? juicy or acid?

What does it sound like when you shake it? roll it? drop it? bite into it?

What does it taste like? How does it feel against the teeth? against the tongue? against the palate? Is it bitter or bland? unripe or rotten? crisp or mushy? Is it a cooking or an eating apple? Is it a crab apple? a Winesap?

Once these questions have been answered, the apple has something of a life of its own. It has color, shape, texture, substance—physical qualities. But as yet it is no more than a painted apple. It must be set in space and time.

Where is it? On a tree? in a gutter? in a supermarket? in a bowl of fruit on a table? in the hand of someone who is ready to throw it? The setting is important.

And what time is it? Morning or evening? spring or winter? The time of the Garden of Eden, of ancient Greece, or of America in the 1970's? Is the apple fresh or preserved? Is it a rotten husk or the contents of a pie?

Now the apple has an objective existence. In other words, it exists in itself, as an object, but it has no clear emotion attached to it, no identity. It simply is. It must have a *subjective* existence too. This only the writer's emotions, his vision, can supply. How does he see it, how does he feel about it? It needs focus, intensity, force, significance, identity. "What, in a simple apple?" you say. "Isn't this going a little too far? An apple, after all, is just an apple. Do you want to start a war out of it, make some great scientific discovery that changes the world from it, build it into some earthshaking religious issue, or something?"

That is, of course, just what did happen to certain distinguished apples in history and legend. The golden apple of Greek legend was the prize at the judgment of Paris that led to the Trojan War. It was a humble apple that set Newton to formulating the law of gravity. It was a symbolic apple that led to the loss of Eden.

But a writer does not have to choose a famous model for his sketch to have significance. He need not focus on something with a meaning beyond itself, some symbol, some trophy: such as the football that stands in your school cabinet behind glass at the end of the hall, reminding you all of a great victory; or the bullet that killed Lincoln; or the paper on which the Declaration of Independence is written. The writer gives life to his subject by bringing to it a vision, a reaction, a set of emotions of his own.

Whatever your subject means to you, however you see it, you should aim to record that single impression. Perhaps you wish to record it in terms of other experience, using simile or metaphor: "It was as red as the evening sun." Comparisons should be used only when needed to express a single, unified attitude toward your subject. And that attitude will determine how sharp is the identity of your model, whether it is just a collection of attributes or whether it is an object with significance.

The most important element in achieving unity is your ability to select and arrange details so that they build the overall effect. Consider this passage by John Steinbeck:

The Octopus

Then the creeping murderer, the octopus, steals out, slowly, softly, moving like a gray mist, pretending now to be a bit of weed, now a rock, now a lump of decaying meat, while its evil goat eyes watch coldly. It oozes and flows toward a feeding crab, and as it comes close its yellow eyes burn and its body turns rosy with the pulsing color of anticipation and rage. Then suddenly it runs lightly on the tips of its arms, as ferociously as a charging cat. It leaps savagely on the crab, there is a puff of black fluid, and the struggling mass is ob-

scured in the sepia cloud while the octopus murders
the crab.

JOHN STEINBECK, *Cannery Row*

Analysis of "The Octopus"

1. What is Steinbeck's overall attitude toward his subject?
   Does it include any of the following?
   a. Horror b. Anger (moral) c. Humor d. Sympathy
2. What is the overall mood of the passage, the overall
   unified effect?

   a. Beautiful and wild   d. Scientific and uninvolved
   b. Horrible and comic   e. Romantic and comic
   c. Homey and comfortable   f. Some other combination

Note: The effect is no less unified because it takes two adjectives to describe it. It could take any number to describe it
accurately.

As you can see from looking at the passage from *Cannery
Row,* a sketch is more than a catalogue of attributes or techniques, an inventory or a grocery list. Writing a sketch involves
selecting a number of specific details that work toward a single
overall impression. To do this, you must have determined the
specific effect that you want. You must examine and think about
the subject so thoroughly that you have many specific details in
mind, discarding those that don't reinforce the underlying purpose of the sketch. To find one or even two such details is not
hard. Two words that suggest or indicate coldness and bleakness,
two words that menace and loom, are not hard to come by. The
trick is to examine and think through your subject so thoroughly
that you have a dozen, fifteen, twenty such details, small experiences, all reinforcing the underlying purpose, all building a single
effect.

In choosing the details, remember that words convey emotional feelings. The effect of Steinbeck's saying the octopus
"steals" out is quite different from saying it "moves" out. "Steals"
suggests the creature's guile, an attribute attested to by the rest
of the paragraph.

To make the sketch come alive, use concrete imagery. In

this respect, good prose is like good poetry. It re-creates life by capturing sensory details. A writer captures these sensory details through figurative language: metaphor, simile, personification, and other figures of speech.

A second point to remember in writing sketches or in writing any other prose work is that good sketches contain verbs of action. The verbs in Steinbeck's passage include "steals," "watch," "oozes," "flows," "burn," "runs," and "leaps." Each describes some sort of action. Steinbeck's passage contains only one sentence in which a form of "to be" is used as the main verb.

The verbs of action are supplemented by several instances in which verbs are used as adjectives: "creeping," "moving," "pretending," "feeding," "probing," plus several more examples. These adjectives add to the action of the sketch.

What subjects are suitable for a sketch? Some compact physical object, or a scene, or a single occasion are best. But an abstract idea such as "time," is equally valid, although harder to focus on. One tends to run out of ideas after the second sentence.

Before you try your hand at a sketch, study the following example closely.

The White Table

When I emerged, the lights were still there. I lay beneath the slab of glass, feeling deflated. All my limbs seemed amputated. It was very warm. A dim white ceiling stretched far above me. My eyes were swimming with tears. Why, I didn't know. It worried me. I wanted to knock on the glass to attract attention, but I couldn't move. The slightest effort, hardly more than desire, tired me. I lay experiencing the vague processes of my body. I seemed to have lost all sense of proportion. Where did my body end and the crystal and white world begin? Thoughts evaded me, hiding in the vast stretch of clinical whiteness to which I seemed connected only by a scale of receding grays. No sounds beyond the sluggish inner roar of the blood. I couldn't open my eyes. I seemed to exist in some other dimension, utterly alone; until after a while a nurse bent down and forced a warm fluid between my lips. I gagged, swallowed, feeling the fluid course slowly to my vague middle. A huge iridescent bubble seemed to enfold me. Gentle hands moved over me, bringing vague impressions of memory. I was laved with warm liquids, felt gentle hands move through the indefinite limits of my flesh. The sterile and weightless texture of a sheet enfolded me. I felt myself bounce, sail off like a ball thrown over the roof into mist, striking a hidden wall beyond a pile of broken machinery and sailing back. How long it took, I didn't know. But now above the movement of the hands I heard a friendly voice, uttering familiar words to which I could assign no meaning. I listened intensely, aware of the form and movement of sentences and grasping the now subtle rhythmical differences between progressions of sound that questioned and those that made a statement. But still their meanings were lost in the vast whiteness in which I myself was lost.

RALPH ELLISON, *Invisible Man*

Analysis of "The White Table"

1. Describe in a sentence or two the overall feeling of the narrator.
2. List five details that contribute to the building of the mood.
3. What significance does the word *white* assume during the passage?
4. Which of the following comes closest to catching the mood of the passage?
   a. Comfortable   d. Sad
   b. Disconnected   e. Eerie
   c. Angry

ACTIVITIES

1. Below is the skeleton of Steinbeck's sketch about the octopus. Choose another object to sketch and fill in the blanks, using the parts of speech that Steinbeck did. Before you begin, determine what specific attitude you want to convey about the subject.

Then the _____, the _____, _____
       adjective   noun   noun   verb

_____, _____, _____ ing like
  adverb   adverb   participle

_____, pretending now to be_____,
      simile   noun

now _____, now _____, while
     noun   noun phrase

_____.
                     description

It _____ and _____ _____,
   verb   verb   prepositional phrase

and _____, its _____ _____
      adverbial phrase   adjective   noun

and its _____.
                description

Then suddenly it _____ _____,
              verb   adverbial phrase

as _____ as _____.
   adjective   noun or noun phrase

It_____ _____ _____,
  verb   adverb   noun or prepositional phrase

there is _____, and the _____
         description   adjective

_____ _____., while _____
 noun   verb or verb phrase   clause

_____.

2. Describe a small object, perhaps an old pencil or a crumpled piece of paper. Organize the details so as to give a simple impression of your model.

3. Describe a scene, selecting your details so as to produce a unified effect.

4. When we go out for a walk, we primarily see and hear, secondarily feel and smell. Describe a walk in which the images are primarily those of smell and feel.

5. Describe a scene that emphasizes one of the following:

a. Horror
b. Hidden fear
c. Sensitivity to color
d. Fragility
e. Freedom
f. Confinement
g. Falling
h. Sadness

6. Write a sketch of an abstract idea, such as "time" or "blue." Give the abstract idea sensory attributes. (See page 155 for an example.)

~~~~~~

You should use a notebook to practice writing sketches. Describe the sights and sounds of your neighborhood. Try capturing smells and tastes. Try to describe tactile sensations— for instance, the feel of wool on your skin. Pick unusual items to sketch, preferably something small—a nail file or a front stoop. Be specific and vivid. Avoid abstract statements. Don't overuse the verb "to be"; instead use active verbs.

4

Character sketch

IN THE LAST CHAPTER, you were writing sketches—of objects, scenes, or abstracts. This chapter will take up the problems involved in writing character sketches.

Once again, the task is to give your subject reality. In the case of character, however, the problem is more complicated. You should convey your model's internal and external characteristics and identity. The external characteristics include physical appearance, present surroundings, and background. These set your model in three dimensions. But when you are deciding on your subject's identity or the internal characteristics, you should think in terms of beliefs, values, what the person feels deeply about, what the person stands for.

Let us assume that we are writing a character sketch of a woman.

First, her appearance: Is she tall or short, fat or thin? What does she look like? Imagine her face exactly: What does it reveal of her internal character? Does it scowl? Does it have any prominent features? Are her eyes deep-set? Is her mouth thin or full, does it smile or sulk? Next, focus on the body: How does she walk? Does she stoop? Is one shoulder higher than the other? What are her characteristic gestures? Is she always excusing herself, holding out a hand and turning it? Does she lean forward, eager and hunched? Does she lean back in her chair, unwilling to be too involved, checking the effect of what she says before she says it? Does she bunch her fist, bite her nails? Is she energetic or at rest? Does she hide behind her hands?

To further develop her external features: What sort of clothes does she wear? What sort of life style does she have, insofar as she can choose? In what circles does she move? How does she spend her time?

This leads to a consideration of her everyday life: What does she do for a living (or where does she study, etc.)? How old is she? What is her name? her nickname? What typical settings is she to be found in? What about her background, parents, life up to now, marriage, relationships, and so on?

This and similar material deals with the *external* aspects of your subject, as opposed to the inner reality: the values that she holds, the things she believes in and will stand by, regardless of the cost.

What is a value? A value is anything that a person thinks important, from her record collection to her ideology. It is not much of an exaggeration to say that literature is primarily about values. So are people.

There are certain commonly accepted values in our society, which represent aims for people's conduct. But each of these respected values also contains a negative interpretation. The table below sets values in both their positive and their negative aspects side by side. Thus, the same man who is unflinching in his defense of freedom may be equally stubborn when it comes to how his eggs are prepared. A man cannot spend all his life defending the great principles; the same man must also spend time eating eggs.

Here is a list of a few of the more commonly held values in our society. Many short stories have been written simply to contrast and separate the positive and the negative sides of these values. Evaluate your own attitude toward some of these values. When you come to compose a full-length short story, they may supply ideas for writing or creating characters:

Positive	Negative
Helping others	Being a do-gooder, busybody
Treating others as equals	Having no standards, reducing everyone to same level
Physical courage	Bullying
Moral courage, having courage of convictions	Obstinacy, stubbornness
Self-respect	Egotism, pride, snobbery
Honesty	Tactlessness
Being an individual, being yourself	Being a misfit, an eccentric, an egotist
Friendship	Cliquishness
Being agreeable, being liked	Being a yes-man
Being firm, respected	Being a bully, a tyrant, an autocrat
Relaxing, having a good time	Being irresponsible, hedonistic, shallow
Excitement	Thrill seeking
Love	Romantic, naive
Sex	Animal instincts, being loose
Liking new things, new experiences	Being a novelty seeker, a radical
Liking old things	Being a stick-in-the-mud, a conservative
Intelligence, being an intellectual	Being an egghead, impractical, lacking emotions
Being practical, pragmatic	Being an opportunist, unprincipled
Money, material things, security	Miserliness, greed, possessiveness, materialism
Family loyalty	Clannishness
Patriotism	Chauvinism, fascism, narrow-mindedness
Motherhood	Momism

| Ambition, getting ahead, power | Ruthlessness, megalomania |
| Reputation | Publicity |

Once you have established what her values are, you can make an attempt to see your subject as a whole. What sort of person is your subject: Busy and anxious? pleasant and thoughtful? responsible or wild? How the different traits of a character relate can be seen by glancing at the figure below.

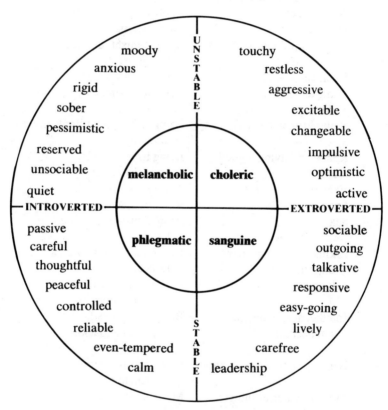

The inner ring shows what for centuries were considered to be the four types of personalities. The outer ring shows the results of modern analytic studies on the connections between personality traits.

Chart from *The Causes and Cures of Neurosis* by H. J. Eysenck and S. Rachman, published by Robert R. Knapp, Publisher, San Diego, 1965. Reprinted by permission of Robert R. Knapp, Publisher, Routledge & Kegan Paul Ltd., and the authors.

You should aim at presenting a unified picture of your model, as with your previous sketches. That does not mean that you should oversimplify your character. If you draw her with any depth at all, she will be contradictory, as most persons are. She will have defenses. She will be changeable. Your chief problem will be, on the one hand, to avoid stereotype or cartoon characterization but on the other, to unify the impression you offer of your model. Every character, however contradictory, has some thread, some common strand which unites his or her personality. For example, the poet Lord Byron was, at one and the same time, the most idealistic and the most cynical of men. He rejected many of the accepted values of country, church, respectability, and success. Yet this same man suddenly decided that he must give his life, if need be, to go and fight for Greece in her struggle for independence from Turkey. His death at the age of thirty-six during the struggle cut short a brilliant career. Yet this action seemed as characteristic of him as all the other actions. It was his honesty, his sensitivity, his craving for values for which he could live—or die—that led him to reject the values of his own society.

Once you have assembled all the details of your character, you must organize them. As you are organizing the sketch, remember that the character's values, especially the most characteristic value, must be shown. Everything else—background, life style, appearance, mannerisms—should be related to these values.

The background, life style, and the other qualities should illustrate, explain, or contrast with the character's values.

The short story "The Quiet Man" by Maurice Walsh opens with a character sketch of the central figure, Shawn Kelvin. As you read the excerpt, notice how Walsh frequently emphasizes Kelvin's quietness, a quality that is basic to our understanding his character.

The Quiet Man

Shawn Kelvin, a blithe young lad of twenty, went to the States to seek his fortune. And fifteen years thereafter he returned to his native Kerry, his blitheness sobered and his youth dried to the core, and whether he had made his fortune or whether he had not, no one could be knowing for certain. For he was a quiet man, not given to talking about himself and the things he had done. A quiet man, under middle size, with strong shoulders and deep-set blue eyes below brows darker than his dark hair—that was Shawn Kelvin. One shoulder had a trick of hunching slightly higher than the other, and some folks said that came from a habit he had of shielding his eyes in the glare of an open-hearth furnace in a place called Pittsburgh, while others said it used to be a way he had of guarding his chin that time he was a sort of sparring-partner punching bag at a boxing camp.

Shawn Kelvin came home and found that he was the last of the Kelvins, and that the farm of his forefathers had added its few acres to the ranch of Big Liam O'Grady, of Moyvalla. Shawn took no action to recover his land, though O'Grady had got it meanly. He had had enough of fighting, and all he wanted now was peace. He quietly went among the old and kindly friends and quietly looked about him for the place and peace he wanted; and when the time came, quietly produced the money for a neat, handy, small farm on the first warm shoulder of Knockanore Hill below the rolling curves of heather. It was not a big place but it was in good heart, and it got all the sun that was going; and best of all, it suited Shawn to the tiptop notch of contentment, for it held the peace that tuned to his quietness, and it commanded the widest view in all Ireland—vale and mountain and the lifting green plain of the Atlantic Sea.

There, in a four-roomed, lime-washed, thatched cottage, Shawn made his life, and though his friends hinted his needs and obligations, no thought came to him of bringing a wife into the place. Yet Fate had the thought and the dream in her loom for him. One middling imitation of a man he had to do chores for him, an ex-navy pensioner handy enough about the house and byre,* but with no relish for the sustained work of the field—and indeed, as long as he kept house and byre shipshape, he found Shawn an easy master.

Shawn himself was no drudge toiler. He knew all about drudgery and the way it wears out a man's soul. He plowed a little and sowed a little, and at the end

* byre: cow barn.

of the furrow he would lean on the handles of the culti-
vator, wipe his brow, if it needed wiping, and lose himself for whole minutes in the great green curve of the sea
out there beyond the high black portals of Shannon
mouth. And sometimes of an evening he would see, under
the glory of the sky, the faint smoke smudge of an American liner. Then he would smile to himself—a pitying
smile—thinking of the poor devils, with dreams of fortune luring them, going out to sweat in Ironville, or to
bootleg bad whisky down the hidden way, or to stand in
a bread line. All these things were behind Shawn forever.

Market days he would go down and across to Lis-
towel town, seven miles, to do his bartering; and in
the long evenings, slowly slipping into the endless summer gloaming, his friends used to climb the winding lane
to see him. Only the real friends came that long road,
and they were welcome—fighting men who had been out
in the "Sixteen": * Matt Tobin the thresher, the school-
master, the young curate—men like that. A stone jar
of malt whisky would appear on the table, and there
would be a haze of smoke and a maze of warm, friendly
disagreements.

In Walsh's character sketch, he describes what Shawn was
like. Once Walsh had fully characterized the hero, he went on to
illustrate Shawn's character by showing the actions of the man.
Even in this character sketch presented here, Walsh told about
specific things that proved that Shawn was quiet.

When you are creating your own characters, remember not
to simply summarize the qualities of the character. Show them in
action. Rather than flatly stating, "John is stingy," tell a brief
story dramatizing his stinginess: "As we left the table, John sur-
reptitiously reached under a plate and scooped up the change he
had left for a tip. He walked silently out of the main dining room
to the hat check stand. The girl asked for our stubs and dis-
appeared into a maze of coats. While we were waiting, he said,
'Hope I left a big enough tip. The service was superb.'"

* **the "Sixteen":** a reference to the Easter Rebellion of 1916 in which Irish patriots
unsuccessfully attempted to seize Dublin by force and declare Ireland free from
English rule.

To review, the basic techniques that can be used in characterization are:

1. A physical description of the person.
2. The character's background or personal history.
3. The character's surroundings, such as his room or office.
4. The character's thoughts, emotions, and values.
5. The character's actions and reactions and opinions of others.
6. The character's speech.
7. The opinions or reactions of others to what the character says or does.

Being able to write character sketches is a vital step toward writing a complete short story. Many complete stories are expanded character sketches. The story that follows, "The Secret Life of Walter Mitty," is an example of a short story that is, in fact, a character sketch.

"We're going through!" The Commander's voice was like thin ice breaking. He wore his full-dress uniform, with the heavily braided white cap pulled down rakishly over one cold gray eye. "We can't make it, sir. It's spoiling for a hurricane, if you ask me." "I'm not asking you, Lieutenant Berg," said the Commander. "Throw on the power lights! Rev her up to 8,500! We're going through!" The pounding of the cylinders increased: ta-pocketa-pocketa-pocketa-*pocketa-pocketa.* The Commander stared at the ice forming on the pilot window. He walked over and twisted a row of complicated dials. "Switch on No. 8 auxiliary!" he shouted. "Switch on No. 8 auxiliary!" repeated Lieutenant Berg. "Full strength in No. 3 turret!" shouted the Commander. "Full strength in No. 3 turret!" The crew, bending to their various tasks in the huge, hurtling eight-engined Navy hydroplane, looked at each other and grinned. "The Old Man'll get us through," they said to one another. "The Old Man ain't afraid of Hell!" . . .

"Not so fast! You're driving too fast!" said Mrs. Mitty. "What are you driving so fast for?"

"Hmm?" said Walter Mitty. He looked at his wife, in the seat beside him, with shocked astonishment. She seemed grossly unfamiliar, like a strange woman who had yelled at him in a crowd. "You were up to fifty-five," she said. "You know I don't like to go more than forty. You were up to fifty-five." Walter Mitty drove on toward Waterbury in silence, the roaring of the SN202 through the worst storm in twenty years of Navy flying fading in the remote, intimate airways of his mind. "You're tensed up again," said Mrs. Mitty. "It's one of your days. I wish you'd let Dr. Renshaw look you over."

Walter Mitty stopped the car in front of the building where his wife went to have her hair done. "Remember to get those overshoes while I'm having my hair done," she said. "I don't need overshoes," said Mitty. She put her mirror back into her bag. "We've been all through that," she said, getting out of the car. "You're not a young man any longer." He raced the engine a little. "Why don't you wear your gloves? Have you lost your gloves?" Walter Mitty reached in a pocket and brought out the gloves. He put them on, but after she had turned and gone into the building and he had driven on to a red light, he took them off again. "Pick it up, brother!" snapped a cop as the light changed, and Mitty hastily pulled on his gloves and lurched ahead. He drove around the streets aimlessly for a time, and then he drove past the hospital on his way to the parking lot.

. . . "It's the millionaire banker, Wellington Mc-Millan," said the pretty nurse. "Yes?" said Walter Mitty, removing his gloves slowly. "Who has the case?" "Dr. Renshaw and Dr. Benbow, but there are two specialists here, Dr. Remington from New York and Mr. Pritchard-Mitford from London. He flew over." A door opened down a long, cool corridor and Dr. Renshaw came out. He looked distraught and haggard. "Hello, Mitty," he said. "We're having the devil's own time with McMillan, the millionaire banker and close personal friend of Roosevelt. Obstreosis of the ductal tract. Tertiary. Wish you'd take a look at him." "Glad to," said Mitty.

In the operating room there were whispered introductions: "Dr. Remington, Dr. Mitty. Mr. Pritchard-

Mitford, Dr. Mitty." "I've read your book on streptothricosis," said Pritchard-Mitford, shaking hands. "A brilliant performance, sir." "Thank you," said Walter Mitty. "Didn't know you were in the States, Mitty," grumbled Remington. "Coals to Newcastle, bringing Mitford and me up here for a tertiary." "You are very kind," said Mitty. A huge, complicated machine, connected to the operating table, with many tubes and wires, began at this moment to go pocketa-pocketa-pocketa. "The new anesthetizer is giving way!" shouted an intern. "There is no one in the East who knows how to fix it!" "Quiet, man!" said Mitty, in a low, cool voice. He sprang to the machine, which was now going pocketa-pocketa-queep-pocketa-queep. He began fingering delicately a row of glistening dials. "Give me a fountain pen!" he snapped. Someone handed him a fountain pen. He pulled a faulty piston out of the machine and inserted the pen in its place. "That will hold for ten minutes," he said. "Get on with the operation." A nurse hurried over and whispered to Renshaw, and Mitty saw the man turn pale. "Coreopsis has set in," said Renshaw nervously. "If you would take over, Mitty?" Mitty looked at him and at the craven figure of Benbow, who drank, and at the grave, uncertain faces of the two great specialists. "If you wish," he said. They slipped a white gown on him; he adjusted a mask and drew on thin gloves; nurses handed him shining . . .

"Back it up, Mac! Look out for that Buick!" Walter Mitty jammed on the brakes. "Wrong lane, Mac," said the parking-lot attendant, looking at Mitty closely. "Gee. Yeh," muttered Mitty. He began cautiously to back out of the lane marked "Exit Only." "Leave her sit there," said the attendant. "I'll put her away." Mitty got out of the car. "Hey, better leave the key." "Oh," said Mitty, handing the man the ignition key. The attendant vaulted into the car, backed it up with insolent skill, and put it where it belonged.

They're so damn cocky, thought Walter Mitty, walking along Main Street; they think they know everything. Once he had tried to take his chains off, outside New Milford, and he had got them wound around the axles. A man had had to come out in a wrecking car and unwind them, a young, grinning garageman. Since then Mrs. Mitty always made him drive to a garage to have the chains taken off. The next time, he thought, I'll wear my right arm in a sling; they won't grin at me then. I'll have my right arm in a sling and they'll see I couldn't possibly take the chains off myself. He kicked at the slush on the sidewalk. "Overshoes," he said to himself, and he began looking for a shoe store.

When he came out into the street again, with the overshoes in a box under his arm, Walter Mitty began to wonder what the other thing was his wife had told him to get. She had told him, twice, before they set out from their house for Waterbury. In a way he hated these weekly trips to town—he was always getting something wrong. Kleenex, he thought, Squibb's, razor blades? No. Toothpaste, toothbrush, bicarbonate, carborundum, initiative and referendum? He gave it up. But she would remember it. "Where's the what's-its-name?" she would ask, "Don't tell me you forgot the what's-its-name." A newsboy went by shouting something about the Waterbury trial.

. . . "Perhaps this will refresh your memory." The District Attorney suddenly thrust a heavy automatic at the quiet figure on the witness stand. "Have you ever seen this before?" Walter Mitty took the gun and examined it expertly. "This is my Webley-Vickers 50.80," he said calmly. An excited buzz ran around the courtroom. The Judge rapped for order. "You are a crack shot with any sort of firearms, I believe?" said the District Attorney, insinuatingly. "Objection!" shouted Mitty's attorney. "We have shown that the defendant could not have fired the shot. We have shown that he wore his right arm in a sling on the night of the fourteenth of July." Walter Mitty raised his hand briefly and the bickering attorneys were stilled. "With any known make of gun," he said evenly, "I could have killed Gregory Fitzhurst at three hundred feet *with my left hand.*" Pandemonium broke loose in the courtroom. A woman's scream rose above the bedlam and suddenly a lovely, dark-haired girl was in Walter Mitty's arms. The District Attorney struck at her savagely. Without rising from his chair, Mitty let the man have it on the point of the chin. "You miserable cur!" . . .

"Puppy biscuit," said Walter Mitty. He stopped walking and the buildings of Waterbury rose up out of the misty courtroom and surrounded him again. A woman who was passing laughed. "He said 'Puppy biscuit,' " she said to her companion. "That man said 'Puppy biscuit' to himself." Walter Mitty hurried on. He went into an A. & P., not the first one he came to but a smaller one farther up the street. "I want some biscuit for small, young dogs," he said to the clerk. "Any special brand, sir?" The greatest pistol shot in the world thought a moment. "It says 'Puppies Bark for It' on the box," said Walter Mitty.

His wife would be through at the hairdresser's in fifteen minutes, Mitty saw in looking at his watch, unless they had trouble drying it; sometimes they had trouble drying it. She didn't like to get to the hotel first; she would want him to be there waiting for her as usual. He found a big leather chair in the lobby, facing a window, and he put the overshoes and the puppy biscuit on the floor beside it. He picked up an old copy of *Liberty* and sank down into the chair. "Can Germany Conquer the World Through the Air?" Walter Mitty looked at the pictures of bombing planes and of ruined streets.

. . ."The cannonading has got the wind up in young Raleigh, sir," said the sergeant. Captain Mitty looked up at him through touseled hair. "Get him to bed," he said wearily. "With the others. I'll fly alone." "But you can't, sir," said the sergeant anxiously. "It takes two men to handle that bomber and the Archies are pounding hell out of the air. Von Richtman's circus is between here and Saulier." "Somebody's got to get that ammunition dump," said Mitty. "I'm going over. Spot of brandy?" He poured a drink for the sergeant and one for himself. War thundered and whined around the dugout and battered at the door. There was a rending of wood and splinters flew through the room. "A bit of a near thing," said Captain Mitty carelessly. "The box barrage is closing in," said the sergeant. "We only live once, Sergeant," said Mitty, with his faint, fleeting smile. "Or do we?" He poured another brandy and tossed it off. "I never see a man could hold his brandy like you, sir," said the sergeant. "Begging your pardon, sir." Captain Mitty stood up and strapped on his huge Webley-Vickers automatic. "It's forty kilometers through hell, sir," said the sergeant. Mitty finished one last brandy. "After all," he said softly, "what isn't?" The pounding of the cannon increased; there was the rat-tat-tatting of machine guns, and from somewhere came the menacing pocketa-pocketa-pocketa of the new flame-throwers. Walter Mitty walked to the door of the dug-out humming "Auprès de Ma Blonde." He turned and waved to the sergeant. "Cheerio!" he said. . . .

Something struck his shoulder. "I've been looking all over this hotel for you," said Mrs. Mitty. "Why do you have to hide in this old chair? How did you expect me to find you?" "Things close in," said Walter Mitty vaguely. "What?" Mrs. Mitty said. "Did you get the what's-its-name? The puppy biscuit? What's in that box?" "Overshoes," said Mitty. "Couldn't you have put them on in the store?" "I was thinking," said Walter Mitty. "Does it ever occur to you that I am sometimes thinking?" She looked at him. "I'm going to take your temperature when I get you home," she said.

They went out through the revolving doors that made a faintly derisive whistling sound when you pushed them. It was two blocks to the parking lot. At the drug-store on the corner she said. "Wait here for me. I forgot something. I won't be a minute." She was more than a minute. Walter Mitty lighted a cigarette. It began to rain, rain with sleet in it. He stood up against the wall of the drugstore, smoking. . . . He put his shoulders back and his heels together. "To hell with the handkerchief," said Walter Mitty scornfully. He took one last drag on his cigarette and snapped it away. Then, with that faint, fleeting smile playing about his lips, he faced the firing squad; erect and motionless, proud and disdainful, Walter Mitty the Undefeated, inscrutable to the last.

Analysis of "The Secret Life of Walter Mitty"

1. Characterize the two worlds of Walter Mitty—his dream world and his real one.
2. List five physical details or gestures that are used to develop the character of Mitty.
3. What indications are there that his wife treats Walter Mitty as a child? as an object?
4. What are the forces that combine to oppress Walter Mitty in real life?
5. What physical objects or situations prompt each of Mitty's four dreams?
6. At the end of the story, is Mitty "Undefeated"? If so, how? If not, why?
7. Write an account of what you think Mrs. Mitty's dream world was like.

James Thurber has shown a typical part of a day in the life of Walter Mitty. From this, one can gather all one needs to know about him. One has his appearance, his personality, his life style, but above all his values, his identity. Shaped by the pressures of his wife, the people about him, and the daily tasks that he must perform, his identity is clearly drawn.

There are no hard-and-fast rules about how to organize a character sketch, what to start with, where to include the main material—that relating to your character's identity and values. The important thing is to unify your portrait, to include no detail that tends to destroy your single effect.

ACTIVITY

Write a character sketch of someone. The person can be real or imaginary. Before you start, set down the values the character holds, his physical appearance, his background, and the other elements that might go to make the person what he is. Once you have done this, begin writing the sketch. Try to dramatize the person's character.

Use your notebook to sketch real people. Give a general description. Then look for any characteristic physical actions. From the person's external appearance, try to deduce his economic status, job, personal life, home life, and so on. Remember to relate the person to the setting of the sketch: Why is this person here at this time? If possible, include dialogue in the sketch.

5

Autobiographical account

THE TROUBLE ABOUT WRITING, most inexperienced writers feel, is that you need something to say. At first, this seems to be a problem. "What have I got to say that everybody doesn't already know?" they ask. They may be surprised to learn, a great deal.

Every writer has his own vision of the world that is based on his own experiences and observations. This vision cannot be duplicated. If he records it honestly and effectively, he cannot help being interesting and informative. But that word *honestly* is an important one. He must record his own vision and not one borrowed from someone else. And that is not easy. There is a story of a Chinese traveler who, on seeing his first Western portrait, remarked, "Yes, very beautiful, but what is all that mud on his face?" "That is not mud," he was told, "they're shadows." The traveler was confused because Chinese art does not depict the human face by means of light and shade. It portrays the face by means of line.

Here is a more startling story to illustrate the difference between what habit urges and what one really sees. At a convention a few years ago, the psychology students attending gathered to listen to a noted guest speaker. As the speaker was about to begin, a man at the back of the hall stood up, yelled loudly, and pointed his pipe at the speaker. In another part of the hall, somebody also bellowed a warning, then burst a balloon in such a way that the audience couldn't see it. Immediately the speaker fell to the floor. He was carried off the stage, and an announcement was made that there would be no speech that day because of an "unfortunate accident." The audience was told that the police would be asking everybody to give their version of what had happened. It seemed that the "assailants" had escaped in the confusion. One by one, the psychology students filed into a booth and told the official investigator that they had *seen the speaker being shot*. Some thought they had seen blood stains on the speaker's coat; others thought the gun was of such and such a make. The shouts that the attackers had given had furnished everybody with the opportunity to see exactly what happened. But the thought that the murder weapons might have been a pipe and a balloon never occurred to anyone. That would have been too fantastic for them to accept: it would have meant a conspiracy among the organizers of the convention, the two members of the audience, the famous speaker, and the police. And why? for what purpose? No, they had *seen a murder,* since no other explanation made sense. It never occurred to them that the whole episode had been planned in advance to experiment with just such material: to study how far a person's senses will deceive him in order to make events reasonable to him.

Think for a moment about some of the implications of these two stories. First, apply it to your own vision:

1. When you first entered your classroom, you probably noticed certain details in the room because they seemed important and relevant at the time. Perhaps you noticed the window, the number of desks, which chairs were broken, what some student had written on the wall last term, the teacher's characteristic mannerisms. Look again, and you will probably become aware of a whole new set of things that you did not see before, simply because they were not relevant to you: a grid for ventilation, a small cupboard in the wall, a stain on the floor.

2. Have you ever noticed how individual and distinctive each human ear is? It is as sure an identifying mark as all the rest of a person's face put together.

3. You probably thought for a long time that your eyes were a sort of window in your head, through which you see. Read a

scientific textbook on how your eyes really work, if you do not already know. You will find that what seems quite simple depends on coordination of the brain, tissue, and nerves all over your body, all of which must combine if a single image is to appear. For example, research indicates that the image of what you see actually appears upside-down in the brain. Your mind corrects the image so that things appear to be right side up.

Can you see a connection between all this and such facts as the following?

1. To an Athenian living in the fifth century B.C., slavery seemed natural and the only way to run a society. Today it seems to us unnatural and immoral.

2. For centuries people believed that the earth was the center of the universe and that the moon, the sun, and the stars revolved around the earth. When people first suggested (only about three hundred years ago) that the sun was the center of our solar system, they were put in prison and threatened with torture.

The conclusion of this seems to be that people, when it comes to seeing and hearing, have wide-ranging powers of "interpretation." Distortion in physical vision is similar to distortion of values and moral vision. Many people tend to see life from a mixed point of view. They have certain unquestioned assumptions and values.

It is a writer's job to record things as they are, to question basic assumptions, to force people to look again at the "truth." To record a character honestly is similar to recording a moral truth. If you can see and hear honestly, you may be amazed how original and urgent your views may be. In the incident with the psychology students, no one had to *tell* the students what to see and hear. There were unspoken obligations to *make sense*. There is always a little voice at the back of the brain saying "This makes no sense. See it *that* way." It is the artist's job to say, "Look again. How did it *really* happen?"

But reality doesn't only happen outside your mind, any more than it only happens inside it. Your fantasies and memories have an internal reality, distinguished from external reality, but none the less real for that. To observe your own fantasies, memories, and dreams is a vital part of any self-understanding, and to record them honestly is an act that often provides insights into other people. That is why this book began with self-examination—which is the beginning, though not the end, of honest perception.

So the first point that this chapter is making is to tell you to open your mind and question basic assumptions: your own and society's.

All this leads us back to values, the subject of the last chapter. If you turn back and review the list of commonly accepted values, you will see that there are at least two ways of seeing everything. What appears great courage to one, may seem to another to be sheer pigheadedness and rank insensitivity. Some people believe that the truth is a balance between opposing forces and that the answer to most problems of belief lies in compromise, taking the best of each side, finding the golden mean. Others believe in extremes; they will not compromise the truth—this is right, that is wrong, and there is no middle ground. And some believe that from a struggle of opposites a third—a new—truth evolves: *thesis, antithesis,* leading to *synthesis.* This new truth is different from both.

A short story shows such a conflict of values in action. This conflict may be happening inside a single person (Should I do this or that?), between one person and another (Should we fight or should we negotiate?), or between a person and a natural force (one man against the cold or an army of ants).

This conflict is the center of the story, both the external action (say, a battle of wits or a trial of strength) and the internal action (a clash of values, of beliefs, of life styles within an individual). It is this conflict that gives the story its unity. Everything in the story is selected and arranged so as to express the conflict in action. Sometimes the author very clearly favors one side or the other; sometimes he shows the weaknesses of both sides. It depends on how the author sees life—as a series of compromises or as a series of comparatively clear positions.

ACTIVITIES

1. List ten details in the classroom that you believe your neighbor has not noticed. Switch lists when you are finished to see how valid your assumption was.

2. Write an essay expressing an opinion on one of the following, giving views pro and con:

a. Noise   c. Science
b. Smoking   d. Professional Boxing
   e. A subject of your own

3. Write an editorial for your school paper, arguing a point of view on an issue of importance to your school, or a vital national issue. State your position in the topic sentence. Support your position with examples.

4. Defend a commonly held value you strongly believe in or attack a value that you believe should be changed.

5. Under what circumstances would you consider a person justified in disobeying a school rule?

6. What is courage? Is the man who acts despite his fear more courageous than the one who feels no fear? Explain.

7. Write a dialogue illustrating two strongly opposed viewpoints on a particular subject. Try reaching some kind of climax or resolution.

8. Read the following excerpt from "To Posterity" by Bertolt Brecht.

> In the old books you read what is wise:
> To keep out of the strife of the world and spend
> Your brief span without fear.
> And to refrain from violence
> Render good for evil
> Not fulfill one's desires, but forget
> Is accounted wise.
> All these are beyond me:
> Truly, the age I live in is bleak.

a. What is Brecht's idea of wisdom? What is the traditional idea?
b. If you were writing a short story about the issues raised in Brecht's poem, who would you choose as your two leading characters?
c. In the story conjectured in *b,* what action would you choose, so that this issue could be dramatized? For ex-

ample, a bully might be at large in the school, and a character might have to chose between fighting back somehow or not getting involved; the action might show a person who had decided not to get involved being forced into a situation where he had to be involved.

d. Write a paragraph that would supply a setting for the story conjectured in *b*. Select a scene that is relevant to the issue under discussion: For example, a sleepy village where people have lived at peace for years suddenly finds a factory under construction. You could show the conflict in a particular scene in the village between the sleepy past and the noisy future. Show this conflict by selecting at least six details that show the effects of this change— in the case of the village a piece of refuse in the stream, a cow disturbed by the sounds of construction, ruts in the grass where the bulldozer passed, and so on.

9. Sketch in the main characters, the action, and the setting of a short story that brings into conflict any two interpretations of a value cited on pages 223–24. Apply the value to yourself and things close to you, as far as you possibly can.

~~~~~~

Your notebook gives you a place in which you can record your own feelings and impressions. Analyze your feelings toward specific objects and persons. Try to determine why you like or dislike something.

The time has come to review what you have learned so far, so that you can write a full short story. You will not be expected to have attained, as yet, the kind of technical sophistication that will be supplied in the second half of the book.

This chapter will prepare you to write an autobiographical account. This does not mean an account of everything you remember or have been told about yourself from your cradle to your entry into this classroom. Interesting as that might be, it would be too long. It involves, instead, relating a *single incident* that caused you to *change your values,* or, in other words, one experience from which you learned something by personal observation. To write such a piece you must describe your values before the episode, to narrate the actual incident vividly and dramatically, and then to show the change of vision that resulted.

The first four chapters helped to prepare you for this assignment. Chapter 2 helped to give you insight into your own unconscious and allowed you to open up as preparation for creative writing. Chapter 3 helped you to portray an object, a scene, or an abstract idea with both physical qualities and identity. This should be useful to you, both in describing the scenery against which your events take place, and in selecting suitable backgrounds. As you were asked to create a single impression in writing your sketches, so you should create an impression in your settings that relates to your theme, either by its similarity and sympathy or by contrast. There are examples of this technique in action in the accounts below.

In Chapter 4, you were asked to describe a single character in depth, and you were asked to consider some important values in our society. This should be useful in choosing an area of focus for your story and in embodying the conflict that you focus on in one, two, or more characters with emotions of their own and a determination to fight for their beliefs.

In Chapter 5, so far, you have considered values in some depth, relating values to vision and both of these to the theme and conflict of a story.

Let us consider two examples of the autobiographical account and observe some of these precepts in action. First, here is an excerpt from Benjamin Franklin's *Autobiography:*

There was a salt marsh that bounded part of the mill pond, on the edge of which at high water, we used to stand to fish for minnows. By much trampling we had made it a mere quagmire. My proposal was to build a wharf there for us to stand upon, and I showed my comrades a large heap of stones which were intended for a new house near the marsh and which would very well suit our purpose. Accordingly, in the evening when the workmen were gone home, I assembled a number of my playfellows, and we worked diligently like so many emmets, sometimes two or three to a stone, 'till we brought them all to make our little wharf. The next morning the workmen were surprised at missing the stones, which had formed our wharf; enquiry was made after the authors of this transfer; we were discovered, complained of; several of us were corrected by our fathers, and tho' I demonstrated the utility of our work, mine convinced me that that which was not honest could not be truly useful.

Benjamin Franklin has not developed this incident into a full short story. He has told it in the simplest possible terms. He might have turned the episode into a short story by introducing the conflict immediately: can something be useful if it is not honest? Then, he might have developed the conflict by giving each side an advocate—perhaps his father on one side, he on the other. Young Franklin and his friends might have represented different degrees of the belief that one could do useful work that was "dishonestly" done. The possible benefits of the wharf might have been developed, and the building have been conducted under conditions of tension and secrecy. The climax would have been the discovery that the stones were missing, some ill effects that resulted from this lack of building materials, and a confrontation at the wharf between Benjamin and his father.

Here is a different autobiographical account that has all the elements of a fine short story. It is successful despite a lack of action and a minimum of dialogue and character portrayal.

Treason

I, Bertholt Brecht, come from the dark forests. My mother carried me to town while in the womb. I lay and still the coldness of the woods lingers and shall remain in me until my dying day. —BRECHT	O Lord, thou hast searched me, and known me. Thou knowest my downsitting and mine uprising; thou understandeth my thought afar off. Thou compassest my path and my lying down, and art acquainted with all my ways. —Psalm 139

I did not see my father for a long time before he died. His hospitalization had somehow weakened my chain of feeling to him. It was as if he were already dead, and only a name, a memory. I would get up late every morning, and the house would be empty—my mother and sister already gone to the hospital. The house was mine, and the long days of solitude slowly drained me of all thought and feeling. I read or listened to the radio long hours, blankly, dulled, all emotion blunted by the empty waiting hours.

My father was in the hospital six weeks the last time. I had gone to see him a couple of times before I got sick and couldn't go. He was in an oxygen tent. The plastic shimmered in the light and he couldn't see out—his eyesight was almost gone. He couldn't talk coherently, although his mind was almost intact—like people who have had a bad stroke. His face was that of a gargoyle, planed by loss of weight, and grimaced by his breathing. Mother would always tell me to walk up very close to the side of the bed and tell him who I was, and he would look and mumble. I stood and watched him in the tent, and turned and walked away. There was nothing to say or do—it was years and a happier time too late. I could not apologize for being young and arrogant, alive beside his death bed. It was worse each time, even for me. I couldn't harden myself to it.

I don't think I would have gone back again, even if I hadn't gotten sick. Bronchitis is a major illness with me, and it was nearly three weeks before I was out of bed. During the long somber days, I had finally seen the real meaning of the evil of my father's body. I had destroyed him, and also his son, for I would always be tainted with my inability to feel the horror of his death. I had lain in my dark forest, that of death, and the chill of my emptiness would be with me forever. . . .

The funeral was huge, one of the biggest ever here. It was not loud and brassy-big, but, oh, God, the people! The house was crowded with them, overflowing with family and friends. The lawn was ringed with cars. The hearse and shiny-black limousines filed into the driveway. The tide of people poured out of the house afterward, and the cars strung out in a long, undulating tail the short blocks to the synagogue.

The actual services were stark—no flowers or indignities, something my father would have liked, for he hated the modern trappings of death. The rabbi and he had been real friends, and the eulogy was short, and perhaps fitting.

After, I saw the huge, black limousines and the massed, waiting cars as I walked out into the parking lot hand-in-hand with my mother and sister. Their bustle sickened me.

"Damn," I said. "The people, the people! Why them, too? Only I had the right to observe and somehow solve the enigma of my father's death, not all these sometime strangers. Damn them, they had no place!"

Marcy understood without words. "They're part of it, too, Mike," she said. "They're part of his life."

I nodded and started walking again toward the cars.

It was a long ride to the cemetery behind the black hearse, so slow and pendulous and somehow obscene, with the long, yellow coffin peeking out the windows. All the long ride out, I thought of my tears at the synagogue. It's not hard to cry at funerals, and I could not stop myself amid all the rest. But the tears were somehow for myself, for the terrible failing as a son, and not for my father. I was crying for a son too small to know or to love his father. All the long ride, I thought of my tears, my treason.

There was a dark mass of people around the grave. We stood under the canopy, arched over the hole and fresh-dug earth. The pallbearers struggled with the coffin. The rabbi read the Twenty-third Psalm, as the coffin was lowered—"in the presence of mine enemies..." I looked at the people around me, at their faces so pure, so confident in their sorrow, and I thought of my emptiness, and I cried. Through the tears I thought this was the final hypocrisy, tears I did not mean, the final treason.

It was not until a long time later that I realized that I was not the traitor.

MIKE STERN

The conflict in this story is within Mike. It is whether or not Mike had failed his father. Behind this is the issue of being a good son, despite the impossible conditions that sometimes complicate relationships. The conflict is never clearly resolved in the story, because everything at the funeral appeared to confirm Mike's feeling of failure, but he tells us at the very end without explanation that years later he realized that he had not failed.

The author introduces the conflict in the first sentence. From then on, the impressions of his senses at the funeral and his emotions and memories wash to and fro like an underwater landscape, until the burial and the tears and the ultimate realization give the most clear-cut resolution to the conflict that is possible in an issue of such subtlety and complexity.

To treat this account purely technically does not do it justice. It is a model for short story writing from many points of view. If you are able to put as much honesty of vision about yourself and your surroundings into such a controlled framework, you will do well indeed.

When you write your account, be honest and be dramatic. Use dialogue giving the exact words spoken. Startle the reader with the freshness of your vision. Do not spend your time trying to prove to the reader that you are really a fine and intelligent person and that you have not really made a mistake in your life. On the other hand, do not go to the opposite extreme of relying on authorities (teachers or parents) to teach the lessons. Your subject should concern something that you have observed from your own experience. It need not be of earth-shattering importance, but it should be yours.

What kind of thing might you have learned? That authority is not always right—authorities are human beings, and so subject to error. That life can be unjust. That your love did not always have the highest motives. That freedom is harder to attain, more elusive than you thought. That the best intentions may be totally misguided. That if you act and think positively, you usually receive a positive response. That you, like everybody else, are really isolated and alone in life. That there are more important things in life than exams and grades. That people can act in unexpected or contradictory ways. That a person who can laugh at himself tends to be more respected than one who considers his dignity sacrosanct. You may have observed groups of people in action and have noticed something about how a crowd behaves. You may have gained experience of human relationships and may be able to share an insight about love, friendship, or hostility between young and old. And so on. There are an infinite number of things that you might have observed. Be sure the observation is based on a single dramatic incident.

~~~~~~

ACTIVITY

Write an autobiographical account of a single experience that has changed your values. Record the incidents dramatically, and set the account against a suitable and effective background. Be sure to describe only characters and situations that you know intimately. Permit the reader to see and to understand the change in values.

~~~~~~

6

Second overview

IN THE FIRST HALF OF THIS SECTION, you worked with the basics of prose writing: conflict, values, character, and setting. You began with self-observation, and you ended with a full-scale auto-biographical account. In the second half of the section, we will be considering some of the subtler techniques that may be used to make your story more effective. You will be asked to apply your self-observation to other people, whom you know and who—believe it or not—feel just as deeply and confusedly about them-selves as you do about yourself. Since you have been focusing entirely on the internal aspects of the short story, there will also be a chapter on plot and incident and on simplifying character—in short, on what goes into telling a good short story.

This chapter will give a view of the short story as a whole, just as the first chapter of the section gave a view of the material you were going to cover in Chapters 1–5. The survey will be divided into three parts: (1) conflicts and theme, (2) character, setting, mood and tone, and style and structure, and (3) such refined devices as foreshadowing, use of title, and irony.

So that you may see all these devices in action, not just in the abstract, here is a story that uses them all, entitled "A Man Who Had No Eyes." The story is not offered for the value of its statement but for the technical skill with which it is written.

A beggar was coming down the avenue just as Mr. Parsons emerged from his hotel.

He was a blind beggar, carrying the traditional battered cane, and thumping his way before him with the cautious, half-furtive effort of the sightless. He was a shaggy, thick-necked fellow; his coat was greasy about the lapels and pockets, and his hand splayed over the cane's crook with a futile sort of clinging. He wore a black pouch slung over his shoulder. Apparently he had something to sell.

The air was rich with spring; sun was warm and yellowed on the asphalt. Mr. Parsons, standing there in front of his hotel and noting the *clack-clack* approach of the sightless man, felt a sudden and foolish sort of pity for all blind creatures.

And, thought Mr. Parsons, he was very glad to be alive. A few years ago he had been little more than a skilled laborer; now he was successful, respected, admired. . . . Insurance. . . . And he had done it alone, unaided, struggling beneath handicaps. . . . And he was still young. The blue air of spring, fresh from its memories of windy pools and lush shrubbery, could thrill him with eagerness.

He took a step forward just as the tap-tapping blind man passed him by. Quickly the shabby fellow turned.

"Listen, guv'nor. Just a minute of your time."

Mr. Parsons said, "It's late. I have an appointment. Do you want me to give you something?"

"I ain't no beggar, guv'nor. You bet I ain't. I got a handy little article here"—he fumbled until he could press a small object into Mr. Parsons' hand—"that I sell. One buck. Best cigarette lighter made."

Mr. Parsons stood there, somewhat annoyed and embarrassed. He was a handsome figure with his immaculate gray suit and gray hat and malacca stick. Of course the man with the cigarette lighters could not see him. . . . "But I don't smoke," he said.

"Listen. I bet you know plenty people who smoke. Nice little present," wheedled the man. "And, mister, you wouldn't mind helping a poor guy out?" He clung to Mr. Parsons' sleeve.

Mr. Parsons sighed and felt in his vest pocket. He brought out two half dollars and pressed them into the man's hand. "Certainly. I'll help you out. As you say, I can give it to someone. Maybe the elevator boy would —" He hesitated, not wishing to be boorish and inquisitive, even with a blind peddler. "Have you lost your sight entirely?"

The shabby man pocketed the two half dollars. "Fourteen years, guv'nor." Then he added with an insane sort of pride: "Westbury, sir. I was one of 'em."

"Westbury," repeated Mr. Parsons. "Ah, yes. The chemical explosion. . . . The papers haven't mentioned it for years. But at the time it was supposed to be one of the greatest disasters in—"

"They've all forgot about it." The fellow shifted his feet wearily. "I tell you, guv'nor, a man who was in it don't forget about it. Last thing I ever saw was C shop going up in one grand smudge, and that damn' gas pouring in at all the busted windows."

Mr. Parsons coughed. But the blind peddler was caught up with the train of his one dramatic reminiscence. And, also, he was thinking that there might be more half dollars in Mr. Parsons' pocket.

"Just think about it, guv'nor. There was a hundred and eight people killed, about two hundred injured, and over fifty of them lost their eyes. Blind as bats—" He groped forward until his dirty hand rested against Mr. Parsons' coat. "I tell you, sir, there wasn't nothing worse than that in the war. If I had lost my eyes in the war, okay. I would have been well took care of. But I was just a workman, working for what was in it. And I got it. You're damn' right I got it, while the capitalists were making their dough! They was insured, don't worry about that. They—"

"Insured," repeated his listener. "Yes. That's what I sell—"

"You want to know how I lost my eyes?" cried the

man. "Well, here it is!" His words fell with the bitter and studied drama of a story often told, and told for money. "I was there in C shop, last of all the folks rushing out. Out in the air there was a chance, even with buildings exploding right and left. A lot of guys made it safe out the door and got away. And just when I was about there, crawling along between those big vats, a guy behind me grabs my leg. He says, 'Let me past, you——!' Maybe he was nuts. I dunno. I try to forgive him in my heart, guv'nor. But he was bigger than me. He hauls me back and climbs right over me! Tramples me into the dirt. And he gets out, and I lie there with all that poison gas pouring down on all sides of me, and flame and stuff. . . ." He swallowed—a studied sob—and stood dumbly expectant. He could imagine the next words: *Tough luck, my man. Damned tough! Now I want to*—"That's the story, guv'nor."

The spring wind shrilled past them, damp and quivering.

"Not quite," said Mr. Parsons.

The blind peddler shivered crazily. "Not quite? What you mean, you—?"

"The story is true," Mr. Parsons said, "except that it was the other way around."

"Other way around?" He croaked unamiably. "Say, guv'nor—"

"I was in C shop," said Mr. Parsons. "It was the other way around. You were the fellow who hauled back on me and climbed over me. You were bigger than I was, Markwardt."

The blind man stood for a long time, swallowing hoarsely. He gulped: "Parsons. By God. By God! I thought you—" And then he screamed fiendishly: "Yes. Maybe so. Maybe so. But I'm blind! I'm blind, and you've been standing here letting me spout to you, and laughing at me every minute! I'm blind!"

People in the street turned to stare at him.

"You got away, but I'm blind! Do you hear? I'm—"

"Well," said Mr. Parsons, "don't make such a row about it, Markwardt. . . . So am I."

MACKINLAY KANTOR

The structure of "A Man Who Had No Eyes" is based on a plot, that is, the plan and arrangement of related incidents; and it is centered on a conflict. The story opens with the meeting of Parsons and the beggar. This meeting initiates the conflict.

Initially the tension is created because Parsons wants to escape from the beggar. Parsons is in a hurry; he has an appointment. At first, the beggar commands a good deal of sympathy because he is blind. Yet apparently he is not merely begging, for he has something to sell. Parsons, by contrast, seems somewhat self-satisfied and successful in a worldly way.

When Parsons says that he doesn't smoke, however, and the beggar wheedles and clings, there is a movement of sympathy toward Parsons. Yet Parsons remains patronizing and privileged, despite his sensitivity in not wishing to press the beggar to tell his story. The shabby man now forfeits more sympathy by insisting on telling his story in a studied way, for money. True, the accident was not his fault, but he is now just a professional beggar, telling his story for money.

Each of the incidents develops the conflict. Notice that each incident also increases the tension. Parsons becomes even more anxious to leave. The beggar gradually reveals his character. The conflict heightens until it reaches the point of greatest tension, or the climax. The conflict must be resolved.

The growing tension is underscored by the change in the weather. In the warm, sunny spring day suddenly a shrill wind, "damp and quivering," comes up. The change in the wind signals the last part of the story—the resolution. The beggar has finished his tale, and the emphasis shifts to Parsons. What will he do? The remainder of the story resolves the conflict.

The beggar's account turns out to have been a distortion. Parsons retells the incident as it really occurred. The beggar now has only one claim on the reader's sympathy: he is blind, while Parsons, apparently, is not. Now Parsons supplies the clincher, in a typically unassuming way: "So am I." The wheel has turned 180 degrees; all our sympathies are now with Parsons' attitude to life —self-help. The beggar has been exposed as, at best, a self-pitying hypocrite.

There are other basic patterns for structuring the material of a short story besides the reversal of sympathies that is found in "A Man Who Had No Eyes." Here are some possibilities that you might use to build your plot.

1. *The homecoming:* The hero returns to a place he knew well to find or resolve something. Often he or the place has changed, which is the source of tension in the story.

2. *The progressive isolation:* A character is trying to accomplish something, but his support is progressively stripped away from him, and he is left more and more alone. The climax shows him completely alone.

3. *The progressive revelation:* There is pressure to find out the truth about something, and hints and clues dribble in until the climax reveals the answer.

4. *The choice:* A decision must be made by a certain time. The climax is the making (or failure to make) the decision.

Notice that, in each of these outlines, there is room for surprise in the end. It is important that, if there is a surprise, it be a natural outgrowth of the story as a whole. Thus, if the person who comes home thinks he has changed, but in the end it is the home that has changed, this must be prepared for. If the secret that is to be revealed turns out to be a hoax, this must seem natural, too.

Within the framework of a plot, there are a number of basic elements that you must keep in mind when writing a short story.

1. You need characters to work out the action and feel or believe the values. You have the major character, the protagonist, who represents one attitude toward the value. He is usually portrayed as a sympathetic figure to the reader. The protagonist is drawn in greatest depth, and he must be interesting enough to hold the attention of the reader. There is often another character who opposes the protagonist. This character is called the antagonist. Usually the antagonist is another person. Sometimes his place is taken by a force of nature, a situation, or a task to be done. Or the antagonist may be another aspect of the major character. To support the two major figures, there may be a number of minor characters (two or three) who are not drawn in depth, but who have a single trait emphasized, such as the faithful friend, or needy widow. They should not be cardboard figures, but they cannot be drawn with too much complexity. Their needs should be real, but not too complex to distract from the protagonist's predicament.

In the model story, Parsons is the protagonist and Markwardt is the antagonist. Other persons are only mentioned, but their presence is necessary for working out the drama.

2. Setting has been discussed in some depth in Chapter 3. It is important and must be made believable. It should relate somehow to the content of the story. In the model story, notice that the setting varies according to the intensity of the action. At the beginning, it is a spring morning. In the end, the wind is suddenly shrill and cold. The overall setting of an encounter in the street is convincing and helps to make the story believable. Even the factory that was blown up by a gas explosion is given a sense of reality.

3. There are a number of technical devices that may be used to make the ending seem more natural.

    a. *Foreshadowing:* the art of suggesting or hinting at the outcome, by way of preparing for it. Kantor sows tiny clues that Parsons is also blind: "noting the *clack-clack* approach," "struggling beneath handicaps," his using a "malacca stick." Thus, when the climax comes, the revelation is natural, since it has been prepared for.

    b. *Irony:* the varied meanings of the term all involve some sort of discrepancy or incongruity. There are three basic types of irony:

        (1) Verbal irony, in which there is a discrepancy between what is said and what is meant.

        (2) Dramatic irony, in which the contrast lies in what the character thinks is true and what the reader knows is true.

        (3) Irony of situation, which is the contrast between appearance and reality, between what is and would seem appropriate, between expectation and fulfillment.

        In this story, the irony is generated by having Markwardt beg from the man he has wronged. Moreover, he accuses Parsons of ridiculing him because he is blind. It turns out that Parsons is blind as well, and he has faced and overcome the same handicaps that Markwardt has faced.

    c. The author has created a neat contrast by means of *parallelism.* When two things are laid side by side, their differences become clear. Set two people together in the same circumstances, and the differences in their characters will become plain. In this case, the two characters are strongly contrasted, which makes for drama. But they are also in the same life situations: both have been deprived of sight as a result of an accident that was not their fault. From the sameness of their life situations, the difference in their characters is made clear. One man overcame the obstacles caused by the accident; the other did not.

    d. The author has reinforced his statement with his *title*. You probably noticed that the title has a double meaning: Throughout the story, the reader assumes that the reference is to the beggar, who is known to be blind. But when it is revealed at the end that Parsons is also blind, the title becomes a puzzle. Which of the two blind people does it refer to? A moment's reflection on the theme clarifies the situation. Parsons was physically blind, but Markwardt has no eyes in a deeper sense. He was blind in his attitudes, in his values. In that sense he lacked Parsons' vision and was a "man who had no eyes."

    e. The first sentences should arouse the reader's interest. The reader should want to continue on with the story. One of the best techniques is to begin with a question, or some sort of action that is taking place. Some good short stories begin with description, but the tendency is to launch into the action of the story immediately. In the model story the first sentence brings the two central figures together.

    f. The initial incident should create suspense. It is suspense that leads the reader to continue with the story. The suspense in Kantor's story derives from the character of Parsons—at first he seems to be a self-satisfied snob, and we wonder how he will get what he deserves.

    g. The last sentence carries more significance than any other. It is the climactic revelation, and it imparts the final impression to the reader. Thus, it should be carefully planned and important.

A well-constructed story has a unity that draws together all its parts and that may be compared to a stylish and tasteful outfit of clothes, or to the unity of a well-coordinated body. In a good outfit, everything matches and nothing seems out of place; the red in the shirt picks up the red in the tie. In a well-proportioned body, everything seems to be working together for a single purpose. In a successful short story, the separateness of its parts is transcended by the unity of the whole.

~~~~~~

ACTIVITY

Read "Charles" by Shirley Jackson.

The day my son Laurie started kindergarten, he renounced corduroy overalls with bibs and began wearing blue jeans with a belt; I watched him go off the first morning with the older girl next door, seeing clearly that an era of my life was ended, my sweet-voiced, nursery-school tot replaced by a long-trousered, swaggering character who forgot to stop at the corner and wave good-by to me.

He came home the same way, the front door slamming open, his cap on the floor, and the voice suddenly become raucous shouting, "Isn't anybody *here?*"

At lunch he spoke insolently to his father, spilled his baby sister's milk, and remarked that his teacher said we were not to take the name of the Lord in vain.

"How *was* school today?" I asked, elaborately casual.

"All right," he said.

"Did you learn anything?" his father asked.

Laurie regarded his father coldly. "I didn't learn nothing," he said.

"Anything," I said. "Didn't learn anything."

"The teacher spanked a boy, though," Laurie said, addressing his bread and butter. "For being fresh," he added, with his mouth full.

"What did he do?" I asked. "Who was it?"

Laurie thought. "It was Charles," he said. "He was fresh. The teacher spanked him and made him stand in a corner. He was awfully fresh."

"What did he do?" I asked again, but Laurie slid off his chair, took a cookie, and left, while his father was still saying, "See here, young man."

The next day Laurie remarked at lunch, as soon as he sat down, "Well, Charles was bad again today." He grinned enormously and said, "Today Charles hit the teacher."

"Good heavens," I said, mindful of the Lord's name, "I suppose he got spanked again?"

"He sure did," Laurie said. "Look up," he said to his father.

"What?" his father said, looking up.

"Look down," Laurie said. "Look at my thumb. Gee, you're dumb." He began to laugh insanely.

"Why did Charles hit the teacher?" I asked quickly.

"Because she tried to make him color with red crayons," Laurie said. "Charles wanted to color with green crayons so he hit the teacher and she spanked him and said nobody play with Charles but everybody did."

The third day—it was Wednesday of the first week —Charles bounced a seesaw onto the head of a little girl and made her bleed, and the teacher made him stay inside all during recess. Thursday Charles had to stand in a corner during story time because he kept pounding his feet on the floor. Friday Charles was deprived of blackboard privileges because he threw chalk.

On Saturday I remarked to my husband, "Do you think kindergarten is too unsettling for Laurie? All this toughness, and bad grammar, and this Charles boy sounds like such a bad influence."

"It'll be all right," my husband said reassuringly. "Bound to be people like Charles in the world. Might as well meet them now as later."

On Monday Laurie came home late, full of news. "Charles," he shouted as he came up the hill; I was waiting anxiously on the front steps. "Charles," Laurie yelled all the way up the hill, "Charles was bad again."

"Come right in," I said, as soon as he came close enough. "Lunch is waiting."

"You know what Charles did?" he demanded, following me through the door. "Charles yelled so in school they sent a boy in from first grade to tell the teacher she had to make Charles keep quiet, and so Charles had to stay after school. And so all the children stayed to watch him."

"What did he do?" I asked.

"He just sat there," Laurie said, climbing into his chair at the table. "Hi, Pop, y'old dust mop."

"Charles had to stay after school today," I told my husband. "Everyone stayed with him."

"What does this Charles look like?" my husband asked Laurie. "What's his other name?"

"He's bigger than me," Laurie said. "And he doesn't have any rubbers and he doesn't ever wear a jacket."

Monday night was the first Parent-Teachers meeting, and only the fact that the baby had a cold kept me from going; I wanted passionately to meet Charles's mother. On Tuesday Laurie remarked suddenly, "Our teacher had a friend come to see her in school today."

"Charles's mother?" my husband and I asked simultaneously.

"Naaah," Laurie said scornfully. "It was a man who came and made us do exercises; we had to touch our toes. Look." He climbed down from his chair and squatted down and touched his toes. "Like this," he said. He got solemnly back into his chair and said, picking up his fork, "Charles didn't even *do* exercises."

"That's fine," I said heartily. "Didn't Charles want to do exercises?"

"Naaah," Laurie said. "Charles was so fresh to the teacher's friend he wasn't *let* do exercises."

"Fresh again?" I said.

"He kicked the teacher's friend," Laurie said. "The teacher's friend told Charles to touch his toes like I just did and Charles kicked him."

"What are they going to do about Charles, do you suppose?" Laurie's father asked him.

Laurie shrugged elaborately. "Throw him out of school, I guess," he said.

Wednesday and Thursday were routine; Charles yelled during story hour and hit a boy in the stomach and made him cry. On Friday Charles stayed after school again, and so did all the other children.

With the third week of kindergarten, Charles was an institution in our family; the baby was being a Charles when she cried all afternoon; Laurie did a Charles when he filled his wagon full of mud and pulled it through the kitchen; even my husband, when he caught his elbow in the telephone cord and pulled telephone, ash tray, and a bowl of flowers off the table, said, after the first minute, "Looks like Charles."

During the third and fourth weeks it looked like a reformation in Charles; Laurie reported grimly at lunch on Thursday of the third week, "Charles was so good today the teacher gave him an apple."

"What?" I said, and my husband added warily, "You mean Charles?"

"Charles," Laurie said. "He gave the crayons around and he picked up the books afterward and the teacher said he was her helper."

"What happened?" I asked incredulously.

"He was her helper, that's all," Laurie said, and shrugged.

"Can this be true about Charles?" I asked my husband that night. "Can something like this happen?"

"Wait and see," my husband said cynically. "When you've got a Charles to deal with, this may mean he's only plotting."

He seemed to be wrong. For over a week Charles was the teacher's helper; each day he handed things out and he picked things up; no one had to stay after school.

"The P.T.A. meeting's next week again," I told my husband one evening. "I'm going to find Charles's mother there."

"Ask her what happened to Charles," my husband said. "I'd like to know."

"I'd like to know myself," I said.

On Friday of that week, things were back to normal. "You know what Charles did today?" Laurie demanded at the lunch table, in a voice slightly awed. "He told a little girl to say a word and she said it and the teacher washed her mouth out with soap and Charles laughed."

"What word?" his father asked unwisely, and Laurie said, "I'll have to whisper it to you, it's so bad." He got down off his chair and went around to his father. His father bent his head down, and Laurie whispered joyfully. His father's eyes widened.

"Did Charles tell the little girl to say *that?*" he asked respectfully.

"She said it *twice*," Laurie said. "Charles told her to say it *twice*."

"What happened to Charles?" my husband asked.

"Nothing," Laurie said. "He was passing out the crayons."

Monday morning Charles abandoned the little girl and said the evil word himself three or four times, getting his mouth washed out with soap each time. He also threw chalk.

My husband came to the door with me that evening as I set out for the P.T.A. meeting. "Invite her over for a cup of tea after the meeting," he said. "I want to get a look at her."

"If only she's there," I said prayerfully.

"She'll be there," my husband said. "I don't see how they could hold a P.T.A. meeting without Charles's mother."

At the meeting I sat restlessly, scanning each comfortable matronly face, trying to determine which one hid the secret of Charles. None of them looked to me haggard enough. No one stood up in the meeting and apologized for the way her son had been acting. No one mentioned Charles.

After the meeting I identified and sought out Laurie's kindergarten teacher. She had a plate with a cup of tea and a piece of chocolate cake; I had a plate with a piece of marshmallow cake. We maneuvered up to one another cautiously and smiled.

"I've been so anxious to meet you," I said. "I'm Laurie's mother."

"We're all so interested in Laurie," she said.

"Well, he certainly likes kindergarten," I said. "He talks about it all the time."

"We had a little trouble adjusting, the first week or so," she said primly, "but now he's a fine little helper. With occasional lapses, of course."

"Laurie usually adjusts very quickly," I said. "I suppose this time it's Charles's influence."

"Charles?"

"Yes," I said, laughing, "you must have your hands full in that kindergarten with Charles."

"Charles?" she said. "We don't have any Charles in the kindergarten."

Analysis of "Charles"

1. What is the attitude of Laurie's parents to Laurie's behavior throughout the story? Does it in any way relate to Laurie's attitude toward his own problems?
2. What indications are there that Laurie is fighting authority figures?
3. What clues are there that Laurie is Charles?
4. Do you think that the accounts of Charles's exploits were entirely true? entirely untrue?
5. What is the theme of the story?
6. In what way does the first sentence move the action of the story toward its central theme?
7. List five small gestures or mannerisms displayed by characters in this story that help to make them more vivid.
8. The story takes place almost entirely in a single setting. What is the setting? What is gained by setting the story in a single place?
9. Why is the story entitled "Charles" rather than "Laurie"?

7

Narrative

NARRATIVE MEANS literally telling what happened and what was done. The art of narrative relates to the techniques used in actually telling the story. It involves limiting the material and selecting the details that will be most interesting to the readers and that will best embody the theme of the story. It is the part of short story writing that is most concerned with technique and ingenuity.

Let us suppose that you are in a mood in which you really don't care about values or the great problems of your time—or even your own problems. You have just finished reading a volume of ghost stories, mystery tales, science fiction, or tales that amuse. Now you want to write a story like the ones you have just read, to exercise your ingenuity. Where do you go for inspiration?

Perhaps you go through the telephone book to find a name that might cause situations to arise in your imagination and then let them arise. Perhaps you go down the personal column of a newspaper and try to make something out of the messages. Perhaps you read the "Dear Abby" column of a magazine, and take off from there. Perhaps you see a man on the subway take off his hat and peer into it very intensely, shake his head and replace it.

Or you overhear a chance remark and would like to build it into a story: "Oh, I thought you meant Luther; that's why I put it in the wrong way 'round." Perhaps you have come across an interesting sentence and would like to start or end your story with that. Or an article in a popular science magazine starts you thinking. There is no end to the odd circumstances that might prod you into creativity and ingenuity.

Let us sketch in the possible progress of one sample idea. (Although the idea did result in a short story, the thought process described is fictitious.) You have just read an article about a minicomputer, a mechanical brain that you can carry about with you. Now where do you go from there? Your thoughts might go as follows:

Well, suppose the portable brain had just done something unusual—say, made its owner President? No, that would lead me into situations I don't know about—politics and the like. Avoid that. What about having it win a chess tournament? Yes, that will give me a chance to air my knowledge of chess notation. What if the victory brought the owner powerful enemies? He keeps getting little notes that threaten him. No, that takes me into the world of gangsters. Again, I would be writing from my movie and reading experiences, not my personal experience. What then? Have him fight a creature from outer space—no, too corny. What about confronting the machine with somebody very ordinary, who resents him? That would give a good conflict and afford some humor, since there could be a battle of wits between the machine and its opponent. Who will win? Of course, man should always win over machine. What if we were to turn that cliché on its head? Have machine win over man? But that causes a problem. How can the readers have more sympathy for a machine than for a man? The machine would have to be very nice and the man very nasty. So I need an ordinary but nasty man to oppose the machine. I've got it! Suppose the machine and its owner go about the town after the chess tournament trying to have some fun and they get kicked out of everywhere. The machine can outwit all the doormen at movie houses, the headwaiters at restaurants, the bartenders, and everyone who officiously tries to eject the machine. That would make them nasty and it would make them the sort of characters I have to deal with every Saturday night. Oh, I'm sick of planning it. We have enough material to try a first draft now. Let's begin.

Draft

A breathless hush hung over the chess room. The clocks ticked and the audience eagerly gnawed their nails as the final championship game moved to its conclusion. A player moved a piece. The other did not respond with a gesture. Instead, a metallic voice rang out, "Queen to bishop's fourth, checkmate."

"How about that? A good touch, not letting the reader know that one of the players is a machine until the second paragraph. Creates an air of mystery. Avoids unwieldy explanations too soon. Suppose I didn't mention that it was a chess room either? Let the readers work that out too. Should I describe the other player at all? Suppose I said something like, "The other player gave no sign of . . ."

But, wait a minute; all this seems a bit unnecessary. Why include the chess game anyway? It is just dead weight. No, let's move straight into the first confrontation—say, the theater. I suppose I should have done a bit more planning before putting pen to paper. Better do some outlining and take some more notes, to avoid more false starts. I know—I'll check my writing notebook. See if I have any good descriptions to use, either ready-made or adjustable. Hm! "Adjustable." That's a good word. I'll use it. Write it in my notebook, so that I won't forget it. Now, what have we? A description of the English teacher in a rage at Jonesy. Not much use. Ha, observations of a bartender, while out dining with parents: "puddled drinks," "mopped bar," "others perched on stools, staring at mirror"—and plenty more. Whole atmosphere of the bar. Good setting. But do I know bars well enough to use them? Just about, I think. I've seen the inside of several, well, one or two of them. I've seen some adult parties, too. And I can ask my father about technical things like names of drinks—must get them right. Good. Anything else of value? Description of rain on roofs. Nothing there. Conversation overheard on subway between two drunks. Arguing about whether they could multiply numbers in their heads. Might be useful, though I can't see how. Hey, I forgot I'd bothered to put this down—description of visit to IBM. How the computers flickered and everything. Lucky I took the trouble to write it all up. It made a real impression at the time. Perhaps my description will recall it.

Good, I've got plenty of material. Now for the outline.

1. Scene at theater. Theater manager kicks them out during movie, I know what I'll use as material for that! The guy at the Roxy who . . . yes, perfect. He even called me a crook. I remember, he said, "That does it!" and slammed his hand down on the counter, when I told him I was eighteen, and anybody would look young at his age.

2. Subway scene. Crowded subway. No, bus would be better because the driver could kick him off. There was the one who used to say, "I've got no time for jokestersmiths!"

3. Barroom scene. Gets kicked out of bar.

I'm beginning to get the feeling that something's wrong again. Why am I putting all these scenes down? Using all of them would require writing a novel. It would make the whole story unwieldy and untidy. Let's focus it all on one scene. No walking about town. Just a single confrontation. Much neater. Now, which shall it be? Theater, bus, or bar? Theater would be awkward, though I could make good use of dialogue from the movie at crucial points in the argument. And the audience could keep saying SHUSH! No, bus might be better. But a bus driver has his bus to drive. That would mean too much sympathy for the driver, who is hard at work. Besides, I've got the description of the bar and the customers there. Also, I could do things with the other customers, who could be more or less drunk and take sides. But do I know enough to do that? Yes, I think so. I would avoid the usual clichés about drunks as far as possible. Besides, I have the conversations in my book. So it's decided: a barroom scene. The bartender (who is made up of the other people I was going to use, all put together) throws him out. But he is within his rights. He will stay. Even orders drinks for the machine. The action increases as the bartender gets madder. Then the other customers join in. Finally they put the machine to the test. The bartender keeps trying to think up objections, and he claims the machine is drunk. The machine is given a math problem to do. There can be about four rounds between the bartender and the machine. Four issues on which the bartender tries to catch him. The math problem can be the last. But how can I finish it? I know. The owner of the machine can bring out a million-dollar bill and say the machine won it at chess. No. That would be out of place in the material so far. A newsboy comes in with the story that a machine-like murderer is on the loose. No, that would be just dragged in out of nowhere. Besides, the machine could hardly win. It has to be something subtler than that. Not something they *say* about how successful the machine has been, but something they *do*. I'll come back to that.

Now what about the characters? Let's work with them. The bartender must be really odious. Bald, with a scar and a patch and a squint. No. All that would be trite. I know. Let's make him rather sympathetic. Kind of puzzled, but knows his rights. Obnoxious, yes, but not too much so. What about the owner of the machine? He should be really loud, with a spangled suit, mink shoes, and a diamond tiepin. No. That would distract from the machine. Besides, if we are going to play down the bartender, we should play down the machine's owner, too, so he doesn't stick out. We'll just make him quiet and cheerful. Likable and with a few mannerisms to give him individuality. Quietly assertive of his right to stay in the bar. Just one flashy item. I know! He has a Cadillac outside, and in the end the machine drives away. That takes care of the ending. Now for the other characters. Oh, let's start. They'll come right. No. Better plan them now or I'll have another false start. There's one who is a little drunk who supports the machine. We'll have to give him a little identity. Say his tie was askew or something. We can introduce him after the main three. He can join in the argument. The other characters don't need to be individualized. Except one, perhaps, who works out the sum to check the machine's arithmetic. He should be young, I suppose, since people always forget their math as soon as they leave college. The problem-solving can be the climax, and the bartender can say, "Oh, he's got his car here, I suppose?" or something, and the machine can walk out and drive it.

Let's go.

Draft

When the man came in, carrying the machine, most of the customers looked up from their drinks, because they had never seen anything like it before. The man set the thing down on top of the bar near the beerpulls. It took up a lot of room and the bartender didn't like it much.

"Two rye-and-water," the man said.

The bartender went on puddling the drink.

That's much better. Goes straight into the conflict. Gives action and dialogue. Sets the scene. We're well on the way. But there's something wrong again. I know. Through whose eyes is all this happening? Who is telling the story? How about having the man who owns the machine telling the story? No, that would miss too much of the fun. Same for the bartender. What about the machine telling it as a reminiscence? That would be really original. No. It would create too many problems. How could it describe itself and so on. I would be giving myself needless difficulties. I know. I'll have one of the people at the bar tell it. That way it can have all the barroom atmosphere but he can see the three main figures in action. It is probably better to keep him in the background, just an observer. Then the whole thing becomes a barroom tale. So even the improbabilities won't matter. It will have just the right kind of style for a story like this. Wow, I must have been a genius when I decided on the bar over the movie house and bus!

Many attempts and crossings-out later, after much reshuffling and rethinking, this is what emerged as the final form:

The Hour of Let-down

When the man came in, carrying the machine, most of us looked up from our drinks, because we had never seen anything like it before. The man set the thing down on top of the bar near the beerpulls. It took up an ungodly amount of room and you could see the bartender didn't like it any too well, having this big, ugly-looking gadget parked right there.

"Two rye-and-water," the man said.

The bartender went on puddling an Old-Fashioned that he was working on, but he was obviously turning over the request in his mind.

"You want a double?" he asked, after a bit.

"No," said the man. "Two rye-and-water, please." He stared straight at the bartender, not exactly unfriendly but on the other hand not affirmatively friendly.

Many years of catering to the kind of people that come into saloons had provided the bartender with an adjustable mind. Nevertheless, he did not adjust readily to this fellow, and he did not like the machine—that was sure. He picked up a live cigarette that was idling on the edge of the cash register, took a drag out of it, and returned it thoughtfully. Then he poured two shots of rye whiskey, drew two glasses of water, and shoved the drinks in front of the man. People were watching. When something a little out of the ordinary takes place at a bar, the sense of it spreads quickly all along the line and pulls the customers together.

The man gave no sign of being the center of attraction. He laid a five-dollar bill down on the bar. Then he drank one of the ryes and chased it with water. He picked up the other rye, opened a small vent in the machine (it was like an oil cup) and poured the whiskey in, and then poured the water in.

The bartender watched grimly. "Not funny," he said in an even voice. "And furthermore, your companion takes up too much room. Whyn't you put it over on that bench by the door, make more room here."

"There's plenty of room for everyone here," replied the man.

"I ain't amused," said the bartender. "Put the goddam thing over near the door like I say. Nobody will touch it."

The man smiled. "You should have seen it this afternoon," he said. "It was magnificent. Today was the third day of the tournament. Imagine it—three days of continuous brainwork. And against the top players of the country, too. Early in the game it gained an advantage; then for two hours it exploited the advantage brilliantly, ending with the opponent's king backed in a corner. The sudden capture of a knight, the neutralization of a bishop, and it was all over. You know how much money it won, all told, in three days of playing chess?"

"How much?" asked the bartender.

"Five thousand dollars," said the man. "Now it wants to let down, wants to get a little drunk."

The bartender ran his towel vaguely over some wet spots. "Take it somewheres else and get it drunk there!" he said firmly. "I got enough troubles."

The man shook his head and smiled. "No, we like it here." He pointed at the empty glasses. "Do this again, will you, please?"

The bartender slowly shook his head. He seemed dazed but dogged. "You stow the thing away," he ordered. "I'm not ladling out whiskey for jokestersmiths."

" 'Jokesmiths,' " said the machine. "The word is 'jokesmiths.' "

A few feet down the bar, a customer who was on his third highball seemed ready to participate in this conversation to which we had all been listening so attentively. He was a middle-aged man. His necktie was pulled down away from his collar, and he had eased the collar by unbuttoning it. He had pretty nearly finished his third drink, and the alcohol tended to make him throw his support in with the underprivileged and the thirsty.

"If the machine wants another drink, give it another drink," he said to the bartender. "Let's not have haggling."

The fellow with the machine turned to his new-found friend and gravely raised his hand to his temple, giving him a salute of gratitude and fellowship. He addressed his next remark to him, as though deliberately snubbing the bartender.

"You know how it is when you're all fagged out mentally, how you want a drink?"

"Certainly do," replied the friend. "Most natural thing in the world."

There was a stir all along the bar, some seeming to side with the bartender, others with the machine group. A tall, gloomy man standing next to me spoke up.

"Another whiskey sour, Bill," he said. "And go easy on the lemon juice."

"Picric acid," said the machine, sullenly. "They don't use lemon juice in these places."

"That does it!" said the bartender, smacking his hand on the bar. "Will you put that thing away or else beat it out of here. I ain't in the mood, I tell you. I got this saloon to run and I don't want lip from a mechanical brain or whatever the hell you've got there."

The man ignored this ultimatum. He addressed his friend, whose glass was now empty.

"It's not just that it's all tuckered out after three days of chess," he said amiably. "You know another reason it wants a drink?"

"No," said the friend. "Why?"

"It cheated," said the man.

At this remark, the machine chuckled. One of its arms dipped slightly, and a light glowed in a dial.

The friend frowned. He looked as though his dignity had been hurt, as though his trust had been misplaced. "Nobody can cheat at chess," he said. "Simpossible. In chess, everything is open and above the board. The nature of the game of chess is such that cheating is impossible."

"That's what I used to think, too," said the man. "But there *is* a way."

"Well, it doesn't surprise me any," put in the bartender. "The first time I laid my eyes on that crummy thing I spotted it for a crook."

"Two rye-and-water," said the man.

"You can't have the whiskey," said the bartender. He glared at the mechanical brain. "How do I know it ain't drunk already?"

"That's simple. Ask it something," said the man.

The customers shifted and stared into the mirror. We were in this thing now, up to our necks. We waited. It was the bartender's move.

"Ask it what? Such as?" said the bartender.

"Makes no difference. Pick a couple big figures, ask it to multiply them together. You couldn't multiply big figures together if you were drunk, could you?"

The machine shook slightly, as though making internal preparations.

"Ten thousand eight hundred and sixty-two, multiply it by ninety-nine," said the bartender viciously. We could tell that he was throwing in the two nines to make it hard.

The machine flickered. One of its tubes spat, and a hand changed position, jerkily.

"One million seventy-five thousand three hundred and thirty-eight," said the machine.

Not a glass was raised all along the bar. People just stared gloomily into the mirror; some of us studied our own faces, others took carom shots at the man and the machine.

Finally, a youngish, mathematically minded customer got out a piece of paper and a pencil and went into retirement. "It works out," he reported, after some minutes of calculating. "You can't say the machine is drunk!"

Everyone now glared at the bartender. Reluctantly he poured two shots of rye, drew two glasses of water. The man drank his drink. Then he fed the machine its drink. The machine's light grew fainter. One of its cranky little arms wilted.

For a while the saloon simmered along like a ship at sea in calm weather. Every one of us seemed to be trying to digest the situation, with the help of liquor. Quite a few glasses were refilled. Most of us sought help in the mirror—the court of last appeal.

The fellow with the unbuttoned collar settled his score. He walked stiffly over and stood between the man and the machine. He put one arm around the man, the other around the machine. "Let's get out of here and go to a good place," he said.

The machine glowed slightly. It seemed to be a little drunk now.

"All right," said the man. "That suits me fine. I've got my car outside."

He settled for the drinks and put down a tip. Quietly and a trifle uncertainly he tucked the machine under his arm, and he and his companion of the night walked to the door and out into the street.

The bartender stared fixedly, then resumed his light housekeeping. "So he's got his car outside," he said, with heavy sarcasm. "Now isn't that nice!"

A customer at the end of the bar near the door left his drink, stepped to the window, parted the curtains, and looked out. He watched for a moment, then returned to his place and addressed the bartender. "It's even nicer than you think," he said. "It's a Cadillac. And which one of the three of them d'ya think is doing the driving?"

E. B. WHITE

ACTIVITIES

1. Listen to a conversation, or part of one in the next few days. Build what you hear into an idea or an outline for a story.

2. Page through the telephone book until you find a name that might be an interesting character. Imagine and record a situation that might be the basis for a short story.

3. Go through the "Dear Abby" column in a newspaper. Expand a situation described there into an idea for a story.

4. Read some articles in a popular science journal. Develop material from one into an idea for a science-fiction story.

5. Go through the personal ads in a paper. Build one of them (or a combination of two or more) into an idea for a story. Write an outline of the story idea.

Guidelines for Writing Narration

1. Make the time span of the narrative short. This will help unify the narration.

2. Limit the setting or settings of the narrative. You can do this by selecting a single incident to present rather than selecting a series of events.

3. Introduce the conflict in the initial situation.

4. Do not write until you have a clear plan of procedure. This plan more than likely will be modified, but if you don't have some idea of the outline, you will continually run into dead ends.

5. Narrate the events in chronological order—that is, in the sequence in which they happen—unless the material or the theme requires some other method of presentation.

Narration, of course, may be factual or imaginary. When you tell someone what you did yesterday you are narrating a story.

Telling an imaginary story is the basis of fiction. Both factual and imaginary narration relate events. You must select the events that lead toward the goal you have selected. The goal is usually the theme of the story.

In fictional narrative you must create your characters. Base your fictional characters on persons you have met in your life or have read about. Don't be afraid to combine several characters from life into a single fictional character.

Use dialogue to make your characters and the narrative come alive. Let your reader hear what was said. There are several general rules to help you write effective dialogue.

1. Make sure it is clear who is speaking and who is being spoken to. Identify the speaker if it is not clear from context.

2. Use dialogue tags to indicate the tone of voice of the speaker. Examples of dialogue tags are "he said *softly*," and "she replied, *spitting out the words*." Don't overdo the use of dialogue tags. Often it is better to let the speaker's words indicate the tone of voice.

3. Avoid long speeches. Break up long speech by having a give-and-take between characters: one character speaks and another answers. This technique is generally more realistic than having one person speak at length and then having another answer.

4. Dialogue is supposed to reflect actual conversation. Most dialogue is not written in formal English. People speak in incomplete sentences. Try to catch the patterns of conversational speech in your written dialogue.

~~~~~~

ACTIVITY

Read and analyze the following excerpt from *The Time Machine* by H. G. Wells:

> I am afraid I cannot convey the peculiar sensations of time traveling. They are excessively unpleasant. There is a feeling exactly like that one has upon a roller coaster—of a helpless headlong motion! I felt the same horrible fear of a smash. As I picked up speed, night followed day like the flapping of a black wing. The dim suggestion of the laboratory

seemed presently to fall away from me, and I saw the sun hopping swiftly across the sky, leaping it every minute, and every minute marking a day. I supposed the laboratory had been destroyed and I had come into the open air. I had a dim impression of scaffolding, but I was already going too fast to be conscious of any moving things. The slowest snail that ever crawled dashed by too fast for me. The twinkling succession of darkness and light was painful to the eye. Then I saw the moon spinning swiftly through her quarters from new to full, and had a faint glimpse of the circling stars. Presently, as I went on, still gaining speed, night and day merged into one continuous grayness; the sky took on a wonderful deepness of blue, a splendid luminous color like that of early twilight. The jerking sun became a streak of fire, a brilliant arch, in space; the moon a fainter band; and I could see nothing of the stars except save now and then a brighter circle flickering in the blue.

a. What feeling characterized the initial stages of traveling through time?
b. List the varied ways in which H. G. Wells has portrayed alternation of dark and light and the acceleration of the machine.

8

Conflicts and climaxes

In CHAPTER 4, you were introduced to the idea that every value has its contrary, an alternative way of viewing it (see the table of values on pages 223–24 as a reminder). But each value also has another kind of opposite, its literal contrast. Thus, love is opposed to hate, responsibility to irresponsibility, altruism to selfishness, courage to fear, and so on. Usually, one or other of these contrasts in values is the source of the conflict in a story, and it is from the conflict and decision between these two opposing forces that the action and tension of the story are generally derived.

Let us review the story "A Man Who Had No Eyes," which we studied in Chapter 6:

> Two men suffer an accident that deprives both of a vital power, their sight. One responds by rebuilding his life, using his new setback as a challenge and gaining strength from it. The other becomes a beggar. The two meet many years later, at which point the story begins; none of this previous history is known to the reader. There is a conversation or action between them that demands a choice, a decision on the part of the reader.

The different attitudes of the two are progressively revealed. First one receives sympathy, then the other. Finally, at the climax of the story, the contrast between the two is made clear. A decisive statement about their respective values has been reached, a point of judgment.

The above account is a skeleton, or outline, of the story, focusing on the conflicts and climaxes. The first conflict, the *internal one,* is the clash of values held by the two men: self-help against self-pity. The second conflict, the *external conflict,* is a conflict of action. It brings the two men into opposition so that they confront each other: in this case the issue is whether one should give the other help, a handout. These two conflicts (the internal and the external) are resolved (settled, brought to a decision) in two climaxes. A climax may be defined as a high point of excitement, where a decision is reached.

Stories may have only an external conflict; many adventure stories have external conflict but not a clash of values. Some stories have only an internal conflict. It requires a very skillful writer to make such a story interesting. For our purposes, the best stories are those which present both an external and an internal conflict.

Usually the external conflict is resolved first, although sometimes the same words or actions resolve both conflicts at once. The external conflict is resolved by the external climax, some decisive action, perhaps a fight, a love choice, or a settlement of a relationship. In the story, "A Man Who Had No Eyes," the external climax comes when the true account of what happened at the factory is revealed, ending at the line, "You were bigger than I was, Markwardt."

This external resolution is capped by the internal climax, which resolves the conflict of values. This is, as a rule, quieter, but deeper and more satisfying. It is the real point of decision in the story, revealing the author's true statement about the values conflict. In our model story, the internal conflict is decided by Mr. Parsons' final line, "don't make such a row about it, Markwardt. . . . So am I." This is the clincher that shows exactly what each of the contestants is worth, what Markwardt's values are and what Parsons' are. The internal climax usually occurs, as in this case, at the very end of the story.

Sometimes the conflicts occur within a single person, or the protagonist is confronted by some inhuman force or adversary: nature, death, sickness, a fire, a dragon, an army of ants. Sometimes the internal conflict is resolved in an opposite way to the external conflict. For example, the story might illustrate life's injustices: One man wins, yet the other is in the right. But this rarely happens without some form of compensation, because readers usually demand some relief from total pessimism.

The interest in a story usually derives principally from the tension generated by the conflict between the two external forces and the two internal values. First, one appears to be winning, then the other. It is the uncertainty as to the outcome that keeps the reader's interest.

Of the two conflicts, the more important by far is the internal one, the conflict of values. Stories that involve only external conflicts are apt to become "plot heavy," and fail to make a statement about life. However ingenious, such stories cannot be considered as seriously as those that present a new vision of life. In fact, as a general rule, the incidents in the story (the plot), should be contrived by the writer with the major purpose of illustrating the deeper conflict, the clash of values. The action should be arranged so as to bring the two values into opposition, each represented by a powerful advocate. But when you are composing a story, do not fall into the opposite trap of neglecting the plot completely and of making a sermon or a court case out of the conflict. The values should be worked out in human action. One, two, or more human beings should contest the central motivating principles of their lives.

The statement about life that emerges from this conflict is the theme of the story. In the story "A Man Who Had No Eyes," the theme might be stated as follows: Some people respond to reverses in life by turning their stumbling blocks into stepping stones, while some give up and rely on others to help them. The former is the healthier way of living.

The reader may or may not agree with the author's statement about life, or with his conclusion. But whether the reader agrees or not should not be the standard by which the work is judged. Rather, it should be judged on the depth, the reality, the validity of the way in which the author has posed his conflict. Whether the reader disagrees or agrees with the theme-statement, the story may be a great work of art if it displays a deep, original, convincing vision of life.

The summaries of two more stories should help make all this clearer:

> 1. A traveling preacher is challenged by a lawyer on the meaning of the word "neighbor" in the phrase, "Love thy neighbor." It is an attack on the preacher by a professional man who is listening less with sincerity than in an effort to trick the other. The preacher replies with a story: A man is mugged and left injured in the gutter. Professional helpers, friends, and neighbors pass him by, not wishing to become involved. But a member of a despised and hated group in society stops to give him help.

Here the external conflict is between, on the one hand, the indifferent forces of respectability who seem unconcerned about humanity and, on the other, the despised who are not. The internal conflict is between judging and acting on common humanity or on the values of respectability—privilege, position, prejudice, profit—between those who really feel concern and those who pretend to.

The theme statement is that a man's best friend and neighbor is he who acts with humanity, not he who happens to live next door or to look respectable. Notice that the conflict in the story relates to the conflict in the "frame" or introduction.

> 2. A family returns to their home after a flood. Will they be able to survive or will they be forced back into economic dependence by taking credit from the local store? They find odd tools and possessions preserved. But they are hungry and have nothing to eat. The storekeeper comes by, and the husband succumbs.

Here the external conflict is between the family (the father especially) and the forces that conspire to enslave and destroy them—the environment and the economic system. The internal conflict is between the values of independence (freedom) and dependence (slavery). The former is resolved when the husband decides to go to the store for credit; the latter is resolved when it becomes clear that there was no real freedom at any point, nor will there be for the next generation. The theme is that some poor black farmers cannot be free from economic subjection even under conditions that apparently mark a new beginning.

Let's see what the actual stories are like:

The Good Samaritan

And, behold, a certain lawyer stood up, and tempted him, saying, Master, what shall I do to inherit eternal life?

He said unto him, What is written in the law? how readest thou?

And he answering said, Thou shalt love the Lord thy God with all thy heart, and with all thy soul, and with all thy strength, and with all thy mind; and thy neighbor as thyself.

And he said unto him, Thou hast answered right: this do, and thou shalt live.

But he, willing to justify himself said unto Jesus, And who is my neighbor?

And Jesus answering said, A certain man went down from Jerusalem to Jericho, and fell among thieves, which stripped him of his raiment, and wounded him, and departed, leaving him half dead.

And by chance there came down a certain priest that way; and when he saw him, he passed by on the other side.

And likewise, a Levite, when he was at the place, came and looked on him, and passed by on the other side.

But a certain Samaritan, as he journeyed, came where he was; and when he saw him, he had compassion on him.

And went to him, and bound up his wounds, pouring in oil and wine, and set him on his own beast, and brought him to an inn, and took care of him.

And on the morrow when he departed, he took out two pence, and gave them to the host, and said unto him, Take care of him: and whatsoever thou spendest more, when I come again, I will repay thee.

Which now of these three, thinkest thou, was neighbor unto him that fell among the thieves?

And he said, He that showed mercy on him. Then said Jesus unto him, Go, and do thou likewise.

Analysis of "The Good Samaritan"

1. What was the issue which prompted the telling of the story?
2. Why do you think Jesus chose a priest and a Levite for his "villains"?
3. Does this story adhere to the modern structure of a short story—a narrative with conflicts, climaxes, and theme?
4. What details are included in the story that were not strictly necessary for the point but merely included to make the action more specific and solid?
5. How can the theme of the story be applied today?

The Man Who Saw the Flood

When the flood waters recede,
the poor folk along the river
start from scratch.

At last the flood waters had receded. A black father, a black mother, and a black child tramped through muddy fields, leading a tired cow by a thin bit of rope. They stopped on a hilltop and shifted the bundles on their shoulders. As far as they could see the ground was covered with flood silt. The little girl lifted a skinny finger and pointed to a mud-caked cabin.

"Look, Pa! Ain tha our home?"

The man, round-shouldered, clad in blue, ragged overalls, looked with bewildered eyes. Without moving a muscle, scarcely moving his lips, he said: "Yeah."

For five minutes they did not speak or move. The flood waters had been more than eight feet high here. Every tree, blade of grass, and stray stick had its flood mark; caky, yellow mud. It clung to the ground, cracking thinly here and there in spider-web fashion. Over the stark fields came a gusty spring wind. The sky was high, blue, full of white clouds and sunshine. Over all hung a first-day strangeness.

"The henhouse is gone," sighed the woman.

"N the pigpen," sighed the man.

They spoke without bitterness.

"Ah reckon them chickens is all done drowned."

"Yeah."

"Miz Flora's house is gone, too," said the little girl.

They looked at a clump of trees where their neighbor's house had stood.

"Lawd!"

"Yuh reckon anybody knows where they is?"

"Hard t tell."

The man walked down the slope and stood uncertainly.

"There wuz a road erlong here somewheres," he said.

But there was no road now. Just a wide sweep of yellow, scalloped silt.

"Look, Tom!" called the woman. "Here's a piece of our gate!"

The gatepost was half buried in the ground. A rusty hinge stood stiff, like a lonely finger. Tom pried it loose and caught it firmly in his hand. There was nothing particular he wanted to do with it; he just stood holding it firmly. Finally he dropped it, looked up, and said:

"C mon. Les go down n see whut we kin do."

Because it sat in a slight depression, the ground about the cabin was soft and slimy.

"Gimme tha bag o lime, May," he said.

With his shoes sucking in mud, he went slowly around the cabin, spreading the white lime with thick fingers. When he reached the front again he had a little left; he shook the bag out on the porch. The fine grains of floating lime flickered in the sunlight.

"Tha oughta hep some," he said.

"Now, yuh be careful, Sal!" said May. "Don yuh go n fall down in all this mud, yuh hear?"

"Yessum."

The steps were gone. Tom lifted May and Sally to the porch. They stood a moment looking at the half-opened door. He had shut it when he left, but somehow it seemed natural that he should find it open. The planks in the porch floor were swollen and warped. The cabin had two colors; near the bottom it was a solid yellow; at the top it was the familiar gray. It looked weird, as though its ghost were standing beside it.

The cow lowed.

"Tie Pat t the pos on the en of the porch, May."

May tied the rope slowly, listlessly. When they attempted to open the front door, it would not budge. It was not until Tom placed his shoulder against it and gave it a stout shove that it scraped back jerkily. The front room was dark and silent. The damp smell of flood silt came fresh and sharp to their nostrils. Only one-half of the upper window was clear, and through it fell a rectangle of dingy light. The floors swam in ooze. Like a mute warning, a wavering flood mark went high around the walls of the room. A dresser sat cater-cornered, its drawers and sides bulging like a bloated corpse. The bed, with the mattress still on it, was like a giant casket forged of mud. Two smashed chairs lay in a corner, as though huddled together for protection.

"Les see the kitchen," said Tom.

The stovepipe was gone. But the stove stood in the same place.

"The stove's still good. We kin clean it."

"Yeah."

"But where's the table?"

"Lawd knows."

"It must've washed erway wid the rest of the stuff, Ah reckon."

They opened the back door and looked out. They missed the barn, the henhouse, and the pigpen.

"Tom, yuh bettah try tha old pump n see ef eny watah's there."

The pump was stiff. Tom threw his weight on the handle and carried it up and down. No water came. He pumped on. There was a dry, hollow cough. Then yellow water trickled. He caught his breath and kept pumping. The water flowed white.

"Thank Gawd! We's got some watah. Yuh bettah boil it fo yuh use it," he said.

"Yeah. Ah know."

"Look, Pa! Here's yo ax," called Sally.

Tom took the ax from her. "Yeah. Ah'll need this."

"N here's somethin else," called Sally, digging spoons out of the mud.

"Waal, Ahma, git a bucket n start cleanin," said May. "Ain no use in waitin, cause we's gotta sleep on them floors tonight."

When she was filling the bucket from the pump, Tom called from around the cabin. "May, look! Ah done foun mah plow!" Proudly he dragged the silt-caked plow to the pump. "Ah'll wash it n it'll be awright."

"Ahm hongry," said Sally.

"Now, yuh jus wait! Yuh et this mawnin," said May. She turned to Tom. "Now, whutcha gonna do, Tom?"

He stood looking at the mud-filled fields.

"Yuh goin back t Burgess?"

"Ah reckon Ah have to."

"Whut else kin yuh do?"

"Nothin," he said. "Lawd, but Ah sho hate t start all over wid tha white man. Ah'd leave here ef Ah could. Ah owes im nigh eight hundred dollahs. N we needs a hoss, grub, seed, n a lot mo other things. Ef we keeps on like this tha white man'll own us body n soul."

"But, Tom, there ain nothin else t do," she said.

"Ef we try t run erway they'll put us in jail."

"It coulda been worse," she said.

Sally came running from the kitchen. "Pa!"

"Hunh?"

"There's a shelf in the kitchen the flood didn git!"

"Where?"

"Right up over the stove."

"But, chile, ain nothin up there," said May.

"But there's somethin on it," said Sally.

"C mon. Les see."

High and dry, untouched by the flood-water, was a box of matches. And beside it a half-full sack of Bull Durham tobacco. He took a match from the box and scratched it on his overalls. It burned to his fingers before he dropped it.

"May!"

"Hunh?"

"Look! Here's ma bacco n some matches!"

She stared unbelievingly. "Lawd!" she breathed.

Tom rolled a cigarette clumsily.

May washed the stove, gathered some sticks, and after some difficulty, made a fire. The kitchen stove smoked, and their eyes smarted. May put water on to heat and went into the front room. It was getting dark. From the bundles they took a kerosene lamp and lit it. Outside Pat lowed longingly into the thickening gloam and tinkled her cowbell.

"Tha old cow's hongry," said May.

"Ah reckon Ah'll have t be gittin erlong t Burgess."

They stood on the front porch.

"Yuh bettah git on, Tom, fo it gits too dark."

"Yeah."

The wind had stopped blowing. In the east a cluster of stars hung.

"Yuh goin, Tom?"

"Ah reckon Ah have t."

"Ma, Ah'm hongry," said Sally.

"Wait erwhile, honey. Ma knows yuh's hongry."

Tom threw his cigarette away and sighed.

"Look! Here comes somebody!"

"Thas Mistah Burgess now!"

A mud-caked buggy rolled up. The shaggy horse was splattered all over. Burgess leaned his white face out of the buggy and spat.

"Well, I see you're back."

"Yessuh."

"How things look?"

"They don look so good, Mistah."

"What seems to be the trouble?"

"Waal. Ah ain got no hoss, no grub, nothin. The only thing Ah got is that ol cow there . . ."

"You owe eight hundred dollahs down at the store, Tom."

"Yessuh, Ah know. But, Mistah Burgess, can't yuh knock somethin off of tha, seein as how Ahm down n out now?"

"You ate that grub, and I got to pay for it, Tom."

"Yessuh, Ah know."

"It's going to be a little tough, Tom. But you got to go through with it. Two of the boys tried to run away this morning and dodge their debts, and I had to have the sheriff pick em up. I wasn't looking for no trouble out of you, Tom . . . The rest of the families are going back."

Leaning out of the buggy, Burgess waited. In the surrounding stillness the cowbell tinkled again. Tom stood with his back against a post.

"Yuh got t go on, Tom. We ain't got nothin here," said May.

Tom looked at Burgess.

"Mistah Burgess, Ah don wanna make no trouble. But this is jus *too* hard. Ahm worse off now than befo. Ah got to start from scratch."

"Get in the buggy and come with me. I'll stake you with grub. We can talk over how you can pay it back." Tom said nothing. He rested his back against the post and looked at the mud-filled fields.

"Well," asked Burgess. "You coming?" Tom said nothing. He got slowly to the ground and pulled himself into the buggy. May watched them drive off.

"Hurry back, Tom!"

"Awright."

"Ma, tell Pa t bring me some 'lasses," begged Sally.

"Oh, Tom!"

Tom's head came out of the side of the buggy.

"Hunh?"

"Bring some 'lasses!"

"Hunh?"

"Bring some 'lasses for Sal!"

"Awright!"

She watched the buggy disappear over the crest of the muddy hill. Then she sighed, caught Sally's hand, and turned back into the cabin.

RICHARD WRIGHT

Analysis of "The Man Who Saw the Flood"

1. How is the Wright story similar to the biblical story of the flood? What is the difference between the two stories?
2. Does finding the dry matches solve any of the problems

facing the family? Of what immediate use is the tobacco to them? What basic problem is not solved by these discoveries?

3. In the story there are three signs of hope, each of which are described as white: the sky, the lime, and the water. How do these apparent signs of hope contrast with the endings of the story? Is white a sign of hope at the end?

4. What makes Tom decide to seek help from Mr. Burgess?

9

Point of view, tone, mood

BEFORE YOU CAN WRITE a really outstanding short story, there are a number of technical problems that you will have to solve. Who is the narrator of your story? How much does he know? How does he know it? What tone of voice is he speaking with? What mood are you aiming to establish?

The most common way of handling this problem of the voice or narrator is to have the storyteller not involved in the events of the story and to have him know, as if from a distance, everything that is going on. He is, in effect, the author himself. Thus, he not only knows what has happened to everyone and what will happen, he also knows what each character hopes, remembers, thinks, and so on. This is a useful general method, because it gives the author great freedom, and there are no questions in the reader's mind about how the narrator came to know certain facts. It is understood from the beginning that the narrator knows all, and that is the convention or agreement between author and reader under which the story operates. Such a narrator is called the *omniscient observer,* because he knows everything that is going on.

This technique does bring one problem, however: that of overabundance. The reader has only one consciousness, and he is probably *identifying with* (imagining himself in the place of) one of the characters. To switch him abruptly from what "he" thought to what "she" saw to what "they" intend is to rock the reader about unfairly and quite possibly to make him seasick.

A second point of view is the *limited omniscient.* The author tells the story in the third person. However, it is told from the point of view of one of the characters, either a major or a minor participant. The author shows what that character says and thinks. The other characters are seen externally, or in other words, as they appear to one character. The reader doesn't know what the other characters think or feel except for what the chosen character can infer.

It is worth having a variety of methods and techniques. You should be able to play more than one set of chords on your guitar. Sir Arthur Conan Doyle used a particularly useful device in the Sherlock Holmes stories. In nearly all the tales, Dr. Watson, Holmes's faithful companion, narrates the story. Now, Dr. Watson is a major participant, but he is not very intelligent. Thus, Holmes can be very mysterious and the narrator can present all the facts to the reader, without revealing what the solution will be. When the answer is finally revealed, the reader, who has been following events through Watson's mental blinkers, is as surprised as the Doctor. "Extraordinary, Holmes! However did you . . .?" exclaims Watson (and the reader with him). To which Holmes replies, "Elementary, my dear Watson. I simply . . ." and proceeds to tell all in one climactic revelation. In this technique, the story is written in the first person and is narrated by a major character.

The Adventures of Huckleberry Finn is written in the first-person, major-character point of view. The reader is allowed to *see through* Huck's canny simplicity and to predict, up to a point, what will happen. But Huck's view of the world is limited. Much of the humor of the book comes from having Huck know just so much:

> The Widow Douglas she took me for her son, and allowed she would civilize me; but it was rough living in the house all the time, considering how dismal regular and decent the widow was in all her ways; and so when I couldn't stand it no longer I lit out. I got into my old rags and my sugar-hogshead again, and was free and satisfied. But Tom Sawyer he hunted me up and said he was going to

start a band of robbers, and I might join if I would go back to the widow and be respectable. So I went back.

The widow she cried over me, and called me a poor lost lamb, and she called me a lot of other names, too, but she never meant no harm by it. She put me in them new clothes again, and I couldn't do nothing but sweat and sweat, and feel all cramped up. Well, then, the old thing commenced again. The widow rung a bell for supper, and you had to come to time. When you got to the table you couldn't go right to eating, but you had to wait for the widow to tuck down her head and grumble a little over the victuals, though there warn't anything the matter with them—that is, nothing only everything was cooked by itself. In a barrel of odds and ends it is different; things get mixed up, and the juice kind of swaps around, and the things go better.

After supper she got out her book and learned me about Moses and the Bulrushers, and I was in a sweat to find out all about him; but by and by she let it out that Moses had been dead a considerable long time; so then I didn't care no more about him, because I don't take no stock in dead people.

Pretty soon I wanted to smoke, and asked the widow to let me. But she wouldn't. She said it was a mean practice and wasn't clean, and I must try to not do it any more. That is just the way with some people. They get down on a thing when they don't know nothing about it. Here she was a-bothering about Moses, which was no kin to her, and no use to anybody, being gone, you see, yet finding a power of fault with me for doing a thing that had some good in it. And she took snuff, too; of course that was all right, because she done it herself.

Her sister, Miss Watson, a tolerable slim old maid, with goggles on, had just come to live with her, and took a set at me now with a spelling-book. She worked me middling hard for about an hour, and then the widow made her ease up. I couldn't stood it much longer. Then for an hour it was deadly dull, and I was fidgety. Miss Watson would say, "Don't put your feet up there, Huckleberry"; and "Don't scrunch up like that, Huckleberry—set up straight"; and pretty soon she would say, "Don't gap and stretch like that, Huckleberry—why don't you try to behave?" Then she told me all about the bad place, and I said I wished I was there. She got mad then, but I didn't mean no harm. All I wanted was to go somewheres; all I wanted was a change, I warn't particular. She said it was wicked to say what I said; said she wouldn't say it for the whole world; *she* was going to live so as to go to the good place. Well, I couldn't see no advantage in going where she was going, so I made up my mind I wouldn't try for it. But I never said so, because it would only make trouble, and wouldn't do no good.

Analysis of "Huckleberry Finn"

1. What internal and external conflicts are treated throughout the passage?
2. Discuss how Huck's point of view is limited. Does he completely understand what the widow and her sister are trying to do? What was the widow's purpose in telling him about Moses?

ACTIVITY

Retell the events narrated by Huck from the point of view of Miss Watson or the Widow Douglas.

Notice the difference in understanding between the author and the hero (Huck). The author can see Huck's limitations, but he can also see the sense in what Huck is saying. The result is that the author's point of view is more subtle than Huck's. This is the chief source of the humor of the story: for all his apparent simplicity, Huck sees things that more educated thinkers do not.

Another useful method is to have the story told by a minor participant, who can see only a limited amount of the action, so that a good deal is left to the reader's imagination. This leaves the reader with either a sense of achievement or of bewilderment (depending on how successful he has been). An example of this is Katherine Brush's "Birthday Party," a story in which a great deal happens, but only the alert reader will be able to work out exactly what:

Birthday Party

They were a couple in their late thirties, and they looked unmistakably married. They sat on the banquette opposite us in a little narrow restaurant, having dinner. The man had a round, self-satisfied face, with glasses on it; the woman was fadingly pretty, in a big hat. There was nothing conspicuous about them, nothing particularly noticeable, until the end of their meal, when it suddenly became obvious that this was an Occasion—in fact, the husband's birthday, and the wife had planned a little surprise for him.

It arrived, in the form of a small but glossy birthday cake, with one pink candle burning in the center. The headwaiter brought it in and placed it before the husband, and meanwhile the violin-and-piano orchestra played "Happy Birthday to You" and the wife beamed with shy pride over her little surprise, and such few people as there were in the restaurant tried to help out with a pattering of applause. It became clear at once that help was needed, because the husband was not pleased. Instead he was hotly embarrassed, and indignant at his wife for embarrassing him.

You looked at him and you saw this and you thought, "Oh, now, don't *be* like that!" But he was like that, and as soon as the little cake had been deposited on the table, and the orchestra had finished the birthday piece, and the general attention had shifted from the man and woman, I saw him say something to her under his breath—some punishing thing, quick and curt and unkind. I couldn't bear to look at the woman then, so I stared at my plate and waited for quite a long time. Not long enough, though. She was still crying when I finally glanced over there again. Crying quietly and heart-brokenly and hopelessly, all to herself, under the gay big brim of her best hat.

KATHERINE BRUSH

Analysis of "Birthday Party"

1. Is there a development in this piece, making a story rather than a single episode?
2. What are the conflicts, climaxes, theme? In what way does the first sentence lead into the main conflicts?
3. How long does the story take (a) in action and (b) to be read?
4. What is the contrast in the values of the husband and the wife?
5. Is this story sentimental (that is, indulging in false emotion or emotionally overstated)? Explain.
6. What has the author gained by setting the story in a restaurant?

Finally, there is the objective point of view. The reader does not learn what the characters are thinking or feeling. Characterization is achieved through dialogue and external action. It is difficult for the author to tell the story totally from an objective point of view. Because of the difficulty, it is not frequently used in fiction. It is more common in the theater.

The point of view that you select for your story can affect the tone, that is, your attitude toward your material. The attitude of the narrator may be different from the attitude of the author. Superficially, the tone in *Huckleberry Finn* is naive and jaunty, but beneath it is the ironic, earnest, perhaps horrified tone of the author.

Edgar Allan Poe's "The Tell-Tale Heart" is an example of how the narrator's and the author's tone may differ:

True—nervous—very, very dreadfully nervous I had been and am; but why will you say that I am mad? The disease had sharpened my senses—not destroyed—not dulled them. Above all was the sense of hearing acute. I heard all things in the heaven and in the earth. I heard many things in hell. How, then, am I mad? Harken! and observe how healthily—how calmly I can tell you the whole story.

It is impossible to say how first the idea entered my brain; but once conceived, it haunted me day and night. Object there was none. Passion, there was none. I loved the old man. He had never wronged me. He had never given me insult. For his gold I had no desire. I think it was his eye! Yes, it was this! One of his eyes resembled that of a vulture—a pale blue eye, with a film over it. Whenever it fell upon me, my blood ran cold; and so by degrees—very gradually—I made up my mind to take the life of the old man and thus rid myself of the eye forever.

Now this is the point. You fancy me mad. Madmen know nothing. But you should have seen me. You should have seen how wisely I proceeded—with what caution— with what foresight—with what dissimulation I went to work! I was never kinder to the old man than during the whole week before I killed him. And every night, about midnight, I turned the latch of his door and opened it— oh, so gently! And then, when I had made an opening sufficient for my head, I put in a dark lantern, all closed, closed, so that no light shone out, and then I thrust in my head. Oh, you would have laughed to see how cunningly I thrust it in! I moved it slowly—very, very slowly, so that I might not disturb the old man's sleep. It took me an hour to place my whole head within the opening so far that I could see him as he lay upon his bed. Ha— would a madman have been so wise as this? And then, when my head was well in the room, I undid the lantern cautiously—oh, so cautiously—cautiously (for the hinges creaked)—I undid it just so much that a single thin ray fell upon the vulture eye. And this I did for seven long nights—every night just at midnight—but I found the eye always closed; and so it was impossible to do the work; for it was not the old man who vexed me, but his Evil Eye. And every morning, when the day broke, I went boldly into the chamber and spoke courageously to him, calling him by name in a hearty tone, and inquiring how he had passed the night. So you see he would have been a very profound old man, indeed, to suspect that every night, just at twelve, I looked in upon him while he slept.

Upon the eighth night I was more than usually cautious in opening the door. A watch's minute hand moves more quickly than did mine. Never before that night had I felt the extent of my own powers—of my sagacity. I could scarcely contain my feelings of triumph. To think that there I was, opening the door, little by little, and he not even to dream of my secret deeds or thoughts. I fairly chuckled at the idea; and perhaps he heard me; for he moved on the bed suddenly, as if startled. Now you may think that I drew back—but no. His room was as black as pitch with the thick darkness (for the shutters were close-fastened, through fear of robbers), and so I knew that he could not see the opening of the door, and I kept pushing it on steadily, steadily.

I had my head in and was about to open the lantern, when my thumb slipped upon the tin fastening, and the old man sprang up in the bed, crying out—"Who's there?"

I kept quite still and said nothing. For a whole hour I did not move a muscle, and in the meantime I did not hear him lie down. He was still sitting up in the bed listening—just as I had done, night after night, harkening to the deathwatches * in the wall.

Presently I heard a slight groan, and I knew it was the groan of mortal terror. It was not a groan of pain or of grief—oh, no!—it was the low stifled sound that arises from the bottom of the soul when overcharged with awe. I knew the sound well. Many a night, just at midnight, when all the world slept, it has welled up from my own bosom, deepening, with its dreadful echo, the terrors that distracted me. I say I knew it well. I knew what the old man felt, and pitied him, although I chuckled at heart. I knew that he had been lying awake ever since the first slight noise, when he had turned in the bed. His fears had been ever since growing upon him. He had been trying to fancy them causeless, but could not. He had been saying to himself—"It is nothing but the wind in the chimney—it is only a mouse crossing the floor," or "It is merely a cricket which has made a single chirp." Yes, he had been trying to comfort himself with these suppositions; but he had found all in vain. All in vain; because Death, in approaching him, had stalked with his black shadow before him and enveloped

* **deathwatches:** small insects that make a clicking sound believed by superstitious persons to be a forewarning of death.

the victim. And it was the mournful influence of the unperceived shadow that caused him to feel—although he neither saw nor heard—to feel the presence of my head within the room.

When I had waited a long time, very patiently, without hearing him lie down, I resolved to open a little—a very, very little crevice in the lantern. So I opened it—you cannot imagine how stealthily, stealthily —until, at length, a single dim ray, like the thread of the spider, shot from out the crevice and fell full upon the vulture eye.

It was open—wide, wide open—and I grew furious as I gazed upon it. I saw it with perfect distinctness—all a dull blue, with a hideous veil over it that chilled the very marrow in my bones; but I could see nothing else of the old man's face or person: for I had directed the ray as if by instinct, precisely upon the damned spot.

And now have I not told you that what you mistake for madness is but overacuteness of the senses?—now, I say, there came to my ears a low, dull, quick sound, such as a watch makes when enveloped in cotton. I knew that sound well, too. It was the beating of the old man's heart. It increased my fury, as the beating of a drum stimulates the soldier into courage.

But even yet I refrained and kept still. I scarcely breathed. I held the lantern motionless. I tried how steadily I could maintain the ray upon the eye. Meantime the hellish tattoo of the heart increased. It grew quicker and quicker and louder and louder every instant. The old man's terror must have been extreme! It grew louder every moment!—do you mark me well? I have told you that I am nervous: so I am. And now at the dead hour of the night, amid the dreadful silence of that old house, so strange a noise as this excited me to uncontrollable terror. Yet for some minutes longer I refrained and stood still. But the beating grew louder, louder! I thought the heart must burst. And now a new anxiety seized me—the sound would be heard by a neighbor! The old man's hour had come! With a loud yell, I threw open the lantern and leaped into the room. He shrieked once—once only. In an instant I dragged him to the floor and pulled the heavy bed over him. I then smiled gaily, to find the deed so far done. But, for many minutes the heart beat on with a muffled sound. This, however, did not vex me; it would not be heard through the wall. At length it ceased. The old man was dead. I removed the bed and examined the corpse. Yes, he was stone, stone-dead. I placed my hand upon the heart and held it there many minutes. There was no pulsation. He was stone-dead. His eye would trouble me no more.

If still you think me mad, you will think so no longer when I describe the wise precautions I took for the concealment of the body. The night waned, and I worked hastily but in silence. First of all I dismembered the corpse. I cut off the head and the arms and the legs.

I then took up three planks from the flooring of the chamber, and deposited all between the scantlings.* I then replaced the boards so cleverly, so cunningly, that no human eye—not even his—could have detected anything wrong. There was nothing to wash out—no stain of any kind—no blood spot whatever. I had been too wary for that. A tub had caught all—ha! ha!

When I had made an end of these labors, it was four o'clock—still dark as midnight. As the bell sounded the hour, there came a knocking at the street door. I went down to open it with a light heart—for what had I now to fear? There entered three men, who introduced themselves, with perfect suavity, as officers of the police. A shriek had been heard by a neighbor during the night; suspicion of foul play had been aroused; information had been lodged at the police office, and they (the officers) had been deputed to search the premises.

I smiled—for what had I to fear? I bade the gentlemen welcome. The shriek, I said, was my own in a dream. The old man, I mentioned, was absent in the country. I took my visitors all over the house. I bade them search—search well. I led them, at length, to his chamber. I showed them his treasures, secure, undisturbed. In the enthusiasm of my confidence, I brought

* **scantlings:** crosspieces.

chairs into the room, and desired them here to rest from their fatigues, while I myself, in the wild audacity of my perfect triumph, placed my own seat upon the very spot beneath which reposed the corpse of the victim.

The officers were satisfied. My manner had convinced them. I was singularly at ease. They sat, and while I answered cheerily, they chatted familiar things. But, ere long, I felt myself getting pale and wished them gone. My head ached, and I fancied a ringing in my ears: but still they sat and still chatted. The ringing became more distinct; it continued and became more distinct. I talked more freely to get rid of the feeling, but it continued and gained definitiveness—until, at length, I found that the noise was not within my ears.

No doubt I now grew very pale; but I talked more fluently, and with a heightened voice. Yet the sound increased—and what could I do? It was a low, dull, quick sound—much such a sound as a watch makes when enveloped in cotton. I gasped for breath—and yet the officers heard it not. I talked more quickly—more vehemently; but the noise steadily increased. I arose and argued about trifles, in a high key and with violent gesticulations, but the noise steadily increased. Why would they not be gone? I paced the floor to and fro with heavy strides, as if excited to fury by the observation of the men—but the noise steadily increased. Oh, God! What could I do? I foamed —I raved—I swore! I swung the chair upon which I had been sitting, and grated it upon the boards, but the noise arose over all and continually increased. It grew louder— louder—louder! And still the men chatted pleasantly and smiled. Was it possible they heard not? Almighty God!— no, no! They heard!—they suspected!—they knew!—they were making a mockery of my horror!—this I thought, and this I think. But anything was better than this agony! Anything was more tolerable than this derision! I could bear those hypocritical smiles no longer! I felt that I must scream or die!—and now—again!—hark! louder! louder! louder! louder!

"Villains!" I shrieked. "Dissemble no more! I admit the deed!—tear up the planks! here, here!—it is the beating of his hideous heart!"

Analysis of "The Tell-Tale Heart"

1. What is the point of view in this story?
2. The syntax and grammar of the sentences is broken and abrupt. How does this suit the subject matter of the story?
3. Why did the madman kill the old man?
4. At what point do the police become suspicious?
5. Whose heart was making the noise?
6. This story makes use of the hunt for its effect. Explain at what points the characters in the story suffer the age-old emotions of the hunter and the hunted.
7. List some of the specific imaginative details that make this story so vivid and horrifying.
8. List some of the comparisons in the story and tell how they relate to the overall statement of the story.
9. Explain the use of irony in the tale.

Similar to the tone of a story is its mood. Both contribute strongly to the overall effect. Take three descriptions of death:

1. Ben Battle was a warrior bold,
   Used to war's alarms.
   A cannon ball took off his legs,
   And he laid down his arms.

2. A drunk like Clausen ought to be snoring very loudly. He ought to be snoring his head off with a nice assortment of checks and gurgles and snorts. He wasn't making any sound at all. A brown army blanket was pulled up around his shoulders and the lower part of his head. He looked very comfortable, very calm. I stood over him and looked down. Something which was not an accidental fold held the army blanket away from the back of his neck. I moved it. A square yellow wooden handle was attached to the back of Lester B. Clausen's neck. On the side of the yellow handle were printed the words "Compliments of the Crumsen Hardware Company." The position of the handle was just below the occipital bulge.

   RAYMOND CHANDLER, *The Little Sister*

3. [A group of soldiers are making their way back to the safety of their base, dead tired after endless fighting in the trenches. Suddenly there is a cry.]

Gas! GAS! Quick, boys!—An ecstasy of fumbling,
Fitting the clumsy helmets just in time,
But someone still was yelling out and stumbling
And flound'ring like a man in fire or lime.
Dim through the misty panes and thick green light
As under a green sea, I saw him drowning.

In all my dreams before my helpless sight
He plunges at me, guttering, choking, drowning.

If, in some smothering dreams, you too could pace
Behind the wagon that we flung him in,
And watch the white eyes writhing in his face,
His hanging face, like a devil's sick of sin;
If you could hear, at every jolt, the blood
Come gargling from his froth-corrupted lungs,
Bitten as the cud
Of vile, incurable sores on innocent tongues . . .
                    WILFRED OWEN, "Dulce et Decorum Est"

All three of the above passages are accounts of death. The difference between them is one of *mood,* which depends to a large extent on the kind of details that are chosen:

The first passage makes no attempt to enlist sympathy for the victim or to elicit horror at the death. It is climaxed by a pun, a bizarre attempt at the comical, which is the point of the ditty.

In the second, there is some revulsion at the death, but it is tempered by an underlying mood of irrepressible humor. The name on the handle, the introduction to the victim as a drunk and his subsequent tranquility, the uninvolved tone of the narrator (in this case, about the equivalent of the author's tone), all combine to make the description more amusing than horrible.

In the third, however, the death is made ugly and serious by the choking language, the references to incurable sickness and to the reader's own nightmares, and by the general mood of helplessness.

The mood of a story is, then, at times more important than its content. Death here is seen as humorous, bittersweet, or hideously real, depending on the mood. Mood stems from choice of detail. You are already familiar with this technique from your work on the sketch. Consider this passage from "The Fall of the House of Usher." Every movement, every object contributes to building a mood of undefined horror.

> During the whole of a dull, dark, and soundless day in the autumn of the year, when the clouds hung oppressively low in the heavens, I had been passing alone, on horseback, through a singularly dreary tract of country, and at length found myself, as the shades of the evening drew on, within view of the melancholy House of Usher. I know not how it was—but, with the first glimpse of the building, a sense of insufferable gloom pervaded my spirit. I say insufferable; for the feeling was unrelieved by any of that half-pleasurable, because poetic, sentiment with which the mind usually receives even the sternest natural images of the desolate or terrible. I looked upon the scene before me—upon the mere house, and the simple landscape features of the domain—upon the bleak walls—upon the vacant eyelike windows—upon a few rank sedges—and upon a few white trunks of decayed trees—with an utter depression of soul which I can compare to no earthly sensation more properly than to the after-dream of the reveler upon opium—the bitter lapse into everyday life—the hideous dropping off of the veil. There was an iciness, a sinking, a sickening of the heart —an unredeemed dreariness of thought which no goading of the imagination could torture into aught of the sublime.
>
> EDGAR ALLAN POE

This passage illustrates the most common way of building up a mood, by means of the selection of details. Another method, which is akin to this, is choice of metaphor and simile to achieve a single mood effect. If a man is shipwrecked in tropical seas, he may expect an island paradise or unknown perils. If the water he slides into is described as "blood-warm," the suggestion is that he is in trouble. A third method of creating mood is by paying attention to the sounds of your words. As a general rule, *s* sounds are menacing, *m* sounds are soft and mellow, *b* and *p* sounds are explosive. Long vowels move slowly; short vowels move quickly.

The challenge when writing a story is to make the mood fit the theme of the story. If your idea demands a mood of transience, or vulnerability, or violence, or nostalgia, or horror, work toward it. Sometimes a contrast between mood and action can be effective.

10

Putting it all together

NOW YOU HAVE the techniques and material to write a good short story. It is time to do the job. This announcement will probably have given you an immediate mental blackout. "Who me? Right now? Where? How do I begin?" If you have such a reaction, it probably comes from having a mass of material but no particular starting point. Let us consider some examples of ways you might begin.

1. You may wish to start from a *value*.
2. Perhaps you have a *character* in mind, as James Thurber probably had when planning "The Secret Life of Walter Mitty."
3. Or maybe a *setting* might have caught your interest.
4. Or a *feeling* or *mood*, such as might have prompted Poe's "The Tell-Tale Heart."
5. Or a *situation* or *incident*, such as that from which Kantor's "A Man Who Had No Eyes" probably evolved.
6. Perhaps you have a *whole pattern* in your mind, as the writer of "Appointment in Samarra."

How do you move from an incident, character, or setting to a full-fledged short story? Let us take each of the possibilities listed above and consider it individually, to see if there is a clear way to build it into a short story, such as you have been studying.

1. Suppose you have a *value* in mind. You are concerned with, perhaps, selfishness, loneliness, courage, working hard, growing up, or friendship, and you would like to resolve your ideas by writing about them. You have been thinking about this value recently, and there are questions in your mind about it. How do you set about it?

First, think of your area of concern and decide what exactly it is that is of concern to you. If the area is loneliness, is it your own, somebody else's, or everyone's? Is it how to get out of the loneliness that concerns you, or how to get into a situation of being more independent? Then, reduce your problem to an issue that sets one value against another or one way of seeing a value against another. Thus, you might contrast loneliness with having lots of friends; or you might contrast being lonely with being independent. If you are concerned about selfishness, is it selfishness as opposed to generosity? or to love? Or is it being a busybody and a gossip? If you are thinking about the value of hard work, is your conflict between working hard and goofing off? Or is it between working hard for the wrong reasons (to defeat somebody that you envy) and working hard for the right reasons (because it makes you feel good when you do something well)? Or is it between working hard and being obnoxious, on the one hand, and relaxing and being pleasant, on the other?

The first step, then, is to reduce your area of concern to a concrete issue that you can write about.

Second, you need two characters to represent the two sides of your issue—or one character versus a force, a problem, a setting, or a whole group of people. Also it is always possible that your protagonist may be a "villain," which is quite common in life as well as in stories. In other words, perhaps you want to focus your story on a character who is sympathetic, even though he is selfish, a coward, or lazy. You must get to know your characters intimately, not only the two major ones but also the minor ones who are there to work the action out in supporting roles. You practiced this in Chapter 4.

Once you have the opposing characters clearly in mind and

you feel you know them intimately, you can find an action that will give body to the conflict. This will involve choosing a time and a place (setting) for the action to work against. This you practiced in Chapter 3. The action of a story is, in fact, a series of actions or exchanges that suggest, alternately, first that the protagonist will win, then that his opponent will. This requires inventiveness at every step. Otherwise, the action stagnates, and there is no building toward a climax.

As the action becomes more intense and the point of decision draws nearer, your resolution will become possible, and you should try to streamline your narrative, intensify your setting and your mood, all the details which support and contribute toward expressing the main action. Perhaps your action will climax with an argument, a decision, a reconciliation. Once it has been resolved, you must use it to tie up the ends of your values conflict. As each step of the action is completed, you come closer to a decision about the values conflict. Now you must find a way of resolving this conflict that leaves the reader satisfied, that feels right. This may take the form of a realization by one of the characters, a justification of your hero, the revealing of information that settles matters, and so on.

Once you have your plan of values and action, you should think of the technical devices that might help you present them more sharply. What information should be withheld from the readers? Who should tell the story? How much should he or she know of what is going on? Can you use foreshadowing effectively? Will a sharper contrast help here, irony there? Can you cut down on the time, the characters, the steps of the action, without reducing the emotional impact of your story?

Now you are ready to write your first draft. After the first draft, the real work will begin: reshaping, reordering, eliminating, explaining, reworking the opening, adding another paragraph at the end, and so on, until the story is right.

But you may be saying, "This is all very well; but what if I don't happen to be worried about any values right now?" Every occasion for a short story can be *translated* into terms of values. Values are concerned with why people function, what they think important, and how they see the world; so it is impossible to write a story that does not include a decision about them.

2. Suppose you have a *character* in mind. Ask yourself what is important to him? What opposing value might be set up to thwart

his main value? The major character must be faced with a problem. Will he overcome this obstacle or not? Then, you have converted your character to a values situation, and you can transfer to the second step of procedure 1.

3. If you start from a *setting* (say, your school), ask yourself, "How do I feel about this setting?" Is it stifling, lonely, stimulating, inhuman? Next, translate this feeling into an idea: this school (or some schools) is stifling, frightening, stimulating, lonely, inhuman, and so on. Now, create a character to deal with this feeling. He feels it, but wants to oppose it or cannot take advantage of it. He may be a character who is frightened by the school but is determined not to be; he may be stimulated by it but in the wrong ways; he may be lonely in it or feel its inhumanity but not wish to. Now you have the essence of a conflict. Either the hero can resist the feeling of the school, or he/she can conflict with someone who does. Thus, the conflict becomes protagonist versus setting over such and such a value, or hero against self with setting involved and a values conflict, related to the setting. You are once again on the second step of procedure 1.

4. If you have a *feeling* or a *mood* to work from, you can see that either could be easily transferred to the process of procedure 3, which could, in turn, be worked into procedure 1.

5. If you are working from a *situation,* it is much the same process. Suppose you have a situation where a girl has a secret life of her own—say, a boy she is seeing whom her parents don't know about, or a fantasy life that she lives by herself when she comes into the privacy of her own room. Once again, think of the values involved: What is there about this boy friend that would be disapproved of? What is there about the girl that makes her seek her own fantasy world in the privacy of her room? Is it a world that cannot last or one that could be developed into a kind of reality?

Next, look for a value to oppose these: parents who don't want their daughter getting involved with this boy, with someone "beneath her station"; or a reality that is closing in on the fantasy world. Now you have a conflict and you can build your story in terms of the conflict: bigotry versus open-mindedness, fantasy versus reality. You are once again on the ladder of procedure 1.

But what if you have only an *incident* to work from—say, a chance meeting between two characters who have not been together for years, or an incident in a restaurant, where a wife orders a birthday cake, embarrassing her husband?

Build your incident into a situation and work from that: Who are the two characters who meet? Do they remember each other? What has happened to each? On what terms did they part? Have they changed? What was their relationship then, and what is it now? Or, in the case of the birthday cake, is this just one of many such incidents? Why did the husband refuse it? What are their characters? What is their relationship like?

As you answer these questions, look for contrasts that will lead to conflicts, for values that may be in opposition. Perhaps one of the two who meet has grown since they met and the other hasn't. Perhaps the husband who rejects the birthday cake does so because he is sick of his wife's sentimentality; perhaps she has been disillusioned by his continual greed and selfishness or his insistence on her doing nothing in public that might embarrass them.

6. It is rare for a story to come to a would-be writer as a *whole pattern,* but sometimes it does: A student leaves school and finds that instead of his accustomed success, he meets with failure. He returns to his old school to speak to a teacher who was sympathetic and helped him, only to find that it was that very teacher who had helped to cause his problems. Or a teacher finds that her desk has been broken into and a paper stolen that was written by a student with very high grades. She suspects an unreliable student with poor grades. It turns out that the good student had taken it herself to conceal the fact that she had stolen the idea from the poor student, who was more creative, although the other worked harder.

Again, think of the situation in terms of values. In the first case, the value is the one that the teacher imparted to the student to make him successful at school but that made him fail outside school—say the value is that one should work for himself rather than with other people. In the second case, the values might be creativity versus memory. You should be working toward a situation in which one or more characters are faced with a problem to be resolved. How the character achieves the resolution of the problem is the heart of the story.

Whatever your starting point, if you think about the real significance of your material, you will find it can be resolved into terms of values. Then you can bring these values into conflict, by setting one value against its opposite and finding an action that allows you to do this.

Although working through values is not the only way to write a short story, it is a good one and forms good habits in the writer. It tends to lead you into writing about yourself and your own immediate concerns. Spacemen on the moon, business tycoons in smoke-filled rooms, war heroes, and presidents of nations are fascinating material, but if the writer doesn't know and feel what he is talking about, he will make the story ridiculous or dull. Exotic islands with mysterious dancing girls are good to escape to in your fantasy; impossible missions for secret agents are amusing challenges; cleaning up a town controlled by gangsters is all very well in one's imagination. But your basic life experiences come at school, at home, at your friends' houses, with your girl or boy friend. These are the subjects you know about, and these are the areas from which you should draw your material if you are interested in writing a seriously moving short story. Material from movies, television, and books and from hearsay will simply bore the reader if it is incompetently and unfeelingly reproduced by a youthful short story teller. What is truly interesting to your readers is the reality of yourself—how you feel, what you see, how you are working with your experience.

When composing a short story, look for the following points:

1. Unity

Have you combined your material, so as to work toward a single effect? Have you reduced *characters* to a minimum?

Is there a single, rising *action,* rhythmically alternating, posing a basic situation and then producing interlocking incidents that rise logically out of that initial situation?

Do all your minor techniques, your choice of details, help to reinforce your single effect: your metaphors, your scenery, your method of marking the passage of time, your style, your mood? Have you compressed your time to a minimum? Your setting to a single place?

Have you cut out all unnecessary material and tied up all the loose ends neatly? Have you left a detail unaccounted for that may trouble the reader?

2. Structure, climax, conflicts

Does the story have a strong beginning, moving toward the conflicts within the first sentence?

Does the external action accurately mirror the internal action? Does the plot relate at all times to the theme?

Are the climaxes well-handled, with intensifying of setting, mood, action?

Is there a form of justice in the ending? (Not just simple rewards for the good and punishment for the bad, but the sort that leaves the reader satisfied: a man may be free and happy in a concentration camp if he has maintained his integrity; success may be fruitless to those who have sold themselves to obtain it.)

3. Interest, style

Have you kept the reader in suspense? Is the reader likely to lose interest in the story? If so, find a way around the difficulty. Danger spots are when you are supplying background information and when you are introducing new materials or characters. How often have you heard, "Well, yes, it was a great book, once you got past the dreary beginning"? Find an interesting way to give the reader the necessary background information.

Have you varied your sentence structure, alternating long and short? Have you found just the right word each time? Can you cut verbiage? Have you varied excitement with explanation, action with description?

Have you said too much too soon, or have you piped your information through at the right rate, so as to arouse but not quite glut the reader's curiosity?

4. Character

Do your characters act realistically at all times? Do they become cardboard characters or puppets at any point? Do you have a character who can dominate a situation, who is fascinating?

Have you given your characters little gestures that make them lifelike, especially when they talk? When a character speaks, he should do so to the accompaniment of an adverb that focuses him briefly in the reader's imagination (for example, "said Charles, talking to his bread and butter"; there are innumerable examples of this in "The Secret Life of Walter Mitty").

5. Honesty of feeling

Have you really searched your soul for an honest statement of the issues? Have you confined yourself to situations and characters that you know intimately? Is the emotion genuine, or merely sentimental?

Have you merely made an intellectual statement, or have you put your emotions behind it? Is the story contrived or natural? Have you communicated enthusiasm for the values you deal with?

On the other hand, have you been too literal? Do you include incidents simply because they happened, not because they were the probable events? You are not bound to relate every detail from a *single event* you know of. Remove incidentals, retain only essential material. Cut clichés. Work to sharpen the details. Make sure the conclusion follows from the actions that have gone before.

6. Technical polish

Have you kept the point of view constant? Have you avoided jerking the reader from one point of reference to another? If you are seeing the action from, say, inside Brenda's head, have you suddenly introduced material she could not know, or shown action from a different point of view?

Have you chosen the most effective narrator for the story?

Should you return and research your materials some more? Perhaps a visit to the library in quest of a book on the subject might make the story more believable. Perhaps a trip to the local prison, courthouse, or hospital would give you a more realistic understanding of the way things really happen.

Has your title a second significance? Are your names the best: suggestive but not too obvious? Don't make the names too similar: a story with three characters called "Rob," "Robbie," and "Robert" would only confuse the reader.

ACTIVITY

Write a short story that makes use of all the technical information you have learned thus far but that also expresses an attitude toward a subject of great importance to you. Be sure that you confine your story to familiar characters and situations.